Creating Great Places

This book provides a bold vision and roadmap for creating great places. Imagining and designing urban environments where all people thrive is an extraordinary task, and in this compelling narrative, Cushing and Miller remind us that theory is a powerful starting point. Drawing on international research, illustrated case studies, personal experiences, as well as fascinating examples from history and pop culture, this practical book provides the reader with inspiration, guidance and tools. The first section outlines six critical theories for contemporary urban design – affordance, prospect-refuge, personal space, sense of place/*genius loci*, place attachment, and biophilic design. The second section, using their innovative 'theory-storming' process, demonstrates how designers can create great places that are inclusive, sustainable, and salutogenic. *Creating Great Places* is an insightful, compelling, and evidence-based resource for readers who want to design urban environments that inspire, excite, and positively transform people's lives.

Debra Flanders Cushing is Associate Professor in Landscape Architecture within the School of Design at Queensland University of Technology in Brisbane, Australia. With expertise in landscape architecture and community planning, Debra worked as a design practitioner before focusing on teaching and research in academia. Debra is passionate about promoting evidence-based design within multi-disciplinary initiatives to create parks and urban environments that better support health and wellbeing for all people, especially children and youth.

Evonne Miller is Professor and Director of the QUT Design Lab in the School of Design at Queensland University of Technology in Brisbane, Australia. Drawing on her background in environmental gerontology and design psychology, her research focuses on creating sustainable, inclusive and age-friendly places. Evonne has published widely in the fields of urban design, population ageing, climate change and sustainability, and is a passionate advocate for creative arts-based participatory research.

Creating Great Places

Evidence-Based Urban Design
for Health and Wellbeing

Debra Flanders Cushing
and Evonne Miller

Routledge
Taylor & Francis Group

NEW YORK AND LONDON

First published 2020
by Routledge
52 Vanderbilt Avenue, New York, NY 10017

and by Routledge
2 Park Square, Milton Park, Abingdon, Oxon, OX14 4RN

Routledge is an imprint of the Taylor & Francis Group, an informa business

© 2020 Taylor & Francis

The right of Debra Flanders Cushing and Evonne Miller to be identified as authors of this work has been asserted by them in accordance with sections 77 and 78 of the Copyright, Designs and Patents Act 1988.

Library of Congress Cataloging-in-Publication Data
Names: Cushing, Debra Flanders, 1974– author. |
    Miller, Evonne, 1977– author.
Title: Creating great places : evidence-based urban design for
    health and wellbeing / Debra Flanders Cushing, Evonne Miller.
Description: New York, NY : Routledge, 2020. |
    Includes bibliographical references.
Identifiers: LCCN 2019036147 (print) | LCCN 2019036148 (ebook) |
    ISBN 9780367257453 (hardback) | ISBN 9780367257460
    (paperback) | ISBN 9780429289637 (ebook)
Subjects: LCSH: City planning—Health aspects. |
    Sustainable urban development.
Classification: LCC HT166 .C8845 2020 (print) | LCC
    HT166 (ebook) | DDC 711/.4—dc23
LC record available at https://lccn.loc.gov/2019036147
LC ebook record available at https://lccn.loc.gov/2019036148

ISBN: 9780367257453 (hbk)
ISBN: 9780367257460 (pbk)
ISBN: 9780429289637 (ebk)

Typeset in Sabon
by Apex CoVantage, LLC

Contents

About the Authors   vii

Introduction: Why Evidence-Based Design?   1

PART I
Six Critical Theories for Contemporary Urban Design   15

  1 Affordance Theory: Take Your Cue   17

  2 Prospect-Refuge Theory: Now You See Me,
     Now You Don't   28

  3 Personal Space Theory: Keep Your Distance!   40

  4 Sense of Place Theory/*Genius Loci*: Locating
     the Magic   54

  5 Place Attachment Theory: Fostering Connections   67

  6 Biophilic Design Theory: The Healing Power
     of Nature   80

PART II
Applying Design Theory to Global Priorities   99

  7 Salutogenic Design: Promoting Healthy Living   101

  8 Child-Friendly Design: Where Young People Thrive   118

  9 Age-Friendly and Inclusive Design: Designing
     for Everyone   138

10 Sustainable Design: Radically Redesigning Our
    Built Environment   160

Conclusion: Creating Great Places through
Theory-Storming   177

Recommended Readings   183
Acknowledgments   190
Index   191

About the Authors

Debra Flanders Cushing is an Associate Professor in Landscape Architecture and the Spatial Discipline Leader in the School of Design at Queensland University of Technology in Brisbane, Australia. With expertise in landscape architecture and community planning with children and youth, Debra worked as a designer in practice before focusing on teaching and research in academia. Her current research focuses on intergenerational parks for physical activity and social engagement, using gamification to promote children's sensory engagement with nature, and the affordances of public art in public spaces. For many years, she taught environment and behavior theories to design and planning students, often embedding them into studio and seminar projects. Debra is passionate about using evidence-based design within multi-disciplinary initiatives to focus on how our environments can better support health and wellbeing for all people, especially those who may be disadvantaged in some way.

Evonne Miller is a Professor and the Director of the QUT Design Lab in the School of Design at Queensland University of Technology in Brisbane, Australia. Originally trained in experimental social psychology, Evonne's expertise is in environmental gerontology and design psychology.

Her research focuses on how to design environments – built, technical, socio-cultural and natural – that better engage and support all users, especially older people in residential aged care. Evonne has published widely in the fields of urban design, population ageing, health and well-being, climate change and sustainability, and is a passionate advocate for creative arts-based participatory research methods. She is a Fellow of the Australian Association of Gerontology, and a founding member of Places for Ageing Australia, a community of designers, educators and age care providers promoting research, innovation and best practice in the design of healthy places for ageing.

Introduction

Why Evidence-Based Design?

Great places don't just happen.

They are created.

Great places are the outcome of deliberate plans and decisive actions, of structured and imaginative thinking, and designers' ability to visualize what is and what might be. This placemaking process is, in many ways, analogous to a game of chess, as seen in Figure 1. Just as a chess master pauses to thoughtfully observe the entire board, a great designer pauses to consider the entire site: to ponder the unique historical, socio-cultural and environmental context, as well as any potential opportunities, surprises and challenges. In any chess game, as in any design process, there are clearly defined patterns, possibilities and paths that tend to predict success but also need to be continuously adapted in response to changing circumstances. Success in both chess and design is, therefore, a calculated mix of art and science. Alongside the imaginative exploration and creative insight that defines art, creating great places where people thrive requires deep engagement with the evidence-based approach of science – the analytical rigor of theory, research and experimentation.

In *Creating Great Places*, we argue that designers need to arm themselves with a comprehensive knowledge of critical design theories and relevant research evidence in order to make informed design choices. Be it the design of a bus shelter, a playground, street intersection, urban plaza, or aged care facility, each and every design decision intertwines to determine whether the experience of a place is positive and memorable or mundane and forgettable. Consider for a moment, the everyday places where you live, work, and play – as well as those you may have helped design. What makes them special – or bland? Have people adapted, reformed or transformed them? Could they have been designed better to begin with?

Imagining and creating places where *all people thrive* is an extraordinary task. It requires built environment professionals – designers, urban planners, architects, landscape architects, developers, policymakers – to more deeply engage with and look through a theoretical lens. If you are a designer, how often do you explicitly integrate the principles of affordance

Figure 0.1 A large outdoor chess board provides an activity to watch and play for intergenerational groups.

Source: Jos Dielis, Flickr CC.

or biophilic theory into your design practice? Do you engage in a constant cycle of design implementation and reflection, or present the client with a return brief that also prompts consideration and discussion of evidence-based best practices such as sustainable, age or child-friendly design? Contemporary practice in urban design increasingly requires a process which ensures places better meet the needs of local users and that diverse voices – children, youth, families, older people, entrepreneurs – are included in the planning of our cities, particularly as they grow. But what about using a theoretical lens – and evidence-based practice? It is only then, when the art and science of design is fully integrated in practice, that we will create the great places that can inspire, excite, support, enable, touch the soul and positively transform peoples' lives.

The Power of Place

Creating great places is critical if we are to manage many of the world's contemporary challenges. From obesity, cancer, attention deficit disorder, depression and dementia, many people are experiencing a reduced quality of life, and governments, organizations, not-for-profits, individuals and families are spending billions of dollars to address and mitigate these issues. In fact, the priorities discussed in Part II – salutogenic design, child-friendly design, age-friendly and inclusive design, and sustainable design, are all part of a broader response to these challenges. Too often, what is missing from discussions about these challenges is the positive impact of quality environments – places designed to afford opportunities for healthy living, not only to help prevent these issues but also to enable people to thrive within their daily lives.

Fortunately, researchers, planners and policymakers have recognized the importance of designing environments and places that do enable people to live healthy lifestyles. Globally, the World Health Organization (WHO) defines health as 'a state of complete physical, mental and social well-being and not merely the absence of disease or infirmity' (WHO, 2017). This state of well-being underpins the concept of salutogenesis, the idea that environments should be health promoting and take a preventative stance, rather than ignoring health issues, or even worse, actually contribute to unhealthy behaviors, sickness and disease. Salutogenic design, discussed in detail in Chapter 7, incorporates the concept of coherence to explain how people read and understand their environment so as to engage in health-promoting activities, and also incorporates place-making principles that enable people to enjoy (and be invigorated by) the places in which they spend their time.

Of the many connections between our physical, mental and psychological health and the environments where we live, work and play, several are more direct and obvious than others. For example, the provision of bicycle and foot paths can directly contribute to an increase in people cycling, walking and running for recreation or commuting. Likewise, the provision of shade structures in sunny locations can contribute to thermal comfort and the prevention of sun burn. Placing pollution limits on factories and industrial buildings can directly improve air quality, reducing asthma and respiratory disease. Yet, many other environmental design interventions are less directly connected to health implications and the impacts take longer to surface. Serious conditions such as cancer or obesity, often take years to manifest, making it harder to pinpoint causal variables. While there is a need for additional longitudinal and experimental research to fully understand how the design of our environments can impact health, the compelling body of evidence to date suggests that we cannot sit back and do nothing. That is not an option.

Today, few people question the connection between smoking and lung cancer. Yet, this relationship required consistent messaging to the public, health officials and policymakers, backed up with decades of research. For something as complex as mental health and sources of stress, much more evidence is needed to help us fully understand how this is linked to a lack of access to natural environments. Given the growing body of evidence confirming the benefits of nature for stress reduction, it is important to advocate for and promote these benefits through quality design. Designing great places is the answer to many of society's 'wicked' problems – from climate change to disconnected communities to our over-reliance on fast food and physically inactive lifestyles. And significantly, as Goldhagen (2017) reminds us, we only have one chance to get the design right – to create a built environment that enables people to thrive, that pulls the younger generations away from technology and into outdoor public places, to be physically active and to interact socially, developing those bonds of social capital that are so important for health and wellbeing:

> Once finished, a new urban area or park or building will likely outlast every person who designed, engineered and built it. It will survive too the people who wrote and adjudicated the codes that dictated its permitting. And it will remain in use long after those who commissioned and paid for it are gone . . . every element – building, landscape, urban area, infrastructure – ought, accordingly, be designed to help us thrive.
>
> (Goldhagen, 2017, pp. 269–272)

Promoting Evidence-Based Design Practice

The built environment disciplines are very much practice-oriented, even today. Students undertake degrees in disciplines such as landscape architecture, architecture, urban design and planning, with the primary goal of gaining professional recognition and skills to create great places. Degree programs for the built environment disciplines, such as landscape architecture, focus on the practical skills involved in site-based problem-solving, an approach that is valuable but can also limit the intellectual growth of the profession (Thwaites, 1998). Other disciplines, such as medicine, geography, psychology, and sociology, have a much more specific theoretical base and research arm. These disciplines have evolved from a practice to evidence-based approach; medicine, for example, was once based on anecdotal connections and professional integrity, but is now completely reliant on research and testing to ensure safety and ethical practices. The design disciplines are on a similar journey. This book focuses on six core theories (with origins predominately in geography, anthropology, sociology and psychology) that we believe should form the basis of contemporary design pedagogy and practice. We refer to them as design theories to recognize their importance to design.

The built environment professions responsible for designing physical spaces where we live, work, and play, do not always rely on research and theory to support their design decisions. Some still rely on intuition, anecdotal information, and their creativity and skill to design good places. Sometimes this is all that is needed and the end-result is brilliantly successful for the intended users. In fact, there are countless examples around the world, with a influential one being Central Park in New York

City, designed by Frederick Law Olmsted and Calvert Vaux in 1857. This park is testament to the creativity and skill possessed by these men, and all the others who contributed to the design. Although they themselves had observed people and studied landscape architecture and architecture, they did not have empirical research to inform or back up their design decisions.

Unfortunately, and far too often, designs of other public spaces are not as successful. There are countless examples of places that have been underused, over-ridden with crime, or inadvertently encourage sedentary lifestyles and unhealthy living. Even Central Park itself faced periods of disrepair, neglect and crime. Fortunately, today it is a well-designed park that provides countless opportunities to be physically active, breath fresh air, relax and destress in a natural setting, socialize with friends and family, learn about art and history, and generally thrive in an otherwise hectic urban environment.

In reflecting on the design process and the importance of research-informed and evidence-based design, there are three key issues. First, the research process in design projects is often informal and not systematic. Most built environment projects involve varying levels of research during multiple stages of the design process, including problem identification, user needs analysis, and site analysis. However, this information is often specific to one project site, and may or may not be collected through rigorous methods that follow traditional research protocols and at the same time, abide by ethical research requirements. The research undertaken during the design process can rely heavily on the anecdotal evidence of clients and designers, and is often informal, and therefore has the potential to be biased and inaccurate. The quality of a design is only as good as the inputs into the decision-making, so professional design needs to more explicitly engage with research-informed and evidence-based theory. Designers (rarely trained in research methods) are sometimes reluctant to do this, concerned that an emphasis on research and science might somehow, as Hamilton and Shepley (2010) explain, 'undermine the art of the design process.'

A second issue regarding the importance of research-informed and evidence-based design is when designers or related professionals champion specific methods causing a critical, long-term impact on the profession, in regards to both research and practice. For example, countless landscape architects are influenced by the work of Ian McHarg (1969) and his systematic overlay mapping method used to analyze site conditions and characteristics. Despite the historical significance of McHarg's method, it is not immune to critique, with some arguing that maps are inherently subjective because someone had to decide what to include and what *not* to include when creating them. The reality is that the overlay mapping method is only as good as the data collected, and this can be flawed and/or misinterpreted. Additionally, design researchers and practitioners often communicate, write for and publish in different places. Hamilton and Shepley (2010) describe how the typical library in an architecture firm will have journals such as *Architectural Record* and *Landscape Architecture*, which rarely publish research. On the other hand, design researchers publish in academic journals such as *Environmental Psychology*, *Environment and Behavior*, or *Landscape Research*, rarely on display in design offices. Crossing these boundaries, and convincing architects and designers that research is not 'dry or dull' can provide an 'opportunity for creative enrichment of the design experience' (Hamilton & Shepley, 2010, p. 241) and is a crucial objective of this book.

Third, it is critical to understand how research informs practice. Although referring specifically to landscape architecture, the following sentiment from Milburn et al. (2003, p.120) is applicable to all of the built environment professions: 'research related to design must achieve both rigor and flexibility to have both credibility in the academy, and applicability to the profession.' Hamilton and Watkins (2009) extend this argument, defining evidence-based design as 'a process for the conscientious, explicit and judicious use of current best evidence from research and practice in making critical decisions, together with an informed client, about the design of each individual and unique project' (p. 9). Each site and design is in some way unique, making the challenge for the designer to engage critically with research theory and findings, and thoughtfully interpret and apply it to each unique site, design and decision-making process.

Why Theory is Important to Design

The theory and research discussed in this book comes predominately from those disciplines that focus on people and understanding how they interact with and are impacted by their environment. Researchers and theorists from disciplines such as sociology, environmental and ecological psychology, social geography, and anthropology often provide important information about humans that are critical for designers to understand – yet is often not communicated in a way that is easily accessible for designers or applicable to a design context.

There are two types of theory: explanatory theory that explains a certain phenomenon; and normative theory, that focuses on what should be. Both are important. And both are critical to informing design decisions. Affordance theory, for example, is the first theory presented in this book and is rather straightforward, essentially arguing that there are visual cues in the environment that can tell people the opportunities there are for actions and how a space can be used. As an explanatory theory, affordance theory helps designers provide effective and varied visual cues to enable well-used and successful places. In this book, therefore, we discuss how designers might use affordance theory and other prominent theories, such as prospect refuge, biophilia, and place attachment, to enhance their design decisions and have a positive impact of their work.

Creating Great Places marks an important transition in the design discourse, squarely placing theory (through a process we label theory-storming) on the agenda for placemaking, urban planning and design practice. For simplicity, this book focuses on six core design theories frequently used in design practice, education and research contexts, theories we believe are important in placemaking and can be easily integrated into design practice. In 2003, Cuthbert claimed that urban design, as a young discipline anchored in professional practice and real world projects, 'has been unable to develop any substantial theory on its own' (Cuthbert, 2003, p. viii). More recently, in his 2017 book *Making Design Theory*, Johan Redström explained a critical change: fifty years ago, a sole practitioner designer working with a few assistants could solve most design problems. These days, the problems are so complex they require large groups of people, with diverse transdisciplinary skills and expertise, as well as the desire to engage deeply with evidence-based practice and theoretical frameworks. The six theories in this book, and their purposeful application to the four real-world priorities of salutogenic, child-friendly, age-friendly inclusive and sustainable design, provides a critical starting point for a new 21st century design discourse.

> Past environments appeared simpler. They made simpler demands. Individual experience and personal development were sufficient for depth and substance in professional practice. While experience and development are still necessary, they are no longer sufficient. Most of today's design challenges require analytic and synthetic planning skills that cannot be developed through practice alone. Professional design practice today involves advanced knowledge. This knowledge is not solely a higher level of professional practice.
>
> (Redström, 2017, p. xii)

How to Use this Book

There are many ways to use this book. If you are interested in understanding the way people interact with the built environment and how our designed spaces impacts daily lives, you can read the book from cover to cover. Since the chapters can stand alone, it is also possible to jump around and read one chapter at a time and not in any particular order. In this regard, this book can be used as a reference book when designing a project or studying a particular theory or phenomenon. In Part I, each chapter examines a specific theory and the associated research to show (1) how it can be applied in design and (2) why it is relevant to understanding the built-environment, drawing on examples from designed environments around the world. As Figure 0.2 illustrates, the chapters in

Design Theory-Storming...

Figure 0.2 Six core design theories.

Source: Clockwise from top right photo: Natalie Wright; NEXT architects/Photography: Rutger Hollander; Vernon Raineil Cenzon on Unsplash; Matthias_Lemm on Pixabay; Mauro Mora, Unsplash, CC; Debra Cushing.

this section include six key theories, each with an associated memorable 'catch-cry' that clearly distills their core focus.

Theory 1: Affordance Theory . . . Take Your Cue

Affordances are opportunities for actions supported by an environment, and communicated through visual cues perceived by people in that environment. These cues are often determined by the surfaces, objects, and layout of the space. Affordances are important in determining how the environment can be designed or manipulated to support (or discourage) various activities and experiences, and depend on the characteristics of an individual. Affordances and subsequent actions often occur together within a particular setting, called a behavior setting. As well as synthesizing the research on affordance theory, this chapter presents examples of designed environments that demonstrate positive and negative affordances.

Theory 2: Prospect-Refuge Theory . . . Now You See Me, Now You Don't

Prospect refuge theory describes the idea that people in public places feel most comfortable when they can observe what is happening around them, while also being slightly protected. Although this theory relates back to the days of hunter gatherers when humans needed to see out into the landscape while being protected from predators, it has important implications today for safety in public spaces, as well as placemaking interventions that involve people watching and performance. This chapter draws on the examples such as the High Line park in Manhattan that offer multiple opportunities for prospect-refuge.

Theory 3: Personal Space Theory . . . Keep Your Distance!

People from different cultures perceive space differently. The term proxemics describes the study of space and how different people conceptualize, use and organize space. First presented by Edward Hall (1966), proxemics explains how intimate, personal, social, and public distances may differ depending on a person's cultural background, gender, age, and relationship with others. For design, it is not only important to understand the cultural context, but also the characteristics of the potential users of the space. This chapter draws on practical examples from public seating, workplaces, and building design – as well as how NASA incorporated personal space and privacy elements into the design of space stations and selection of astronauts – to highlight the importance of considering human spatial needs in design practice.

Theory 4: Sense of Place Theory/Genius Loci . . . Locating the Magic

In a society where efficiency, regularity and standardized design can be the norm, creating quality built environments, that celebrate a unique sense of place or genius loci, is more important than ever. Sense of place theory is the concept that every natural environment has a unique sense of place and character with which people can identify and be intrigued. This character can and should be the starting point of a designed environment, ensuring that this unique character is not lost or hidden, but is celebrated and reinforced. This chapter describes inspiring examples of places from across the globe, from Shanghai to Seattle, illustrating how thoughtful design practice can celebrate the unique qualities of a place.

Theory 5: Place Attachment Theory . . . Fostering Connections

Place attachment theory explains why people develop emotional bonds with specific places, often a treasured landscape from their childhood or other significant place-based life experience. Understanding why and how people have developed attachments to places and using that knowledge during the design process, can aid in the creation of better places that people will use and enjoy, take ownership of, and thrive in. This chapter particularly highlights the importance of understanding cultural and indigenous perspectives (and voices) on place attachment, and the importance of understanding, respecting and integrating a community's attachment to place into the design process.

Theory 6: Biophilic Design Theory . . . the Healing Power of Nature

Humans have evolved with nature and therefore have an innate preference for being with other living things, including plants and animals. To illustrate how designers can better engage with this theoretical concept, our discussion of biophilic design details three international examples at very different scales – from biophilic urbanism throughout Singapore to the biophilic design of hospitals and pedestrian bridges. Closely linked to biophilia is attention restoration theory and related research that substantiates the importance of access to nature in today's fast-paced, over-stimulating urban environment. This chapter synthesizes key research findings which show nature to be truly healing, with the presence of nature linked to reductions in crime rates, domestic violence, the duration of hospital stays and the amount of medicine patients need.

Applying Design Theory to Global Priorities

Many of these theories are inter-related and when used together help explain how people interact with their environment. The chapters in Part II illustrate this, focusing on four key global priorities:

- salutogenic design;
- child-friendly design;
- age-friendly and inclusive design; and
- sustainable design.

Salutogenic Design . . . Promoting Healthy Living

It is becoming increasingly important to design places that enable people to live healthy lifestyles. Salutogenec design focuses on creating health promoting environments that are preventative rather than reactive. The salutogenic model incorporates the sense of coherence, which is a person's ability and motivation to deal with stresses in life, and which relies on the resources provided by the environment to encourage healthy activities. Salutogenic design incorporates placemaking principles to enable people to enjoy and be invigorated by the places in which they spend their time. As well as examples and images of salutogenic places, this chapter unpacks the characteristics of coherence and how actively engaging with cutting-edge research findings alongside established design theories encourages healthy living.

Child-Friendly Design . . . Where Young People Thrive

Communities are focusing more on the needs of children, youth and families, and global policies now recognize the rights of young people to have a healthy environment in which to live, play and work. A significant body of research which supports child-friendly cities has been oriented to designing public spaces, improving independent mobility, enhancing access to the natural environment, and providing opportunities for life chances more generally. For example, a key area of importance is safety and well-designed walking and cycle paths that effectively and efficiently connect residential areas to parks, public spaces, schools, and community amenities. Access to nature and the opportunities to play safely outside are other critical areas of research that provide evidence for improving environments for young people. Drawing on examples of child-friendly environments, this chapter identifies the key features of places that can have a positive impact on growing up – and how explicitly engaging with evidence-based theory facilitates the design of great places, particularly for young people.

Age-Friendly and Inclusive Design . . . Designing for Everyone

Universal design focuses on inclusivity, rather than isolating people or groups. Ideally, universal design principals form part of the design intent and process from the beginning and are seamlessly incorporated into the environment or building. Yet, more often than not, places need to be retrofitted to be universally accessible and the solutions are not always elegant or even practical. Global population ageing has focused attention on the importance of age-friendly inclusive design, of creating homes, places and spaces that enable people with disabilities and older people to 'age in place.' By 2020, people aged over 65 years will outnumber children – and innovative design has a significant role to play in improving their quality of life, independence and mobility. From access and social inclusion, well-lit and wide footpaths, signage and street furniture, to slowing traffic and prioritizing walkability, design decisions affect whether everyone can easily use our public spaces. Discussing concepts such as design for dementia, this chapter outlines innovative examples of evidence-informed design that engages our senses (color, touch, texture, smell, sound) and the importance of creating attractive public spaces that welcome and support people of all abilities. Supported by best-practice examples, this chapter establishes a clear design problem, brief and challenge: how can we create great places for all, using evidence-based design theory.

Sustainable Design . . . Radically Redesigning Our Built Environment

Tackling climate change will require a disruptive, radical rethink of how we design places, with this chapter investigating key emerging trends in sustainable design. These responses all argue for moving beyond *reducing* the environmental impact of a building, product or place to actively *putting back more* than is taken in the construction and operation. Drawing on examples from London, Pittsburgh, Oslo, Adelaide and Vancouver, we illustrate how the process of designing for restorative and regenerative sustainability means adopting a triple bottom line, systems-thinking, and circular design perspective, grounded in biomimicry, cradle-to-cradle, and a broader social impact perspective. Design, through relevant evidence and theory, can be a powerful force for positive action on climate change.

Working towards Evidence-Based Design Practice

Creating great places is increasingly a global policy priority, given the large body of research which consistently links the quality of our urban built environment – the buildings, streetscapes, and greenspace – to our health, wellbeing and overall quality of life. Our lives are situated in, and shaped through, everyday interactions with place. Yet, as designers know all too well, the process of design is complex. Careful decisions must be made about site selection, configuration, density, orientation, building footprint, open space design and amenities, and the choice of materials, colors, furnishings. Designing places to foster health and wellbeing, across different socio-culturally diverse neighborhoods in different climates, countries and contexts, is not an easy or straightforward task. We can rely on the wonderfully inspiring work of urban design theorists (e.g. Jane Jacobs, Jan Gehl and William Whyte), the current work of organizations such as Project for Public Spaces (PPS.org) in New York City, and the increasing popularity of concepts such as tactical urbanism, design justice, participatory and humanitarian design.

Still, renowned architectural critic and educator Sarah Williams Goldhagen recently concluded that 'boring buildings and sorry places are nearly everywhere we turn' (Goldhagen, 2017, p. 30). A similar passionate, persuasive plea for urban designers, architects and planners to rethink their design practices and methodologies is a key aim of this book. What's more, advanced level books documenting classic design theory – alongside examples in practice – are rare. In practice, designers do not often turn to evidence or theory as a source of inspiration. There are rarely conversations about how to use affordance, prospect-refuge or place attachment theories, or the most recent research findings, as a tool to visualize, adjust, adapt, and improve the design of places.

Creating Great Places addresses this critical practice-theory knowledge gap, arguing that designers need to explicitly reengage with theory. By systematically covering design theories, and directly linking these to examples of practice from across the globe, this book serves as a design theory toolkit – showing design educators, researchers, practitioners, and students how the informed use of evidence and theory helps create great places where people really can thrive. It serves as a critical reminder to those shaping our urban spaces, especially design practitioners, to explicitly use theory in their design process – for example, to think about how design decisions (and a place) might look differently if the lens of personal space theory, or affordance theory, or biophilic design is adopted.

We have labeled this approach, of thinking about a design problem through the lens of different theories, 'theory-storming' (described in detail in Part II). The notion of 'theory-storming' was inspired by Edward de Bono's (1985) Six Thinking Hats which challenges people to think differently – for example, by adopting a green hat of creativity (possibilities, alternatives and new ideas); a red hat of feelings, hunches, and intuition; a black hat of judgement; a yellow hat of brightness and optimism; or a white hat of information known or needed– this book challenges designers to think differently about designing, and to explicitly adopt the different conceptual lenses of six theories. Just as designers might engage in a design charrette or critique, our hope is that this book might more deeply embed theory into practice through a *theory-storming* approach.

This book seeks to shift the dialogue, to inform and change the conversation so that engaging critically with research theory and findings becomes a standard part of design practice. Encouraging designers to think differently, in an imaginative, conceptual and evidence-based way, is a strategy to foster placemaking practice that supports health and wellbeing.

References

Cuthbert, A. R. (2003). *Designing Cities: Critical Readings in Urban Design.* Chichester: Wiley.

de Bono, E. (1985). *Six Thinking Hats: An Essential Approach to Business Management.* New York: Little, Brown & Company.

Goldhagen, S. W. (2017). *Welcome to Your World: How the Built Environment Shapes Our Lives*. New York: HarperCollins.

Hall, E. T. (1966). *The Hidden Dimension*, New York: Anchor Books.

Hamilton, D. K. & Shepley, M. (2010). *Design for Critical Care: An Evidenced-Based Approach*. Oxford: Elsevier.

Hamilton, D. K. & Watkins, D. H. (2009). *Evidence-Based Design for Multiple Building Types*. New York: Wiley & Sons.

McHarg, I. (1969). *Design with Nature*. Garden City, NY: Natural History Press.

Milburn, L.-A., Brown, R., Mulley, S. & Hilts, S. (2003). Assessing Academic Contributions in Landscape Architecture. *Landscape and Urban Planning* 64: 119–129.

Redström, J. (2017). *Making Design Theory*. Cambridge, MA: The MIT Press.

Thwaites, K. (1998). Landscape Design is Research: An Exploration. *Landscape Research* 23(2): 196–198.

WHO. (2017). Constitution of WHO: Principles. Retrieved from www.who.int/about/mission/en.

Part I

Six Critical Theories for Contemporary Urban Design

In Part I, we provide an overview of six theories that are critical for urban design pedagogy and practice. These theories have their origins predominately in geography, anthropology, sociology and psychology. We refer to them throughout the book as design theories to recognize their importance to design. To provide a more complex picture of each theory, we discuss a wide variety of the supporting research evidence. In many cases we also include real-world examples of how this theory can be used in the built environment. Together these theories provide a solid foundation for delving into the four complex global priorities discussed in Part II.

1   Affordance Theory
Take Your Cue

People perceive and interpret different cues in the environment in order to understand the opportunities for action that are supported within that environment. These cues are predominately visual and indicate whether that environment is conducive to a specific activity, if it presents obstacles, or if it prevents the activity from happening entirely. The activities are the *affordances* offered by that environment.

Countless scenes from the 1970s sitcom *Mork and Mindy* portray Mork, an alien from Ork played by Robin Williams, using everyday items in unsuspected ways. Sitting on his head in an armchair, laying across the back of the sofa and wearing a surgeon's mask as a hat were just some of the antics portrayed by the show to get a laugh. But in reality, they demonstrate that intended affordances can be misinterpreted, or actually expanded if we look at them from a different perspective. Although Mork was an alien, he was in some ways no different than a child, or foreigner, first encountering cultural objects and learning how to use them. This scenario reminds us that designing the cues can be critical to the activities that occur, and reinforces the importance of affordance theory for creating great places.

Theoretical Origins of Affordance Theory

Affordance theory was first introduced by perceptual psychologist J. J. Gibson to explain how we perceive our environment and the actionable properties of the spaces around us (Gibson, 1986; Norman, 1999). Our efforts to understand the environment can be instinctive and also purposeful. We perceive and process cues in order to understand the elements in our environment with which we can potentially interact, and then make a choice whether to actually complete those actions we perceive. In this sense, every person is both 'a perceiver *of* the environment and a behaver *in* the environment' (Gibson, 1986, p. 8) and therefore designers must take both into account.

Although Gibson coined the term, it was Donald Norman, a cognitive scientist with an engineering and mathematical psychology background, who helped us understand its relevance for design. Norman's question 'When you first see something you have never seen before, how do you know what to do?' (Norman, 1999, p. 39) has broad appeal to all areas of design. When we first go into a public space that is new, perhaps in a foreign country, how do we know how to act, or what we are allowed and encouraged to do? What cues can designers provide that communicate this information in a subtle but clear way?

In most situations, we don't simply look at the spaces we inhabit, but we evaluate them in terms of a specific purpose or activity (Min & Lee, 2006). Research suggests that we often prefer places that afford the functions that are important and meaningful to us, and are not afforded by other places (Hadavi et al., 2015). These perceived affordances may actually be more important than the physical attributes of a space in influencing – if and how much – we prefer particular settings. For example, when shown photos of park features and asked about their preferred spaces, 68% of the participants focused on the affordances they perceived (what they could do in the space), rather than on which park elements were portrayed (Hadavi et al., 2015, p. 26). Similarly, research on children's preferences for neighborhood spaces found that when a park was deemed important, it was because it supported behavioral opportunities (e.g. shade and nooks for private gathering, paths for bicycle riding, and open areas for sports) (Min & Lee, 2006). And in some cases, affordances are unanticipated, as was the case for a tree in a playground in Sweden which provided opportunities for climbing and other child-friendly activities, outshining the purpose-built play equipment (Laaksoharju & Rappe, 2017).

The affordances that are perceived and actualized in a particular setting often depend on the characteristics of the individual (Heft, 2010). Children and foreigners may have a lack of experience with various cultural activities and social norms, a lack which may impact their use of space and the cues they require. It is equally important to recognize the specific characteristics that we all have as humans, as these can determine how we perceive a space and the activities we participate in. For example, physical characteristics such as height, weight, age and ability will impact what we do in a space. Understanding who is or will be using the space is important in determining which cues need to be provided and which affordances offered.

We perceive our environment at varying scales and forms, and it is this perception that may alter the affordances available. These forms are not separate from each other, but are 'nested' within other forms (Gibson, 1986, p. 9). For example, a leaf is nested within a tree, which is nested along a row of street trees, which may be nested within a leafy neighborhood. However, the form and scale that is relevant to us as an observer depends on many factors, including our vantage point and personal characteristics. If you are standing under a tree in the rain, the size and shape of the individual leaves may be the most important factor in terms of how dry you stay. But if you are viewing the same tree from your car looking down the street, an individual leaf is no longer as relevant, and it is the grouping of trees that creates an aesthetically pleasing space, and a comfortably shaded street.

Similarly, it is important to recognize abstract concepts of permanence, persistence, and change, in reference to the layout and elements that we can perceive within the environment (Gibson, 1986). In a temperate climate, those same trees may lose their leaves in the fall and winter, changing the look and feel of the street, but also perhaps allowing sun to come in and warm up an otherwise cool space. If your house was on that street and the trees afforded privacy for an upstairs bedroom window in the summer, this may dramatically change in the winter and you have to pull the curtains more often to prevent people seeing in. The affordances provided by the trees that are constantly evolving create a dynamic space that may alter our activities. In sustainable urban design practice, discussed in Chapter 10, the affordances of tree selection, height and placement are considered to help optimize human thermal comfort in commercial office buildings – deciduous trees are purposely selected to provide shade in hot summer months, but also to allow the winter sun to penetrate.

Ensuring the Cues Match the Affordances

Cues are critical and 'the art of the designer is to ensure that the desired, relevant actions are readily perceivable' (Norman, 1999, p. 41). Therefore, it is the job of the designer to understand how people will perceive and interpret cues. This is especially true if certain actions are more desired than others or if specific actions are meant to be deterred.

Cues to actions in urban places are often determined by the surfaces, objects, and layout of a space. Some cues are 'natural signals, naturally interpreted, without any need to be conscious of them' (Norman, 1988). This natural interpretation can be the result of the shape of an object. For example, a round door handle or knob is designed to turn. When you see one, you expect to be able to turn the handle and pull the door open. It is because of the way your hand fits nicely around the door handle and your arm is in a better position to pull, rather than push, that your hand-to-handle fit makes sense. This cue is natural and there is no need for signage to indicate otherwise. Similarly, when a door has only a flat metal plate attached to it the natural action is to push the door open. There is nothing to actually hold onto in order to pull. Again, this is a natural cue that doesn't require signage. Yet, when designers work outside of these natural cues and natural actions, things can get difficult, or sometimes embarrassing if you first push a door that has a sign on it saying pull. And let's be honest, we have all done it.

Mapping cues with affordances should be an important step in the design of urban spaces, but doesn't always happen in practice. Norman (1988) discusses the concept of mapping actions to their effects in relation to lighting controls. For example, think about a dimmer switch for ceiling lights that is a single button on a slider moving up and down. If you move the button up, the light gets brighter, if you move it down, it dims until it shuts off completely and the button is at the bottom. This action/movement would be a natural mapping since the action conceptually matches the result.

This mapping can occur, and should occur, at multiple scales. For example, trash bins located in a public place can be mapped in multiple ways. First, the design of the bin should naturally afford throwing trash away. For most designs this means a top that pushes in and swings back into place, or perhaps has a hole that is located on an angle. This affords one-handed use, prevents the top from being taken off and left off, and protects the trash inside from being rained on. The design, however, could also make it easy for animals to get into the trash. If you have ever travelled in bear country in the USA, you'll know that many national parks have bear-proof trash bins that open outward. These are not as intuitive, and definitely not designed for one-handed use, but they do prevent bears from getting in. At a larger scale, a trash bin within the context of an urban space requires other cues to be mapped. Locating them near a food stall or picnic area is important since that is where people will be producing trash. Similarly, placing them at the exit of a movie theatre is an ideal location for people to discard their empty popcorn boxes. Or they can be placed at the entrance to a museum or other important building if people are not allowed to bring food or drinks in with them.

Mapping cues with affordances can also be a useful exercise when designing public spaces that require pedestrian wayfinding. For example, a series of pathways that afford walking from A to B needs to include cues when there are turns or choices. Clear wayfinding cues are particularly important for people with dementia or autism, as discussed in Chapter 9. If you consider the route you use regularly to walk to the store or to your office, or perhaps less frequently to the entrance of a major tourist attraction within a large city, there are a number of cues that you follow. Even when you know the route, there are always choices you make that determine which way you go. It is often the job of a designer or planner to make the route intuitive and clear, and with more complex journeys this is harder to accomplish. Yet, subtle, or not so subtle, cues can lead people in certain directions and get them to where they want to go. Elements such as arbors and gates such as the one shown in Figure 1.1, and design characteristics, such as hierarchies, colors and materials, can provide cues in the environment without relying on signage.

Cues are also important for affordances which are standardized, and can be quite useful in some situations. For example, in certain countries

Figure 1.1 A bougainvillea covered arbor affords a comfortable walking experience and is a recognized city icon at Southbank Parklands in Brisbane,
Australia.

Source: Debra Cushing.

Figure 1.2 A sign painted on a Sydney street indicates which way to look before
crossing.

Source: Debra Cushing.

like Australia and England, you drive and walk on the left. Knowing this is important for safety reasons when driving or cycling, but also in terms of comfort and courtesy when you are walking on a busy sidewalk. When people from countries such as the United States, who drive and walk on the right, visit Australia or England, they usually realize these differences at a macro-level, especially if they rent a car. But they can underestimate how significant the difference is when doing something like crossing the street and looking the wrong way for oncoming traffic. In some cases, a sign is necessary to remind people of the differences for safety reasons. Figure 1.2 shows a reminder painted on a busy urban street in Sydney, Australia. With many one-way streets and international visitors from countries that drive on the right side of the road, cues like these are especially useful in an urban environment.

Perceived versus Real Affordances

Designers can really only influence perceived affordances, or the cues that people see in an environment. What people actually do with an object or in a space is often beyond the influence of the designer. One simple example is a standard dining chair. A furniture designer will focus on height, material, form, color, and other characteristics of the chair that will signal to an adult that it is ideal for sitting at a table. That is the typical and probably the most basic perceived affordance for a chair. But in actuality, an adult can stand on the chair to reach up high, they can put a couple of chairs together to form a bench for laying down, they can use one as a side table next to a bed, they can hang clothes on the chair back, they can prop it under a door handle to keep the door from opening, or they can hold onto the back to steady themselves when doing lunges or yoga poses. If these actions are completed, they represent the actualized affordances. A good designer may in fact think of all of these affordances, but might see them as secondary to the primary affordance of sitting comfortably at the dining table.

When given that same chair, a small child may perceive different affordances. Depending on their age, they may create a fort underneath the chair, or use it as a table when sitting on a stool or the floor. These affordances may not be apparent to an adult unless they have observed how children interact with chairs. Being able to anticipate both the perceived and actualized affordances when designing a chair is somewhat inconsequential as long as the chair is able to serve its main purpose. When designing other spaces and objects, however, anticipating all affordances may be crucial.

Other types of affordances include a false affordance, which is an apparent affordance that does not have a real function. For example, a seat next to a fountain in the lobby or courtyard of an office building that is always wet may not actually be a feasible place to site. People in business suits working in the building do not want to sit there for obvious reasons. Yet, a similar seat next to a fountain on the boardwalk or promenade of a sunny beachfront community may be more acceptable, and perhaps afford a place to cool off when the fountain splashes.

A hidden affordance is one that you wouldn't perceive unless you knew it was there or were creative enough to think of it. For example, if you are not a skateboarder and don't watch skateboarding, you wouldn't necessarily know what elements in an urban plaza are ideal for grinding, ollies, catching air or doing a noseslide, whereas a skateboarder might see a handrail and automatically see the possibilities for doing tricks. Unfortunately for skateboarders, councils are not always open to skateboarding in urban spaces when there are potential conflicts with other people and often introduce barriers or constraints to prevent those affordances. Barriers can also be placed strategically in urban environments to prevent people from sitting on walls or to prevent homeless people from lying on benches, as described briefly in Chapter 3. In some cases, these barriers can actually lead to creative work arounds to maintain the affordance.

Preventing Affordances

There are generally three types of constraints that will prevent someone from taking action: physical, logical and cultural (Norman, 1999). Physical constraints can either be present in the environment (e.g. a closed road or sidewalk) or a characteristic of the person (e.g. a person with a broken leg who cannot climb stairs). A logical constraint requires reason (e.g. a path that continues around a bend, which you cannot see but logically you understand that it will keep going rather than stop). Cultural constraints are conventions specific to a cultural group and are often learned (e.g. knowing to push the button at a crosswalk to get a walk signal or understanding how to call an elevator and take it to a specific floor).

Some people will find ways to overcome constraints. An example that we often see in urban parks is a desire line, a pathway that wasn't specifically designed into or afforded by the space, but is created by the people using it. We often see evidence of this when an open grass area or landscape planting is worn from people walking on it, to get from A to B in a more direct manner than the formal path allows. The people who designed and created the space didn't anticipate the paths people wanted to follow, which is almost always the most direct route. Instead they created a barrier that was easily overcome, enabling people to create a desire line or worn path within the landscape, such as the one shown in Figure 1.3. Although a thorough understanding of how people move

Figure 1.3 This scene in NYC's Central Park shows a clear desire line where people have taken a short cut down the hill.

Source: Debra Cushing.

through space will help preempt these desire lines, sometimes good design means making an adjustment afterward rather than increasing or reinforcing the barriers. For example, desire lines are commonly generated by large numbers of students taking shortcuts across open areas on university campuses in the US, which have large lawn areas or quads. When maintenance staff are responsive and willing to adjust, rather than obstinate, these desire lines eventually become official pathways and are maintained as such.

Behavior Settings and Programming

Affordances and the subsequent actions that occur together within a particular place can be referred to as a behavior setting (Heft, 1989). These settings often include the assembly of people, activities, and objects within small-scale social situations (Popov & Chompalov, 2012). For designers, understanding how affordances can be combined within a behavior setting is a key aspect of programming a space to ensure it successfully accommodates the intended users and activities.

Programming a space or building can sometimes be a confusing concept. It is critical to design spaces that effectively afford activities that do not conflict with each other. It is also critical to ensure they are successfully used both for what is intended and for other activities that arise. Programming a space within an urban setting requires knowledge of the potential activities and the needs of the people using the space. An urban plaza intended to accommodate outdoor concerts may require a raised area or stage for performers, a large open area for seating, a power source for lighting or electrical instruments, storage for seats or other equipment, a place to offer refreshments, bins for the garbage generated, nearby parking, restroom facilities, and countless other amenities. The location of these elements in relation to each other is critical. Space needs to be provided if there will be a long queue for the restrooms or food. Likewise, if people need to leave early, they don't want to walk in front of the stage and interrupt the experience for others. Careful programming of all of the affordances in a space is therefore critical to creating a great place.

Another example is the design of community parks to afford opportunities for physical activity. How can we design spaces that afford exercise and get people active? In many parts of the world there is an obesity epidemic. As many as three in four people do not get enough daily physical activity. Designing spaces that are appropriate for exercise is the first step. The spaces also must be free from smog, safe from traffic and crime, and not too exposed to the elements. Then there are cues that can determine whether people actually do the exercise. For example, a fit person can run anywhere. But someone who is not used to running, may be more inclined to do it only if there is a purpose-built multi-use path with mileage markers, signs about the benefits of running, shaded areas, and other cues that indicate clearly that the space is perfect for running. Thinking about affordances for different people is a good strategy for creating a salutogenic environment, a topic discussed in depth in Chapter 7.

Multiple Affordances in One Setting

As a behavior setting, places should be designed to offer multiple affordances, with the objects or elements within these spaces also designed for multi-use. Research on the affordances of trees in a garden setting determined that children use trees as building materials to construct huts, nests and furnishings, and to demarcate an area; as play props to represent food, tools, weapons, and toys; for decoration to beautify spaces and clothing; and simply for climbing (Laaksoharju & Rappe, 2017). While these activities may not always be appropriate in public spaces in busy urban settings, it is important to recognize that accommodating multiple affordances can sometimes lead to a richer, more enjoyable experience within a space.

The Project for Public Spaces organization, based in NYC, developed a concept called the 'Power of 10+' (PPS, undated) to suggest that places with more affordances are more effective. This concept works at multiple scales, with the place scale focusing on affordances. A successful public place should have at least 10 things for people to do. These 10 things should ideally be layered, some occurring at the same time, and some at different times. And some planned affordances should be unique and reflect the culture and heritage of that place. Capitalizing on the unique qualities of a specific place ties into the concept of *genius loci* or sense of place discussed in Chapter 4.

A space that offers multiple affordances is usually considered ideal. Anything single-use is out. In fact, CNN reported that 'single-use' is the 2018 word of the year, as chosen by the *Collins English Dictionary* (Kolirin, 2018). Although single-use is more typically used in reference to plastic bags and water bottles that are used once and thrown away, it is equally appropriate for urban spaces. Designing so that something can be used by multiple people, at multiple times of day and for multiple purposes is critical, particularly in a time when resources are scarce and urban densification is real. We no longer have the luxury of letting spaces sit unused for periods of time, not to mention that unused spaces can become unsafe areas attracting crime, and are simply uninviting.

The multi-use idea is ideally portrayed within the 'Complete Streets' concept, which highlights street design that affords multiple activities for many different people in one space. We've all seen streets designed only for cars, where pedestrians and cyclists risk their lives when trying to share the road, or walk along the side. To counteract this, the Smart Growth America organization promotes complete streets that include multiple affordances to accommodate multiple activities. The program suggests the provision of 'sidewalks, bike lanes (or wide paved shoulders), special bus lanes, comfortable and accessible public transportation stops, frequent and safe crossing opportunities, median islands, accessible pedestrian signals, curb extensions, narrower travel lanes, roundabouts, and more' to create streets that are more complete than the car-only designs (Smart Growth America, undated).

Understanding Affordances to Make Places Better

Affordance theory can ensure that urban design is both aesthetically pleasing and functional. It is relevant to countless contexts and is especially relevant when designing urban spaces for people to use effectively, safely and to benefit their wellbeing. Not only do activities need to be accommodated, people need to be given cues for which activities are possible, so they actually participate. It is not enough to think that 'if we build it, they will come' as they did in the *Field of Dreams* baseball movie. We need to send out proper invites through the use of strategic and intuitive cues that give people direction and let them know what is possible.

Creating great places requires designers to understand the limitations and barriers people face when trying to do activities in urban spaces, both simple and complex. Understanding how they will interpret the cues for these activities is critical, and depends on both the designed environment and their personal characteristics. In Chapter 9 we discuss the concept of age-friendly inclusive design which focuses more specifically on designing places that accommodate different needs and abilities. And, as the following chapter illustrates, while designers are quite comfortable with the language of affordance, they are much less fluent with the well-known, but under-researched theory of prospect-refuge.

References

Gibson, J. J. (1986). *The Ecological Approach to Visual Perception*. Mahwah, NJ: Lawrence Erlbaum Associates. (Originally published in 1979.)

Hadavi, S., Kaplan, R. & Hunter, M. C. (2015). Environmental Affordances: A Practical Approach for Design of Nearby Settings in Urban Residential Areas. *Landscape and Urban Planning* 134: 19–32.

Heft, H. (1989). Affordances and the Body: An Intentional Analysis of Gibson's Ecological Approach to Visual Perception. *Journal for the Theory Social Behavior* 19(1): 19–30.

Heft, H. (2010). Affordances and the Perception of Landscape: An Inquiry into Environmental Perception and Aesthetics. In C. W. Thompson, P. Aspinall & S. Bell (Eds.), *Innovative Approaches to Researching Landscape and Health*. Abingdon: Routledge, 9–32.

Kolirin, L. (2018). Single-Use is Collins' Word of the Year for 2018. Retrieved from https://edition.cnn.com/2018/11/06/health/word-of-year-scli-intl/index.html

Laaksoharju, T. & Rappe, E. (2017). Trees as Affordances for Connectedness to Place – a Framework to Facilitate Children's Relationship with Nature. *Urban Forestry and Urban Greening* 28: 150–159.

Min, B. & Lee, J. (2006). Children's Neighborhood Place as a Psychological and Behavioral Domain. *Journal of Environmental Psychology* 26: 51–71.

Norman, D. A. (1988). *The Design of Everyday Things*. New York: Currency Doubleday.

Norman, D. A. (1999). Affordance, Conventions, and Design. *Interactions* (May/June): 38–43.

Popov, L. & Chompalov, I. (2012). Crossing Over: The Interdisciplinary Meaning of Behavior Setting Theory. *International Journal of Humanities and Social Science* 2: 19.

PPS. (undated). The Power of 10+. Retrieved from www.pps.org/article/the-power-of-10

Smart Growth America. (undated). What are Complete Streets? Retrieved from https://smartgrowthamerica.org/program/national-complete-streets-coalition/publications/what-are-complete-streets

2 Prospect-Refuge Theory
Now You See Me, Now You Don't

Prospect-refuge theory describes the concept that people in public spaces feel most comfortable and prefer spaces that allow them to observe what is happening around them, while also being slightly protected. They have *prospect* (or views outward), while also having a sense of *refuge* (or protection).

In the 1950s classic thriller *Rear Window* by Alfred Hitchcock, Jeff played by James Stewart, is confined to a wheelchair in his Greenwich Village apartment in New York City. His rear window looks out onto the courtyard of the apartment building and gives Jeff an idle vantage point through which to watch the activities of his neighbors, while being obscured in the safety of his own apartment. Although staged for cinematic drama, this is a prime example of prospect-refuge. Jeff can see what his neighbors are up to, even when they are up to no good, without them seeing him.

Theoretical Origins of Prospect-Refuge

Prospect-refuge theory is arguably one of the most well-known environmental preference theories, and used most often in architectural, interior design, landscape architecture and urban design disciplines (Dosen & Ostwald, 2016; Senoglu et al., 2018). It is also probably one of the most straight-forward and easiest to remember, due in part to the catchy phrase associated with it 'see without being seen' (Appleton, 1996, p. 66). It is a critical theory for designers to better understand how people might feel in a space in regards to the spatial arrangement of seating and activity areas.

Prospect-refuge theory was first coined by British geographer Jay Appleton in his book, *The Experience of Landscape*, first published in 1975 (revised edition 1996). Although not a landscape architect or urban designer, Appleton's book is considered a seminal work about landscapes and has significantly influenced urban design thought and practice. Prospect-refuge theory references our hunter–gatherer evolutionary beginnings, when people needed to see out into the landscape while being protected from predators. Today, it has important implications for safety

Figure 2.1 The iconic Salk Institute in La Jolla, California was designed by architect Louis Kahn and is a classic representation of prospect-refuge.

Source: Natalie Wright.

in public spaces, as well as placemaking interventions that involve simple people watching, public events, and performances. The theory suggests that we prefer environments that offer both prospect and refuge because they make it possible to anticipate threats and opportunities and, therefore, protect ourselves from harm (Singh & Ellard, 2012).

To better understand prospect-refuge, let's start with an example from everyday life. If you have ever been walking or cycling on a mixed-use pathway that has a blind corner, it can be uncomfortable, if not downright scary. We often feel the need to peer around the corner – with caution – in case there is another cyclist coming the other way. We do *not* have good prospect-refuge. We can't see what is coming, and we have very little escape if we need to get out of the way quickly. We are not protected, but are vulnerable. Or at least we *feel* vulnerable, which is just as important. In cases when this is unavoidable, designers use techniques such as mirrors to give people a view of what is coming around the bend. And industrial designers have actually created a new 'smart helmet' that uses video streaming technology to give riders advance warning of impending hazards.

Appleton explains how our innate qualities and behaviors influence how we explore the environment and choose places that enable us to complete certain tasks. This is similar to affordance theory described in Chapter 1. A non-human animal, on the other hand, tends to prefer environments that satisfy all of its needs. As Appleton describes:

> aesthetic satisfaction, experienced in the contemplation of landscape, stems from the spontaneous perception of landscape features which, in their shapes, colors, spatial arrangements and other visible attributes, act as a sign-stimuli indicative of environmental conditions favorable to survival, whether they really *are* or not.
>
> (Appleton, 1996, p. 62; emphasis in original).

These landscape preferences can be considered together to form the basis of *habitat theory*. Habitat theory relates the human observer to the perceived landscape in a similar way to the animal with its habitat, asserting that 'satisfaction which we derive from the contemplation of this environment, and which we call 'aesthetic,' arises from the spontaneous reaction to that environment as a habitat, that is to say as a place which affords the opportunity for achieving our simple biological needs' (Appleton, 1996, p. 63). More simply, we have a preference for places that provide what we inherently need as humans.

Aligned with habitat theory, but more directly focused on certain actions, prospect-refuge theory specifically addresses our biological needs that are met by exploring, observing, escaping, and shelter-seeking. As Appleton explains, 'the ability to see without being seen is an intermediate step in the satisfaction of many [biological] needs, the capacity of an environment to ensure the achievement of *this* becomes a more immediate source of aesthetic satisfaction' (Appleton, 1996, p. 66; emphasis in original). The aesthetic impact of the environment could be discussed in terms of evolutionary circumstances related to humans' 'deep-seated behavioral mechanism.' The environment underlies the preference to find pleasure in landscapes that offer points of vantage, and also furnish security or refuge from hazards (Clamp & Powell, 1982, p. 7). For example, if given the option, people generally prefer to sit around the edge of a space – so their backs are protected and are partially covered.

Prospect versus Refuge

Designers need to consider the choice and arrangement of objects and site elements so that they symbolize prospect *and* refuge. What is intended by the designer and what is perceived and experienced by people using a space can differ. How a space is designed and which elements are included can determine whether people feel comfortable and safe. The balance of symbols and whether they form a prospect-dominant or refuge-dominant environment is also important (Appleton, 1996).

Sometimes multiple elements representing one aspect, such as refuge, can reinforce each other. Consider for example, the romantic notion of a cottage in a wooded grove. Both the cottage and the woodland each represent a refuge, and when seen together reinforce this idea. However, the woodland may also conceal hazards by limiting prospect and/or limiting movement, so the lines between prospect and refuge become slightly blurred and depend on the specific situation and characteristics of the user, such as gender, age, and experience.

A refuge can be symbolic in terms of function, origin, substance, accessibility and efficacy (Appleton, 1996). In terms of scale, it also needs to be proportionate to the person using it for protection or shelter. For example, a bus shelter needs to provide protection from the weather, enable pedestrians to walk by, be protected from traffic on the adjacent road, and still fit within the context of the sidewalk or footpath. Likewise, the shelter must afford a view of the approaching bus and other relevant hazards in order to effectively serve its purpose. If people need to constantly peer around the shelter or move out of it to get a clear view, it is not an effective refuge, even when it is a recognized symbol of a refuge. Chapter 9 continues this bus shelter example, evaluating it using the theory-storming approach.

Within a design context, the concept of refuge can be limiting, since it implies that there is a need to retreat from danger or trouble. Some researchers prefer a more inclusive concept of shelter. Hudson (1992) suggests that a shelter functions as protection from both animate and inanimate objects, and that protection from inanimate objects such as the weather, is probably a more common consideration in public spaces today. Shelters are often seen in the modern urban landscape as gazebos, awnings, balconies and verandas, among others. When designed well, these types of shelters include prospect, which can be a panorama or vista. A *panorama* is a wide view from a good vantage point, usually from high-points in the landscape or from the tops of buildings or structures. A *vista* is a view that is constricted, often by the arrangement of objects. A vista into a park could be created, for example, by placing hedges on either side of a gate, blocking the view into the park other than through the gate.

The quality of the view is also dependent on the amount of light that allows people to take advantage of prospect. Whether there is ample light at the location of the viewer, as well as the location of what is being viewed, are important considerations. Designers must also consider how to focus a person's attention on a view and strategically choose what is being viewed. Determining what is hidden from view can be an important design decision when there is something unsightly in the vicinity, or a delightful opportunity if there is a unique or interesting view to be had.

The ability and freedom of movement is especially important during the assessment of hazards, offering the opportunity to move between key positions within the prospect-refuge scenario. Impediment hazards discussed above often restrict movement. The opportunity for movement must also be perceived by the person, as we discussed in relation to affordance theory in the last chapter. Ideally, opportunities for movement are obvious, such as a pathway that connects two areas and leads directly through an impediment (such as a gate within a wall). And according to prospect-refuge theory, those places which offer both will be preferred.

Implications for Health and Wellbeing

Although prospect-refuge can be considered an easy theory to comprehend, it has complex implications for health and wellbeing within urban spaces. Once understood, we start to see the theory in action everywhere. And ideally, we start to understand how important it is for people who use these urban spaces on a daily basis. It not only impacts safety and security, both perceived and actual, but also our ability to socialize. Good use of prospect-refuge theory facilitates our desire to spend time in public spaces that are engaging and enriching, enabling us to be part of a community.

People have an inherent need to feel safe in urban spaces. Fear of crime or hazards can often overshadow other human needs and can limit people's activities and daily lives (Cinar & Cubukcu, 2012). The urban environment often presents two types of hazards:

- *Incident hazards* are those which threaten a person's wellbeing and come from an external incident. They can be animate, such as from other people, or inanimate, such as hazards posed by inclement weather.
- *Impediment hazards* are those which prevent the freedom of movement and do not directly pose a 'threat' to the survival or wellbeing of a person. Impediment hazards can be natural, such as a thick cluster of vegetation that you cannot walk through, or artificial, such as a wall or busy highway (Appleton, 1996).

How people perceive the hazard is critical for designers to determine the use of public urban spaces, and is influenced by both the personal characteristics of the individual and the physical environment. Prospect-refuge theory encourages designers to be mindful of people being able to see approaching danger and having a place of refuge to hide or protect themselves from that danger. These dangers can include being attacked or mugged, but can also relate to traffic, falling objects, and weather related dangers. It is important to remember that feeling safe and being safe are not the same thing, but are both important. Consider a child who is scared of a dancing shadow on their wall. They are intensely scared by what they see, imagining it is something sinister or evil. In reality, the shadow is the result of a street light shining through a partially closed curtain, swaying with the breeze from an open window. Until the child realizes and accepts this, the reality is of little consequence. To seek refuge from the perceived danger, the child might hide under the bed or in a small space where they feel protected but still have a view out, as seen in countless suspense thrillers. For them, prospect-refuge enables them to feel safe (and perhaps get a good night sleep) regardless of whether they are actually in any danger.

It is the concept of probabilistic functionalism that researchers say enables people to extract relevant information from nearby cues to appraise their environment (van Rijswijk, Rooks & Haans, 2016). These appraisals are subjective. People will appraise the cues in their immediate or proximate surroundings to decide whether a place is safe or not for them, and individual characteristics such as gender, often impact feelings of safety. For example, a hiding spot in an urban park can be perceived as positive or negative depending on whether someone is the potential victim or potential offender (van Rijswijk et al., 2016). Women have also reported increased perceptions of danger in environments with higher levels of entrapment (Blöbaum & Hunecke, 2005). If urban environments are to be considered inclusive, as we discuss further in Chapter 9, then it is critical that individual and group characteristics be considered in any design and planning process.

Yet, it is impossible to understand and address the different personal characteristics of all potential users, especially when these may be in conflict. Research suggests that 30% of the perceptions of safety of night-time urban environments can be attributed to personal characteristics. The other 70% is attributed to the environmental characteristics. Designers can directly address these environmental characteristics, which often include the layout of a space. For example, higher levels of entrapment were associated with lower perceived environmental safety and when people judge an environment as a place that represents entrapment (limiting their ability to flee the scene or seek help from passers-by), they will often perceive a space to be unsafe (van Rijswijk et al., 2016). In contrast, higher levels of prospect and outlook were positively associated with judgments of environmental safety, evidence that prospect-refuge theory is important to understand when designing safe urban spaces.

However, there is perhaps a fine line between entrapment and refuge. The dark alley scenario seen on countless crime shows is a case in point. An actor playing either a criminal or potential victim, runs into a rather dark alley only to find a wall or fence at the end of it, which requires serious parkour skills to climb or jump over. Yet Paley Park, the well-known pocket park in New York City, is an example of a refuge that works. If you consider the layout of the space, seen in Figure 2.2, you might think it would create feelings of entrapment. In fact, it is a very popular and well-used park because it also includes design features that enhance

Figure 2.2 Because of the design characteristics of Paley Park in New York City, it does not induce feelings of entrapment.

Source: Kathia Shieh.

the quality of the space, including a lighted waterfall on the back wall, windows from neighboring buildings that overlook the space, and a gate that closes at night. And despite its small size, it is wider than a typical alleyway which creates a more inviting space.

Safety is also addressed through CPTED (crime prevention through environmental design), an approach first discussed by criminologist, C. Ray Jeffrey as early as 1971, and further developed by criminologist Tim Crowe (1994). The CPTED principles align with prospect-refuge theory. The concept of defensible space, developed by architect Oscar Newman (1996), further reinforces the need for both prospect and refuge to ensure safety in cities. Newman evaluated different housing scenarios, combining the concept of prospect-refuge, surveillance, and territoriality with other concepts such as access control, lighting, and regular maintenance, to design safer housing developments.

Similar to the role of viewing within a prospect-refuge scenario is the concept of natural surveillance. Natural surveillance of a public space refers to people observing or watching over that space informally, without the use of security cameras. Although, this may conjure images of Gladys Kravitz, the extremely nosy neighbor with the irritating voice on the 1960s American sitcom *Bewitched*, it is actually the idea that people are able to observe what is happening in a space which can serve as a crime deterrent. In her classic book *The Death and Life of Great American Cities*, Jane Jacobs (1961) discussed this concept as 'eyes on the street' to highlight the importance of having neighbors and community members watch over a space.

Implications for Placemaking and Social Engagement

Countless cities globally are currently focused on placemaking strategies to reinvigorate urban areas and to encourage a greater sense of community. Designing spaces that do this can feel like trial and error at times, borrowing successful strategies that work in some cities, only to find they don't work as well in other contexts. As designers, however, we must actively engage with the best evidence-based practice and research as a way to foster great places. Regardless of the site-specific design elements, providing opportunities for prospect and refuge are key to creating a successful urban space where people want to spend time. An iconic front porch on a busy residential street, commonly promoted in new urbanist principles, offers a great example of prospect-refuge designed to enable people to observe their street and engage in friendly conversation with their neighbors. This design can also be seen in the sidewalk cafes of Paris that look out to busy pedestrian areas, perfect for people watching while sipping cappuccinos and eating croissants. Elevating this concept to the High Line park in New York City sees a viewing platform provide the ultimate prospect of street life in the Chelsea neighborhood, as shown in Figure 2.3. It is simply a great place to watch people. And as William H. Whyte matter-of-factly pointed out in his classic film *The Social Life of Small Urban Spaces*, people like to watch other people (Whyte et al., 2012).

As a park built on an abandoned elevated rail line, the High Line park is a great example of prospect-refuge and its popularity is testament to the importance of this theory. Offering countless opportunities for prospect, including views of the Statue of Liberty, Freedom Tower, the Hudson River, the Whitney Art Museum, and many typical New York City streets in Manhattan, the park affords a different experience of New York City that is not common for a park (Cushing & Pennings, 2017). Although the sense of refuge is less prominent, it is still provided by plantings, walls from adjacent brick buildings, and subtle changes in elevation throughout the park. The recent undulating residential building constructed next to the park on West 28th Street, designed by the late architect Zaha Hadid, also puts the concept of prospect-refuge to the test. With large windows facing the High Line, park visitors can catch a glimpse into the high-end condominium units at the same time that residents of the building can gaze onto the park from the protected vantage point of their unit. This perhaps raises important questions about how we can best use this theory in urban design.

Figure 2.3 The High Line park in New York City offers a viewing amphitheater at 10th Avenue that affords an ideal prospect-refuge experience.

Source: Debra Cushing.

Prospect-Refuge for Children

Although it may be difficult to address all user needs with a single design, it is important to recognize vulnerable populations that are more at risk of feeling or being unsafe or uncomfortable in an urban environment. Chapter 8 discusses some of these considerations in more detail, but here we briefly focus on prospect-refuge theory in relation to young people.

If you remember your childhood, or have a child yourself, you probably know that preschool age children like to create secret spaces or refuges. My favorite was creating a fort in our living room with sofa cushions, blankets, dining room chairs, and a broomstick to act as a tent pole. Or you may observe children getting more enjoyment from playing with and hiding inside a large box that a toy came in, than from the actual toy itself. Research shows that children as young as three years understand secret hiding places and have expressed a desire to play in places that offer shadows where they can be hidden from view and feel safe (Corson, Colwell, Bell & Trejos-Castillo, 2014; Colwell et al., 2016). These spaces offer refuge from adults or older children, giving them a sense of security and safety and the freedom to play loudly, offering more of a psychological barrier, than a physical one. This use of space supports the notion that children prefer spaces where they can remain separate from adults and where they can be selective about who they let into their secret places. They often want autonomy and could even use 'magic powers' to create a sense of not being seen by adults. Such behavior suggests that safety for young children includes being seen by adults, but pretending not to be seen. With either a playful or serious intent, *now you see me, now you don't* becomes the motto for children in this context.

Understanding how children perceive and use space is important for designing spaces that are inclusive and supportive. Designing child-friendly cities means asking the question (as we do in Chapter 8) about how we translate children's preferences for refuge into urban design solutions, given that young people still need adult supervision and are often more at risk to everyday hazards, such as traffic.

Digging Deeper: Investigating Prospect-Refuge in Urban Spaces

Using research to better understand how people interact with, use and feel about the urban environment is a critical step in creating better places. Designers, planners and policymakers can partner with skilled researchers at universities or other research institutes to gather empirical evidence in order to support future design and planning decisions. It is important to use appropriate and innovative methods that really do elucidate new information and verify, or perhaps discount, assumptions that are often made. Some of these methods are presented below, acknowledging that these examples are far from comprehensive.

An analysis of 30 studies that investigated prospect-refuge theory using social science methods showed that most asked participants to rate images or other stimuli for aspects such as preference and comfort (Dosen & Ostwald, 2013). Approximately half of the 30 studies used real environments and half used virtual environments that were computer generated. Of those that used real environments, only two took participants on-site and incorporated actual conditions. Other considerations for this type of research include sample size and participant characteristics, the influence of design style represented in the images, and the amount of time participants were allowed to view the images or scene. In all cases, best practices should be followed when designing a study to evaluate prospect-refuge theory, focusing on the desired outcome and the limitations of each method.

One popular method is photo-elicitation, used by van Rijswijk et al. (2016) to better understand the level of environmental safety of urban environments. The researchers used a large set of photographs previously judged on prospect, concealment, and entrapment and calibrated by a panel of judges, to ask a series of five-point scale questions. For example: *How good or poor an overview do you have over this environment?* This method helps us better understand how a person may perceive and compare environments they may potentially encounter, enabling a researcher to keep constant the variables related to personal characteristics of the participants and environmental conditions, such as weather.

Recognizing the Importance of Prospect-Refuge

Prospect-refuge theory is a critical theory for understanding and designing places that people find most comfortable. The perception and reality of safety are both equally important for people's wellbeing. Having a view of what is around us, and being somewhat protected from hazards, enables us to feel comfortable and less vulnerable in urban spaces. Environments that offer good prospect-refuge can also afford community engagement, opportunities for people-watching and public performances, while also being generally neighborly. In the next chapter, we turn our attention to personal space theory.

References

Appleton, J. (1996). *The Experience of Landscape*. Chichester: Wiley and Sons.
Blöbaum, A. & Hunecke, M. (2005). Perceived Danger in Urban Public Space: The Impacts of Physical Features and Personal Factors. *Environment and Behavior* 37(4): 465–486.

Cinar, E. & Cubukcu, E.(2012), The Influence of Micro Scale Environmental Characteristics on Crime and Fear. *Procedia – Social and Behavioral Sciences* 35: 83–88.

Clamp, P. & Powell, M. (1982). Prospect-Refuge Theory under Test. *Landscape Research* 7(3): 7–8.

Colwell, M., Gaines, K., Pearson, M., Corson, K., Wright, H. & Logan, B. (2016). Space, Place, and Privacy: Preschool Children's Secret Hiding Places. *Family and Consumer Sciences Research Journal* 44(4): 412–421.

Corson, K., Colwell, M. J., Bell, N. J. & Trejos-Castillo, E. (2014). Wrapped Up in Covers: Preschoolers' Secrets and Secret Hiding Places. *Early Child Development and Care* 184(12): 1769–1786.

Crowe, T. (1994). Understanding CPTED. *Planning Commissioners Journal* 16: 5.

Cushing, D. & Pennings, M. (2017). Potential Affordances of Public Art in Public Parks: Central Park and the High Line. Urban Design and Planning: *Proceedings of the Institute of Civil Engineers* 170(6): 245–257.

Dosen, A. S. & Oswald, M. J. (2013). Methodological Characteristics of Research Testing Prospect-Refuge Theory: A Comparative Analysis, *Architectural Science Review* 56(3): 232–241.

Dosen, A. S. & Oswald, M. J. (2016). Evidence for Prospect-Refuge Theory: A Meta-analysis of the Findings of Environmental Preference Research. *City, Territory and Architecture* 3(4): 1–14.

Hudson, B. (1992). Hunting or a Sheltered Life: Prospects and Refuges Reviewed. *Landscape and Urban Planning* 22: 53–57.

Jacobs, J. (1961). *The Death and Life of Great American Cities*. New York: Random House.

Newman, O. (1996). *Creating Defensible Space*. Washington, DC: US Department of Housing and Urban Development Office of Policy Development and Research.

Senoglu, B., Oktay, H. E. & Kinoshita, I. (2018). An Empirical Research Study on Prospect– Refuge Theory and the Effect of High-Rise Buildings in a Japanese Garden Setting. *City, Territory and Architecture* 5(3): 1–16.

Singh, P. & Ellard, C. (2012). Functional Analysis of Concealment: A Novel Application of Prospect-Refuge Theory. *Behavioural Processes* 91: 22–25.

van Rijswijk, L., Rooks, G. & Haans, A. (2016). Safety in the Eye of the Beholder: Individual Susceptibility to Safety-Related Characteristics of Nocturnal Urban Spaces. *Journal of Environmental Psychology* 45: 103–115.

Whyte, W., Kanopy & Municipal Art Society of New York (2012). *The Social Life of Small Urban Spaces: A Film*. Subiaco, WA: Kanopy [distributor].

3   Personal Space Theory
Keep Your Distance!

Personal space theory, also known as proxemics, is the study of how people use the physical space surrounding their body. It is the language of space, and our innate need to keep a certain physical distance from others.

Of the 7.7 billion people living on Earth, more than half live in cities. Whether in high-density apartments, sprawling suburbs, or chaotic informal settlements, our experience of cities can vary dramatically. Whether we live in Las Vegas, Jakarta or Melbourne, however, we each carry an invisible 'personal space bubble' that helps us negotiate space. This instinctive invisible protective zone, memorably described by neuroscientist Michael Graziano (2018) as the 'bad breath zone, the duck-and-flinch buffer,' explains why we tend to feel uncomfortable when a stranger sits too close on crowded public transportation and why we tend to stand closer to our good friends, than our boss. How we perceive, manage, behave and feel in physical space is the essence of personal space theory. This chapter documents why and how personal space theory remains very relevant for designers, drawing on practical examples from public seating, workplaces, and building design.

The Origins of Personal Space Theory

The first to observe the concept of personal space, in animals, was zoo biologist and animal psychologist Haini Hediger (1908–1992). The successive director of the Bern, Basel, and Zurich Zoos, Hediger observed that animals are bound by a myriad of invisible natural space-time limitations that restrict their territory and behavior. Animals naturally maintained a remarkably constant distance between one another and seemed to communicate through non-verbal body movements, behaving differently depending on their distance from other animals. Hediger's concepts of biological social distance, flight distance, defense, and personal space in animals, outlined in *Wild Animals in Captivity* (1950), established the theoretical foundation for subsequent human social distance theories.

Cultural anthropologist and cross-cultural researcher, Edward T. Hall (1914–2009), was especially intrigued by Hediger's concepts. Hall taught intercultural communication skills to American diplomats, and

Figure 3.1 Maintaining personal space is challenging in dense urban settings, whether on public transit or crossing a busy street in Santiago, Chile.

Source: Mauro Mora, Unsplash, CC.

had observed similar cross-cultural patterns in human spatial behavior. North and South Americans, for example, would mistakenly interpret each other as being too 'pushy' or 'cold' for simply standing either too close or too far away. Hall subsequently explored the micro-level aspects of space, time and culture in several seminal books including *The Silent Language* (1959) and *The Hidden Dimension* (1966). Hall coined the term 'proxemics,' which he defined as the 'study of how man[1] unconsciously structure microspace – the distance between men in the conduct of daily transactions, the organization of space in his house and buildings, and ultimately the layout of his towns' (Hall, 1963, p. 1003).

In *The Hidden Dimension*, Hall persuasively argued that space speaks as loudly as words, with meaning communicated by the distances people establish between themselves and others. Hall made two core arguments, which today are the basis for our understanding of personal space. First, spatial interpretation is generally hidden and outside our conscious awareness (hence the title of his book, *The Hidden Dimension*). Second, all people implicitly learn the rules and cues about space from their culture, with expectations and individual personal space boundaries culturally determined. Hall identified four distinct interpersonal zones: intimate, personal, social and public, which continue to provide important guidance for contemporary designers. How Hall visualized personal space as a series of invisible spheres, progressing from intimate to public interactions, is illustrated in the list of zones and Figure 3.2 below. Understanding this language of space is critical for designers since as Hall explained, 'if one sees man surrounded by a series of invisible bubbles which have measurable dimensions, architecture can be seen in a new light' (Hall, 1966, p. 121). A notable limitation of Hall's spatial taxonomy was that it was developed from a North American cultural context. However, as the next section describes, despite some individual and cultural nuances, this spatial pattern generally holds. Hall also originally separated each zone into close and far phases, a distinction rarely used in subsequent research.

- **Zone 1: intimate distance.** Within half a meter (15–45 cm, 6–18 inches), this space is for loved ones only. At this distance, the close presence of the other person is unmistakable and at times, overwhelming – you

Intimate Distance   Personal Distance   Social Distance

'drawing is not to scale

Manspreading   She-bagging

Figure 3.2 Visualizing and protecting space boundaries – 'manspreading' and 'she-bagging.'

Source: Sketch by Ama Hayyu Marzuki.

can see, feel, smell, hear and touch the other person's body. This is the distance of trust, affection and intimacy; for whispering, touching, embracing, comforting, love-making, and protecting. People normally only enter this intimate distance zone with permission, and are people we are emotional close to (family, lovers, close friends). To enter this close space without permission is an aggressive act.

- **Zone 2: personal distance.** From 0.5 to 1.2 meters (45–120 cm, 1.5–4 feet), personal distance is 'arm's length.' It is for interactions among family and friends. When seated in such close proximity to strangers (for example, on an airplane or train), this close contact often makes us feel a little uncomfortable.
- **Zone 3: social distance.** From 1.2 to 4 meters (4–12 feet), this social distance space is for everyday interactions with acquaintances such as co-workers in business meetings, or groups in social settings. At this distance, interactions are more formal and the voices are louder.
- **Zone 4: public distance.** Greater than 4 meters (12 feet+), this is the distance of the lecture hall, large meetings and with powerful individuals. It is considered the distance at which you can safely ignore another person. In a glance, people can see the whole body, but have to speak louder and cannot pick up subtle nuances.

Being within someone's personal space boundaries can be either positive or negative. For example, the phrase 'to be in someone's face' is often used as a threat. United States President Donald Trump is an example of someone who frequently breaks conventional personal space norms with his close physical positioning making people feel uncomfortable. During the second 2016 presidential debate, he frequently invaded Hillary Clinton's personal space, standing unusually close to her. Our personal space boundaries function as an invisible zone of safety around our bodies. When others intrude our personal space, without our permission, we feel uncomfortable and anxious.

Consider your own experiences and instinctive behaviors in very crowded public spaces. In a packed elevator, do you stand quietly, avoid eye contact and look at your feet? When a stranger invades your public space at a function, standing and talking very close to you, do you instinctively step back? The last time you were in an airport-waiting lounge, what seat did you select? Did you try to sit apart from other waiting passengers, claiming 'your space' by placing your belongings on an empty seat beside you? (she-bagging in Figure 3.2).

The quintessential example of personal space theory is how we behave on public transportation. All free seating rows will only have one person on them, unless people are travelling in groups. It is only when every row has one occupant that strangers will start to sit next to each other. Our instinctive responses in each of these situations illustrate how personal space theory and proxemics remains an important, often invisible force shaping the rhythms, flows, activities, and experiences of everyday life.

Thinking Territorially

Space, and the claiming and marking of defensible public space through devices, is also an indicator of cultural norms, situational factors, and power. Territoriality is a behavior that indicates a person's control over an area, using invisible or visible boundaries. It reflects a basic need to have a space, with Sommer (1969) identifying four territorial categories: public, home, interactional and body. Public territory includes the places in which everyone has free access, such as streets and parks. Boundaries are often unmarked, so people may mark out their own territory with personal items such as bags, books, coats and water bottles. Lying across a park bench, putting down a picnic blanket or rug, or leaving your drink bottle on a table when you briefly move away are all examples of marking out your territory and physically 'claiming your space' in public spaces. The bottom image in Figure 3.2 illustrates how men and women use both their bodies and possessions to claim their territory on public transportation: 'manspreading' (men occupy two seats by widening their legs) and 'she-bagging' (women reserve space with their handbags).

The second category, home territories, are when groups take over a specific space; think of the 1980s American sitcom *Cheers* where a small group of friends regularly gathered at their local Boston bar. Similarly, on the 1990s television show *Friends*, the Central Perk cafe was a popular third space home territory. The third category is interactional territories, which includes social gatherings with specific boundaries and rules such as book clubs or writing groups. The final category is body territory – the personal space immediately surrounding us, our invisible boundaries. People might identify and claim body territory by having a preferred seat in a café, local library, or within their own home. Territoriality, essentially people's need to signal perceived space ownership, is an extension of personal space theory onto and through objects, things and places. The nature of these boundaries, and users' personal space requirements, must inform designers' decisions regarding the size, shape, scale and proportions of a place.

The Size, Regulation and Flexibility of Personal Space

Before deeply delving into how personal theory should inform design practice, however, we first briefly review the research in this space. A common critique of Hall's spatial taxonomy is that it was predominantly developed from a North American lens, drawing on personal experiences and stories of cross-cultural encounters. Scholars from a range of disciplinary fields, including anthropology, sociology, psychology, communication, geography and design, have systematically explored notions of personal space, proxemics and territoriality in multiple contexts and cultures. This large body of research suggests that the invisible personal space 'bubble' exists, but the 'size' varies depending on factors such as nationality, culture, ethnicity, personality, gender, age, degree of acquaintance, location and situation.

Culture is a significant predictor of preferred physical distances, with personal space in Mediterranean, Arab, and Latin American cultures substantially smaller than in Northern European and North American cultures. As well as socio-cultural norms, recent research suggests psychological and ecological variables (including wealth and environmental factors, such as the temperature of the inhabited region, parasite stress and population growth rate) also influence cultural patterns of preferred interpersonal distances. One study assessing hypothetical space boundaries asked 8,943 participants from 42 countries to indicate on a simple graphic how close another person (a stranger, friend or more intimate relation) could be during a conversation for things to remain comfortable. Participant gender and average country temperature predicted preferred social distances, with women and people in colder countries preferring a greater distance from strangers (Sorokowska et al., 2017).

Using unobtrusive observations from time-lapse digital photography, Ozdemir (2008) investigated interpersonal distances for shopping mall users in Turkey and the United States. Recording over three thousand interpersonal distances, he showed that pairs in Turkish malls interacted more closely than those in U.S. malls, while the largest interpersonal distance was between adolescents interacting with other adolescents. Memorable experimental studies have also documented the use of space in men's urinals. Researchers varied how close a confederate stood to another, and then measured the speed and duration of urination; the closer the confederate, the greater the delay in urination (Middlemist, Knowles & Matter, 1976). Similarly, when a confederate was seated closer (one foot versus five or ten feet) to a water fountain, male college students were less likely to drink from the fountain and also drank less (Barefoot, Hoople & McClay, 1972). These examples highlight how, even when we may not be consciously aware of it, personal space theory impacts our everyday behaviors.

Individual differences, such as personality, experience of PTSD (posttraumatic stress disorder), and autism spectrum disorder (ASD), also affect the size, regulation, and flexibility of personal space. Extroverts have smaller personal distance zones than introverts. An extravert may be more comfortable with people standing closer to them, while an introvert may select a secluded safe space in the corner (see Chapter 2 for prospect-refuge theory). Spatial proximity predicts friendships; people who sit close to each other at work or live near one another are more likely to become friends (Festinger, Schachter & Back, 1950). Recent research studying the experience of shared student accommodation linked design features that encourage unintentional social interactions (e.g. a shared common area and a lack of en suite bathrooms) with stronger interpersonal bonds and wellbeing (Easterbrook & Vignoles, 2014). Psychiatric and developmental disorders also change how people regulate personal space. Male war veterans with PTSD, physically abused children, and children with ASD have significantly larger personal space boundaries, can misinterpret spatial social cues, and do not appropriately moderate others' interpersonal distance (see for example, Gessaroli et al., 2013).

Designing with the Language of Space

This large body of research is an important reminder that creating great places requires an appreciation of personal space theory. The design of spaces can either pull people apart or bring them together, with great places meeting our different needs for intimacy, personal connection, socializing and gathering, and being alone. While Hall observed that both fixed (immobile properties of space, such as walls, doors and windows) and semi-fixed features (moveable elements, such as furniture, chairs and tables) affected our perception and use of personal space, British psychiatrist Humphry Osmond was the first to identify that specific spatial arrangements either encourage or discourage social interaction. Osmond coined the phrases *sociofugal* (separating people) and *sociopetal* (bringing people together). Sociofugal space is grid like, designed to keep people apart, such as lecture hall seating, church pews or library carrels), while sociopetal space is radial, purposely intimate, and designed to bring people together. At a larger scale, the sociopetal design of interconnected spirals, rings, and funnels in New York City's Washington Square Park is a good example of purposely fostered social interaction. At a smaller scale, think how the chairs in your manager's office might be arranged in a welcoming sociopetal semi-circle to encourage a friendly conversation, or opposite each other in a sociofugal arrangement to reinforce the hierarchy.

In his later work, Osmond collaborated with environmental psychologist Robert Sommer to test these ideas. Their redesign of a day room in the psychiatric facility doubled the frequency of interpersonal interactions. In his classic 1969 book *Personal Space: The Behavioral Basis of Design*, Sommer reflects on the power of design and furniture arrangements to influence social behavior, arguing that buildings should be built first for function and usefulness, rather than for form or aesthetics. Sommer's observation-based, cross-disciplinary spatial research emphasizes the importance of evidence-based design for public buildings and spaces. Observing seating patterns and behaviors across settings as diverse as prisons, aged care, schools, airports and hospitals, Sommer attests people have an innate need for privacy, and will find it, using corners, alcoves, a 'broom closet, fire escape, or toilet stall' (Sommer, 1969, p. 93). Memorably describing airports as the most sociofugal places in society, Sommer laments how the layout of inflexible institutional rows of chairs in waiting spaces is designed to separate rather than connect. A glance around your local airport will likely confirm a significant change in contemporary spatial design practices; modern airports are much less sterile and soulless, typically featuring flexible furniture, alongside creative biophilic and sustainable design practices (see Chapters 6 and 10).

The importance of proxemics for interior design practice is emphasized in Linda Nussbaumer's book, *Human Factors in the Built Environment* (2013) where she explains how interior designers must avoid creating environments that penetrate intimate space boundaries. For example, interior designers need to ensure cocktail tables in bars are not so close together that they disrupt private conversations (intimate zone), and use chairs, rather than sofas, in waiting rooms so that people can separate themselves from strangers (a public zone). Material choice will also differ, depending on the zone. Small scale pieces, intricate details, and unique or precious materials are most suited to intimate personal spaces, enjoyed by owners. Materials used in social spaces must be more durable, to suit a wide range of activities and intended users, while materials in public spaces must consider issues of public safety and durability. Materials in office workspaces for example, must withstand spilled coffee and heavy bags; childcare centers must be age-appropriate and cater to high energy young children; high-traffic hospitals have unique needs for durability, cleanliness and wellbeing.

The nature of the activity, our unique individual characteristics, and our body dimensions combine to determine the design elements required to support our response and movement through space. In his reflective book *The Language of Space*, Lawson describes the delicate challenge of designing for human distance in reception areas, such as a doctor's waiting room. The distance between the receptionist and seats for waiting need to be close enough to allow occasional friendly conversation, yet far enough to allow the receptionist to work without being considered rude by waiting visitors. The spatial layout, specifically the distance and chair arrangement, determines how people will interact; yet, it is so rarely considered that one of Lawson's hobbies is photographing poorly designed reception spaces.

Personal space and territoriality are such critical design considerations that they even inform the selection process for astronauts and the design of space stations. A technical report for NASA emphasized that the opportunity to withdraw from other people was essential for psychological wellbeing. Architectural guidelines for the space station also highlighted the importance of privacy in spaceflight environments, including visual and acoustic privacy promoted by walls and doors that removed sights and sounds; physical privacy through the distribution of people in physical space; olfactory privacy through sanitation and air filtration systems; and relatively light colors were recommended for interior walls to create an impression of spaciousness (Harrison, Caldwell & Struthers,

1988). Interestingly, this report stated that 'cultural determinants of personal space and territoriality cannot be ignored in the design process,' with Recommendation 59 noting, 'Do not select individuals with unusual personal space requirements.'

Personal space theory, in essence, is a reminder to keep the spatial needs of the user at the forefront during the design process. Whether designing the placement of furniture in a room, seating on public transport, or the length of a public bench, conscious consideration of personal space theory helps create 'containers to accommodate, separate, structure and organize, facilitate, heighten and even celebrate human spatial behaviour' (Lawson, 2001, p. 4).

Personal Space in Public Space Seating and Gender-Sensitive Park Design

Traditionally utilitarian in design, the humble public seat or park bench is an important feature in our public realm and the archetypal symbol of public space. Best practice public space policy, and the works of urban design theorists William H. Whyte and Jan Gehl, remind us that thoughtfully designed street furniture (benches, seats, ledges, walls and planters) help create a sense of community and foster positive social interactions. At their best, public benches are welcoming and are tangible symbols of a democratic, friendly and people-centered place where free, accessible and equitable public space is provided for all. Public benches can also be an example of hostile architecture; many cities add extra dividers to prevent rough sleeping, as officials in Shandong province in eastern China have installed coin-operated park benches where sharp steel spikes rise and retract

The classic park bench, composed of simple wooden slats and metal arms, has evolved to reflect society's changing values. Smart benches, which seamlessly integrate Wi-Fi, solar panels, lighting and phone charging stations, are increasingly appearing in our public spaces. These benches can monitor atmospheric conditions, including air quality, and even activate built-in fans to cool people. Public seats also implicitly and explicitly convey other social norms. From 'buddy benches' where a school child can sit to indicate they need a friend, to a bench in the Netherlands that displays weight as a tool to motivate gym memberships, the design and use of the outdoor seat is evolving.

The most useable public seating, which incorporates an understanding of anthropological physical dimensions (height, weight, sitting height, buttock-knee height, knee front and back heights, thigh clearance), will respect individual personal space bubbles and enable people to maintain an appropriate distance from strangers. The photographs in Figure 3.3 clearly illustrate how the simple seats in Helsinki are spaced just slightly apart, enabling people on a snowy winter day to maintain personal space

Figure 3.3 Seats – in sub-tropical Hong Kong, snowy Helsinki and suburban England.

Sources: Evonne Miller (Hong Kong); Charlotte Teagan (Helsinki), The Friendly Bench™ (England) with permission, © 2019.

boundaries. Similar spacings are evident in the round seating on an over-cast day in Hong Kong, where two strangers easily share the same space. In the distance, a row of color plants on stairs delineates one side for entering the temple and the other for leaving. The features and shape of the surrounding landscape, including grass, ledges and steps, also invite secondary seating. As people tend to feel uncomfortable sitting face-to-face with a stranger, the seats do not face each other and the array of seating options enable people to easily sit closer with friends or further apart from strangers. Missing are arm rests, which help people with restricted mobility or visual impairment sit down and get up, providing security and stability.

Building on the idea of the 'buddy' bench which explicitly invites a stranger to invade an individual's private space, Lyndsey Young an independent designer from Leicestershire launched the 'Friendly Bench' in 2018. The bottom image in Figure 3.3 illustrates how this curb-side community garden with integrated seating explicitly tells users (primarily the elderly, lonely, and socially isolated) that conversation and connection are both desired and welcome. Critically, as Gehl noted in *Life Between Buildings*, people feel exposed and uncomfortable in the middle of open spaces (prospect-refuge theory) so the integrated vegetation provides a sense of security.

Spatial thinking also informed the re-design of popular inner-urban public parks in Vienna. As Chapter 7 discusses, contemporary park design must meet the recreational and social needs of multiple user-groups – parks are play spaces for children, workplaces for parents, hang out spaces for youth, and sportsgrounds and meeting places for older retirees. Yet, Austrian research identified that tween girls (aged 10 to 13) tended to withdraw from parks and public open spaces, in part because of 'male' spatial and functional design patterns. In response, pioneering gender-sensitive park design in Vienna re-engaged these tween girls, and increased the number of overall users. After workshops to identify girls' preferences, St. Johann Park and Einsiedlerpark (now Bruno-Kreisky-Park) were re-designed to feature multi-functional play areas, tranquil zones, wider walking trails and lighting, with football cages converted into activities (badminton and volleyball courts) that appealed to both girls and boys of all ages. The addition of simple 4 × 2-metre wooden platforms on the grass successfully created 'islands of appropriation, and by situating these carefully between the existing trees they also create centers for spatial units within the park' (Jorgensen & Licka, 2012, p. 232). The success of the project, frequently cited as an exemplar of best practice, means gender-sensitive planning for recreation spaces is officially part of Venna Park Design guidelines. And, as the excerpt below explains, thoughtful consideration of individual differences in the space use often has significant impact on health and wellbeing, as does thinking with prospect-refuge theory:

The presence of women in green areas, parks, and squares increases markedly if their appropriation wishes are taken into account. If, for example, pleasant refuges are available, if the design itself and rules of use impose quieter appropriation patterns, if a sense of security prevails, and if the aesthetic and atmospheric standards (apparently more precious to women than men) are met, then women will not only be present in greater numbers but there will be considerably fewer gender-specific differences in behavior. Women are far less present or congregate in peripheral areas where open spaces are designed more for movement-intensive activities or self-presentation before others.

(Harth, 2007)

Designing for Personal Space in Workplaces and Buildings

The look and feel of the contemporary office workplace has transformed over the last decade from individual offices and workplaces, to open-plan and unassigned 'hot desks'. Both architectural and psychological privacy is needed, in terms of visual and acoustic isolation, as well as control over ones' accessibility to others. Unfortunately, the design of open workplaces often impedes, rather than facilitates employee happiness and productivity, a view supported by a growing body of research. Common complaints include how easy it is to be distracted, how hard it is to get any individual work done and the simple sensory challenges of working in close physical contact with many others, who have different personalities, hygiene practices, and spatial expectations. Clearly, many of the stresses of contemporary work environments are because people's personal space is being compromised, with co-workers now often seated close to or in the intimate range. The best design starts with a deep consideration of how people will actually use space. Architect Frank Gehry's design of an academic building for MIT in particular was guided by how he thought people would use the space to seek out (or avoid) social interactions:

> They will have a building for seven departments that need to talk with each other. The reclusive ones among them will find ways of interacting and the building will function to facilitate that interaction. It's simple. Just putting the cafeteria in the middle and putting their breakout spaces in view of the cafeteria means they can see when other professors are going to lunch and say, 'Oh God, I'd like to talk to that guy. He's going to lunch, I'm going to go to lunch.' It's that dumb, and I think it's going to work that simply.

(Gehry, 2004, p. 24)

This awareness of personal and social space needs is also evident in the practice of Chinese architect and 2012 Pritzker Architecture Prize Laureate Wang Shu. Recalling the design of one high-rise apartment building (the Vertical Courtyard Apartments, 2002–2007, in Hangzhou, China), Wang Shu described how he gave every family a small courtyard and every 10 families a small public courtyard, as a way to build neighborhood connections. In personal space terminology, this is the provision of both private personal space and social space. Wang Shu recently visited the building and observed people using the space differently: he was disappointed to note the public courtyard on the ground floor was empty and unused, with much dust. On the fifth-floor courtyard, however, a young child was doing his homework there and on the eleventh floor, it had become a beautiful garden, with flowers and trees. This example from China illustrates how different people will use the same space very differently.

The Continuing Need for Personal Space Theory

Proxemics, and the need to cater and then design for many and varied personal space preferences, is clear from these brief examples. However, a thought-provoking dress highlights the continuing need to address personal space. Media artist Kathleen McDermott created a motorized 'personal space' dress, with an expanding hemline, in response to being frequently crowded on public transportation. While such extreme fashion items are unlikely to become an everyday feature in our urban environment, this dress serves as a unique reminder of the 'invisible' bubble each of us carries around with us. To create great places, designers must thoughtfully engage with personal space theory and ensure that human spatial needs are considered. In the next chapter, we explore the importance of listening to the site and searching for the unique sense of place – the *genius loci*.

Note

1. In his writings, as was the convention at that time (around 50 years ago), Hall uses the term 'man' to refer to both men and women.

References

Barefoot, J., Hoople, H. & McClay, D. (1972). Avoidance of an Act which Would Violate Personal Space. *Psychonomic Science* 28(4): 205–206.

Easterbrook, M. J. & Vignoles, V. L (2014). When Friendship Formation Goes Down the Toilet: Design Features of Shared Accommodation Influence Interpersonal Bonds and Well-being, *British Journal of Social Psychology* 54(1): 125–139.

Festinger, L., Schachter, S. & Back, K. (1950). *Social Pressures in Informal Groups: A Study of Human Factors in Housing*. Oxford: Harper.

Gehry, F. (2004). Reflections on Designing and Architectural Practice. In R. J. Boyland & F. Collopy (Eds.), *Managing as Designing*. Stanford, CA: Stanford University Press, 19–35.

Gessaroli, E., Santelli, E., di Pellegrino, G. & Frassinetti, F. (2013). Personal Space Regulation in Childhood Autism Spectrum Disorders. *PLoS ONE* 8(9): e74959.

Graziano, M. (2018). *The Spaces Between Us: A Story of Neuroscience, Evolution, and Human Nature*. Oxford: Oxford University Press.

Hall, E. (1959).*The Silent Language*. New York: Doubleday

Hall, E. (1963). A System for the Notation of Proxemic Behavior. *American Anthropologist* 65(5): 1003–1026.

Hall, E. (1966). *The Hidden Dimension*. New York: Doubleday.

Harth, A. (2007). Open Space and Gender: Gender-Sensitive Open-Space Planning. *German Journal of Urban Studies* 46(1). Retrieved from www.difu.de/publikationen/open-space-and-gendergender-sensitive-open-space.html

Hediger, H. (1950). *Wild Animals in Captivity*. London: Butterworths Scientific Publications.

Jorgensen, A. & Licka, L. (2012). Anti-planning, Anti-design? Exploring Alternative Ways of Making Future Urban Landscapes. In A. Jorgensen & R. Keenan (Eds.), *Urban Wildscapes*. New York: Routledge, 221–236.

Lawson, B. (2001). *The Language of Space*. New York: Routledge.

Middlemist, R. Knowles, E. & Matter, C. F. (1976). Personal Space Invasions in the Lavatory: Suggestive Evidence for Arousal. *Journal of Personality and Social Psychology* 33(5): 541–546.

Nussbaumer, L. (2013). *Human Factors in the Built Environment*. London: Fairchild Books.

Ozdemir, A. (2008). Shopping Malls: Measuring Interpersonal Distance under Changing Conditions and across Cultures. *Field Methods* 20: 226–248.

Sommer, R. (1969). *Personal Space; the Behavioral Basis of Design*. Englewood Cliffs, N.J: Prentice-Hall.

Sorokowska, A. et al. (2017). Preferred Interpersonal Distances: A Global Comparison. *Journal of Cross-Cultural Psychology* 48(4): 577–592.

4 Sense of Place Theory/*Genius Loci*

Locating the Magic

Genius loci is Latin for the spirit of the place. In contemporary design practice, it is the adept and respectful designer who genuinely understands, connects with, and highlights the unique and distinctive history, environment, climate, topography, culture, or traditions of a place.

Contemporary urban design is often criticized for being banal, generic and 'place-less,' disconnected from its unique site, context, and neighborhood. Consider the lyrics of 'Little Boxes,' a 1962 song by American folk/blues singer-songwriter and political activist, Malvina Reynolds. Her lyrics lament the urbanization and rows of cookie-cutter development houses (little boxes) lining the hills of the San Francisco Bay Area. If the song sounds familiar, you may also remember it as the theme song for the television show *Weeds* (2005–2008), which depicted the exploits of recently widowed, suburban mom Nancy Botwin as she sold marijuana to pay the bills in her middle-class, very homogenized neighborhood. In contrast, great places challenge this cookie-cutter aesthetic through a genuine dialogue and connection with the unique *genius loci* of a site – the spirit of the place, seen in the distinctive history, environment, climate, topography, traditions and culture.

Generic urban design practice is very different from purposeful design and architecture that is powerfully connected to the unique sense of place. From the distinctive domed rooftop and decorated spires of Saint Basil's Cathedral prominently positioned in Moscow's Red Square, the cobblestone streets and terracotta walls of Italy, the colorful fishing shacks in Scotland's Isle of Skye, the ever-changing graffiti-filled laneways in Melbourne, or the High Line park perched above the Manhattan streets in New York City, the design of great places *always* draws inspiration from and references the unique local context, creating a strong sense of identity.

Terminology: Sense of Place Theory versus *Genius loci*

This chapter explores the origins and importance of the theoretical concept 'sense of place,' often described in practice as *genius loci*. This term originates from Roman mythology, and is the protective spirit or guardian

Figure 4.1 Zalige bridge in the Netherlands – when in flood.
Source: © NEXT Architects, photography by Rutger Hollander.

deity of a place. In religious iconography, the 'spirit of the place' was
often depicted as a snake – a guardian angel for a place, rather than a person. Landscape design history attributes the modern revival of this term
to eighteenth century British poet and translator Alexander Pope, a passionate gardener who encouraged garden designers to consult the genius
(the spirit) of the place for design inspiration. The following lines from
his poem 'Epistle IV, to Richard Boyle, Earl of Burlington' illustrate this:

> Consult the genius of the place in all;
> That tells the waters or to rise, or fall;
> Or helps th'ambitious hill the heav'ns to scale,
> Or scoops in circling theatres the vale;
> Calls in the country, catches opening glades,
> Joins willing woods, and varies shades from shades,
> Now breaks, or now directs, th'intending lines;
> Paints as you plant, and, as you work, designs.
> (Pope, 1731, lines 57–64)

The concept of *genius loci* has been replaced by the broader term '*sense
of place*' – how we perceive a place. Drawing on a wide array of theoretical perspectives, methodologies and approaches, researchers from a

diverse range of disciplines (including geography, anthropology, urban sociology, planning, architecture, landscape architecture, urban design, interior design and environmental psychology) have investigated 'sense of place,' variously defined as place meaning, place identity, place experience, people-place interactions, and placemaking. This large body of scholarly literature documents the concept of place as both physical and psychological, since the physical landscape or place becomes an important part of a person's identity (Jacobs, 1961; Lynch, 1981). Place attachment, as we discuss in Chapter 5, is the emotional bond between people and places, while place meaning is the symbolic meaning people ascribe to places (Carmona et al., 2010; Stedman, 2002, 2003; Seamon, 2018; Relph, 1976).

People's understanding of what a place is and represents is influenced by a wide-array of tangible and intangible socio-cultural, political-historical, spatio-temporal and physical factors. In his groundbreaking book *Place and Placelessness*, geographer Edward Relph (1976) argued that space must be explored in terms of how people experience it. He identified three core pillars that combine to create a sense of place: physical setting, meaning, and activities. Urban design theorists have subsequently extended Relph's conceptualization, outlining a complex list of design qualities, features, experiences and interactions that contribute to and enhance a sense of place in the public realm – including street life, cafe culture, opening hours, sensory experience, symbolism and memory, vitality, safety and diversity (Canter, 1977; Carmona et al., 2010; Montgomery, 1998).

There is, of course, no universal checklist for creating great places where people can thrive – as designers and urban planners know all too well, real places are unpredictable, complex and messy (Carmona et al., 2010, p. 122). What we do know, as Trancik (1986) has observed, is that people do have an innate need for a 'relatively stable system of places in which to develop themselves, their social lives, their culture. These needs give man-made space an emotional content – a presence that is more than physical' (p. 113).

In her pivotal writings about place, geographer Doreen Massey reminds us how place is always under construction, and is neither fixed nor spatially bound. Place reconnects people with each other, through 'articulated moments in networks of social relations and understandings' (Massey, 1994, p. 154). A deep exploration of this placemaking literature, geographical imagination, and the politics of place is beyond the scope of this chapter, but what is important to highlight is that questions of space and place are always personal, local and global. Place is a multidimensional, well-researched and often contested term, with American landscape writer J. B. Jackson (1994) criticizing the phrase 'sense of place' for being so general and broad that it means very little:

'Sense of place' is a much used expression, chiefly by architects but taken over by urban planners and interior decorators and the promoters of condominiums, so that now it means very little. It is an awkward and ambiguous translation of the Latin term *genius loci*. In classical times it means not so much the place itself as the guardian divinity of that place. . . . in the eighteenth century the Latin phrase was usually translated as 'the genius of a place,' meaning its influence. . . . We now use the current version to describe the atmosphere to a place, the quality of its environment. Nevertheless, we recognize that certain localities have an attraction which gives us a certain indefinable sense of well-being and which we want to return to, time and again.

(Jackson, 1994, pp. 157–158)

In this chapter, we purposely use the theoretical concept and term '*genius loci*' as a means to amplify the unique atmosphere and distinctive design features of a place – rather than the broader behavioral or social science lens emphasized in the 'sense of place' discourse. As a praxis-based discipline, designers must maintain a deep geographical sensibility and remain aware that ideas occur within unique socio-political contexts. Great design means consciously pausing and listening for the unique *genius loci* of the site, and as the examples that follow illustrate, this process requires deep, thoughtful and critical engagement with the physical site, local residents, and awareness of future use and users. Great design also demands a future-focused mindset, driven by a deep awareness that the attitudes and values of both individuals and societies change over time (Jive´n & Larkham, 2003). Deeply reflecting on, searching for and amplifying the *genius loci* is one strategy to raise awareness of these values and foster the creation of great places.

The Theoretical Origins of *Genius Loci*

Genius loci is a powerful force, present in all the places we live, work, and play. It engages our senses, awakens memories, and fuels aspirations, enlivening 'our present by reminding us of our past and anticipating our future' (Nivala, 1996, p. 1). Norwegian architectural theorist and historian Christian Norberg-Schulz has written extensively about *genius loci*. Drawing on Heidegger's ideas of 'being' and 'dwelling,' Norberg-Schulz asserts the ontological importance, the originality and uniqueness of every place. He encourages designers to 'dwell' within, respect and befriend a site, so as to identify all its unique surrounding elements and qualities. Ponder, for example, how sand is an important place element for the Arab, just as water is for the Dutch, snow for the Norwegian, and sun for the Australian. Natural and man-made elements, such as topography and landscape (e.g. rivers, mountains, and forests), cosmic order (e.g. climate, sky, light, and the time of day), and architecture and cultural landscape elements influenced by ideas, values, and beliefs, shaped by history, all intertwine in varying ways to form the distinctive character of a site. The *genius loci* is *always* uniquely different.

In his thought-provoking book *Genius loci: Towards a Phenomenology of Architecture*, Norberg-Schulz (1980) documented how the three cities of Rome, Prague and Khartoum have all preserved their *genius loci*. Prague, for example, engenders a strong sense of mystery; Rome a sense of long history, and eternal presence; and Khartoum reflects a powerful natural order, 'the horizontal expanse of the barren desert country, the slow movement of the life-giving Nile, the immense sky and the burning sun . . . and the bustling, colourful life of the city' (Norberg-Schulz, 1980, p. 113). When a design or building is aesthetically isolated and disconnected from the place to which it belongs (its *genius loci*), then a fragmented and meaningless environment is created. The essence of *genius loci* is how well the human-made structures in our built environment, through the tangible design language of materials, patterns, textures, color, scale, function, form and proportion, convey an understanding of local context, of the unique cultural, societal, and historical values.

Every city has a unique pattern and scale, which is reflected in the prevailing architectural styles, materials and colors. In several beautifully evocative books, architectural theorist Juhani Pallasmaa describes how buildings and cities are powerful connectors to our past. Thoughtful design means locating, preserving and amplifying the unique meaning, character, particularity or distinctiveness of a site. Heritage is often a central feature of *genius loci*, with design practices often privileging memories, along with imaginations of place.

Internationally, the cultural and historical significance of place is acknowledged by the Burra Charter (the Australia ICOMOS Charter for Places of Cultural Significance), which advocates maximizing the cultural significance of places by identifying 'aesthetic, historic, scientific, social or spiritual value.' Experiencing historic buildings, as Pallasmaa poignantly explains in *Eyes of the Skin*, enables time and space to stand still and fuse into a singular elemental experience: the sense of being.

> Architecture emancipates us from the embrace of the present and allows us to experience the slow, healing flow of time. Buildings and cities are instruments and museums of time. They enable us to see and understand the slow passing of history, and to participate in time cycles that surpass individual life. Architecture connects us with the dead; through buildings we are able to imagine the bustle of the medieval street, and picture a solemn procession approaching the cathedral. The time of architecture is a detained time; in the greatest of buildings time stands firmly still.
>
> (Pallasmaa, 1996, p. 52)

Our perception of the surrounding world is always experiential, as we see, hear, touch, smell, taste, and feel. This experience is mediated by physical and emotional experiences, memories, aesthetic responses, history, politics and culture, as well as the temporality of our interactions with the environment. And, as *genius loci* is frequently the intangible manifestation of the site, this unique sensory experience might be interpreted differently by different people or at different times of day and night, varying during different weather and seasons. People's experiences with and perception of a site are ever changing: places can be vivid, active and exciting, or dull and dark, all varying due to time and context. Drawing from a range of different cultural contexts and design scales, the following examples illustrate why engaging with *genius loci* is an essential aspect of creating great places.

Identifying the *Genius loci* of Iconic Buildings and Places

Iconic buildings often amplify their unique *genius loci* both implicitly and explicitly. Look, for example, at the Temppeliaukio Church (Rock Church), built by architect brothers Timo and Tuomo Suomalainen in 1969. One of Helsinki's most popular tourist attractions, this building is timeless because the design responds to the unique identifying element of the place, rock. The interior of the church was excavated and built into the rock. The interior color scheme is based on the shades of granite: red, purple, and grey. The sanctuary floor is located level with the highest street, meaning visitors easily enter without the need for stairs, a wonderful example of universal design in practice. The roof is seemingly a floating copper-plated dome, connected to the natural rock wall by 180 window panes that shine natural light into the space. By using the natural geometry of the rock, the crevice alter area is illuminated more than other parts of the sanctuary, creating a deep feeling of lightness, harmony, and peacefulness.

How Industrial Heritage Contributes to *Genius loci*

Notable urban landscapes often have a strong dialogue with the local context. Perhaps the most well-known example is the widely-acclaimed design of The High Line in New York City, a park created from a decommissioned elevated industrial railway. The park includes elements from the site's original use, such as the railway ties, to eloquently reference the important history of the place, sparking curiosity and educating people about the transformation of the Chelsea neighborhood in Manhattan. Similarly, Gas Works Park (GWP) in Seattle, designed by landscape architect Richard Haag in 1971, was considered a ground-breaking design at the time, and is now an American National Historic Landmark. A highly respected 'elder' of landscape architecture, Haag is primarily known for his advocacy of bioremediation and reuse of industrial remains. Instead of erasing a historical moment by removing the giant relics of the coal and gas plant, Haag chose to celebrate this unusual industrial relic in his design of a 20.5-acre public park. The contrast between the rusted gas reservoirs and its location on a bright green hill are clearly evident in Figure 4.2. As Haag recalls below, he initially found the gas works landscape confronting, given its hazardous appearance, though after a few site visits, very quickly realized the large gas reservoir towers needed to be preserved; without them, the site would be just another flat field. Maintaining the structures was a conscious link to the industrial heritage; it was his explicit recognition of the *genius loci* that embraced meaning, scale, prospect, and refuge of the site.

> I had some really romantic ideas about it. I thought it was a place of great beauty and mystery, after I got over my initial shock of wandering around through all the soot and the smells and everything. Well, when you do site planning . . . one of the things you have to do when you do this *genius loci* thing is find out what the site has, what mystery, what the spirit is and what are the most sacred things on the site. So very soon I decided that those big towers were that . . . but I thought my god, if you just push all this in the lake or cut it down as one of the early mayors wanted to do, why what would you have here, you know, just a flat field and that's all.

Figure 4.2 Gas Works Park in Seattle demonstrates a distinct *genius loci*.
Source: Shannon Satherley.

So climbing up on the mound is a prospect, but going down in among the towers could be refuge, or going inside of the towers. So, there's a lot of that yin-yang going on there: up and down, and structure and softness. But there's not a lot of planting, and that's because I felt that nowhere else in the city do you get such a strong sense of space and light and openness, sky and water, reflections. So it's purposely under-planted . . . it's really important then to take the land when you can in between there and make it very sensuous and a sculptural form against the hardness of the architecture and the beauty of those cylinders and cubes and all the great geometry left from that industrial age. So each plays a kind of a complementary, but complementary by being opposite experiences, visually and tactilely and so on. And certainly those structures give meaning and scale to the site.

> (Haag, cited in Satherley, 2016, pp. 117–118)

GWP is noteworthy for several reasons. First, GWP took a new approach to post-industrial reclamation, challenging many people's ideas about public parks and the place of industrial remains. Haag's progressive proposal recommended not removing the polluted soil from the site, but 'cleaning and greening' the park through bioremediation and carefully selected plants. He led the fight to save some of the industrial structures, which were redesigned for different active uses: the exhauster-compressor building became a children's play barn, and the historic boiler house became a picnic shelter. While Haag argued for the prominent industrial feature, the massive generator towers, to become climbing and lookout platforms, other political priorities mean they remain inaccessible behind fences. They do however remain on site as a visible celebration of our industrial past. Second, Haag's vision for GWP was that the park should evolve through people's interaction with the landscape, rather than being dictated by a master plan. Haag achieved this interaction by providing the standard public meetings, as well as providing an on-site office, inviting the City Council and the public to do what he had done: physically interact with the landscape in order to discover its 'genius' (Way, 2013; Satherley, 2016).

Genius loci in Chinese design

The unprecedented speed and magnitude of urban development processes in China, one of the oldest and largest urban civilizations in the world, has seen 90% of traditional buildings demolished over the past few decades. In response, Chinese architect and 2012 Pritzker Architecture Prize Laureate Wang Shu (2015) argues that preserving memory and respecting the identity of a place must become a priority. Challenging the creation of a repetitive and anonymous modern urban environment, and loss of urban memory, are several high profile adaptive reuse projects that have retained a historical, cultural, and traditional 'rootedness' with place. Drawing on the *genius loci* of these industrial sites, architectural firm Atelier Deshaus led two notable projects with distinct and grounded urban character. In Shanghai, the largest grain silos in Asia (the 80,000-ton silos on Minsheng Wharf, Pudong District) were transformed into an exhibition space, with the existing architectural typology purposely retained. Both the exterior and interior of the original silos were untouched, with connection to the waterfront position on the Huangpu River highlighted via exterior hanging elevators and reflective stainless steel panels on the underbelly.

Further along the banks of the Huangpu River, the old Laobaidu coal bunker is now the site of the Long Museum West Bund. Respecting the *genius loci* of this site, the most prominent remnant of the site's industrial heritage is now the center of the building – the large coal-hopper unloading bridge, 110 meters long, 10 meters wide and 8 meters high. It frames the museum's entrance, provides a temporary exhibition space and is an attractive outdoor space, accessible even when the museum is closed. The site is powerfully infused with memory, with the history of a primitive, savage allure completely captivating every visitor (Interior Designer, 2016). Both projects purposely and artistically amplify the history, drawing on the *genius loci* of the site to create powerful unintentional monuments of contemporary industrial heritage that respect the spatial character and cultural identity.

The *Genius loci* of Nordic Architectural Identity

To end our discussion of *genius loci*, we return to the important work of Christian Norberg-Schulz. In his 1996 book *Nightlands: Nordic Building*, Norberg-Schulz provides an evocative insight into the very distinctive Nordic architectural identity, where the *genius loci* emphasizes an almost mythic geography where nature (especially wood and water), light and darkness, and a timeless quality, all combine. This unique Nordic *genius loci* is seen in the Oslo Opera House, an iconic Scandinavian building depicted in the top image of Figure 4.3. As well as the openness and horizontality, the defining feature is the sloping white marble roofscape growing out of the harbor waters. Reminiscent of an iceberg or floating glacier, visitors are encouraged to 'walk on the roof' of this large public plaza. Designed by Norwegian architects Snøhetta, this flagship project encapsulated waterfront regeneration and symbolically reconnected the city to the fjord. It exemplifies what Timothy Beatley (2014) terms blue urbanism, fostering connections with the ocean by 'allowing visitors to virtually touch and dip into the surrounding aquatic world' (p. 68). Snøhetta also designed the beautiful Norwegian Wild Reindeer Center Pavilion, located on a rocky hilltop in Hjerkinn, which

Figure 4.3 Responding to the *genius loci* of the site – Oslo Opera House, a surfboard bench on Australia's Gold Coast and the Zalige bridge in the
Netherlands.

Source: Ellen Marie Sæthre-McGuirk (Oslo); Debra Cushing (Surfboard bench); ©NEXT
architects/Photography: Jeroen Bosch.

draws on the surrounding natural, cultural and mythical landscape. This education center is the size and shape of a shipping container with one long glass wall facing Mt. Snøhetta (and passing herds of reindeer). The undulating pine timber recesses in the rear wall, mirror the wood and curves of the surrounding mountains, inviting visitors to sit or lean as they contemplate the spectacular landscape inside this cave-like space. These buildings are uniquely memorable because of their sense of place, their *genius loci*: a strong and unique connection to the surrounding Nordic landscape.

Cold climates often have a distinctive *genius loci*. British-Swedish architect Ralph Erskine, known as the Arctic Architect of Modernism, is renowned for sensitively developing built form in response to the unique climatic, cultural and geographic conditions of cold places. His 1948 design of the Swedish mountain ski Borgafjäll Hotel, for example, was inspired by the surrounding geology, topographic locality and seasonal activities, with guests able to ski off the roof, directly onto the slopes. An integral part of Erskine's design philosophy was to work closely with the future inhabitants, to ensure their needs were met. He explained:

> I try to base my work on that seasonal rhythm of the north, which I find so enthralling, and form communities which encompass all its richness of contrasting experiences. I hope that we architects could give such a dwelling a form, make a space with a potential for contentment. But in the final count it is the inhabitants who will give the same dwelling its meaning and will change our architectural space to place.
>
> (Erskine, 1968, p. 165)

The *Genius loci* of Everyday Objects

Whether it is a focus on the local history, preserving industrial heritage, or connecting with distinctive features of the natural environment (the ocean in blue urbanism, the rock in Temppeliaukio Church, the ability to ski off a hotel roof), designing great places that resonate and feel authentic starts with a deep understanding and appreciation of the unique local context – the *genius loci*. Figures 4.1 and 4.3 show how even the design of more functional and potentially mundane structures, such as roads, bridges, walkways, toilets and elevators, can be made more special and memorable when *genius loci* is a core consideration. Toilets in New Zealand often have a unique sense of place: the 'toilet with a view' overlooking a lake on top of the MacKinnon Pass on the Milford Track; the ship-shape cubicles in Matakana referencing the local boat-building industry: and, the laser-cut steel 'shrouds' of toilets in Redwoods Forest in Rotorua which fuse the traditional Maori *kowhaiwhai* pattern with imagery of extinct or endangered native birds (one of six finalists in the 2014 World Architecture News Small Spaces Awards).

The sense of place also inspired the innovative design of pedestrian bridges that connect people experientially with bats or the changing weather patterns, as Zalige bridge does in the Netherlands (discussed in Chapter 6). Designed by Next architects and built on flood plains, this pedestrian bridge in an urban river park embraces the dynamic changing river landscape, and experientially responds to the impact of changing weather patterns from climate change. The middle image in Figure 4.3 shows the bridge on a fine sunny day; Figure 4.1 shows the bridge during rain – the simple stepping stones have multiple affordances, visual barriers and seats when the weather is fine and an intermitted access path over the water during wet weather. The innovative experiential design won the 2018 Dutch Design Awards, and was described as 'something that could only by pulled off by the Dutch,' a reference to how the design embraces the *genius loci* of the site – the changing water.

Genius loci can also guide the smallest of design decisions too, as we see in the bottom image of Figure 4.3 – a public bench, opposite the Gold Coast beach in Australia, in the shape of a surfboard. The benches are also nicely spaced, reflecting an awareness of personal space theory, although the vegetation behind does a poor job of providing refuge and safety from the street behind. What we see in these different examples of varying scale, scope and context, is how great places are created from a deep awareness, respect and empathy for the unique *genius loci*.

The Enduring Legacy of Design

We are what we build: our buildings, spaces and places reflect our values, and are the enduring legacy we leave for future generations. Instead of leaving a legacy of 'little boxes,' urban planning practice and architectural design must be more ambitious and adopt a conscious *genius loci* approach to preserve, celebrate and activate the distinctive and cherished components of a place. As we show throughout this book, creating great places requires a complex understanding of multiple theories. Focusing on the unique *genius loci* is a good place to start.

Designs that capture the sense of place and *genius loci*, are often those special places to which we more easily become attached. Our next chapter discusses place attachment theory to further this discussion of people and place bonds.

References

Beatley, T. (2014). *Blue Urbanism: Exploring Connections between Cities and Oceans*. Washington, DC: Island Press.

Canter, D. (1977). *The Psychology of Place*. London: Architectural Press.

Carmona, M., Tiesdell, S., Heath, T. & Oc, T. (2010). *Public Places – Urban Spaces: The Dimensions of Urban Design* (2nd edition). Burlington, VT: Elsevier Science.

Erskine, R. (1968). Architecture and Town Planning in the North. *Polar Record* 14(89): 165–171.

Interior Designer. (2016). *Chinese Architecture Today*. Beijing: Chinese Architecture and Building Press.

Jackson, J. B. (1994) *A Sense of Place, a Sense of Time*. New Haven, CT: Yale University Press.

Jacobs, J. (1961). *The Death and Life of Great American Cities*. London: Vintage Books.

Jivé'n, G. & Larkham, P. J. (2003) Sense of Place, Authenticity and Character: A Commentary, *Journal of Urban Design* 8(1): 67–81.

Lynch, K. (1981). *A Theory of Good City Form*. Cambridge, MA: MIT Press.

Massey, D. (1994). Introduction to Part III: Space, Place and Gender. In D. Massey, *Space, Place, and Gender*. Minneapolis, MN: University of Minnesota Press, 177–184.

Montgomery, J. (1998). Making a City: Urbanity, Vitality and Urban Design. *Journal of Urban Design* 3: 93–116.

Nivala, J. (1996). Saving the Spirit of our Places: A View on Our Built Environment. *UCLA Journal of Environmental Law and Policy* 15(1): 1–56.

Norberg-Schulz, C. (1980). *Genius loci, Towards a Phenomenology of Architecture*. New York: Rizzoli.

Norberg-Schulz, C. (1996). *Nightlands. Nordic Building*. Cambridge, MA: MIT Press.

Pallasmaa, J. (1996). *The Eyes of the Skin*. New York: John Wiley & Sons.

Pope, A. (1731[1966]). Epistle to Lord Burlington. In H. Davis (Ed.), *Pope: Poetical Works*. London: Oxford University Press, 314–321.

Relph, E. (1976) *Place and Placelessness*. London: Pion.

Satherley, S. (2016) Identifying Landscape Meanings: Images and Interactions at Gas Works Park. PhD thesis, Queensland University of Technology.

Seamon, D. (2018). *Life Takes Place: Phenomenology, Lifeworlds and Placemaking*. New York: Routledge.

Shu, W. (2015). Interview – Searching for a Chinese Approach to Urban Conversation. In F. Bandarin & R van Oers (Eds.), *Reconnecting the City: The Historic Urban Landscape Approach and the Future of Urban Heritage*. Oxford: Wiley Blackwell, 103–107.

Stedman, R. C. (2002). Toward a Social Psychology of Place: Predicting Behavior from Place-Based Cognitions, Attitude, and Identity. *Environment and Behavior* 34: 561–581.

Stedman, R. C. (2003). Is It Really Just a Social Construction? The Contribution of the Physical Environment to Sense of Place. *Society and Natural Resources* 16(8): 671–685.

Trancik, R. (1986). *Finding Lost Space*. New York: Van Nostrand Reinhold Co.

Way, T. (2013). Landscapes of Industrial Excess: A Thick Sections Approach to Gas Works Park. *Journal of Landscape Architecture* 8(1): 28–39.

5 Place Attachment Theory
Fostering Connections

Place attachment theory describes the emotional bonds people have for places where they had significant life experiences, where they grew up, or where they developed personal relationships and social networks. The emotions can range from appreciation, pleasure, fondness, and respect, to concern and responsibility for a place.

Many people have attachments to the places where they live. This can be especially true for indigenous or native groups such as Indigenous Australians, Maori in New Zealand, Native American Indians in the United States, and First Nations peoples in Canada who have a special connection with the land. Yet, no matter our background or heritage, we almost all experience attachments or connections to certain places in our past or present that are meaningful. These attachments can be important for our wellbeing in order to ground us, to give us special memories, and can influence where we choose to live or spend our vacations. Place attachment theory describes this symbolic relationship that an individual or group has with a place, often derived from an experience that is valued by cultural, sociopolitical, or historical sources (Low, 1992).

Theoretical Origins of Place Attachment

The book *Place Attachment*, edited by Irwin Altman and Setha Low (1992), carefully considers the unique emotional experiences and bonds that people develop with places. The theory of place attachment has evolved from a predominately psychological concept about people's knowledge and understanding of their environment, to one that encompasses a sociological perspective and includes variations in culture and social issues. Crossing multiple disciplinary boundaries and being quite complex, place attachment theory has been a topic of considerable research, representing a complicated web of individual and group experiences that occur over a lifetime. Our attachments can impact how we think and feel about our environment.

Figure 5.1 Locks placed on a bridge represent the attachment that people feel toward a place or people they associate with the place.

Source: Matthias_Lemm CC.

To describe how people develop place attachment in terms of cultural aspects of the built environment, Low created a typology with six different symbolic links between people and place: *genealogical links* through history or family; linkages developed because of *loss* of land or destruction; *economic links* developed through land ownership or inheritance; *cosmological links* through religious or spiritual connections; links developed through *pilgrimages*; and *narrative links* through stories and place naming (Low, 1992, p. 166). These cultural connections with place can essentially be sorted into social, material, and ideological factors, and help determine how people build connections with place.

Emotion and feeling are central to the concept of place attachment with emotions often integrated with knowledge, beliefs, behaviors, and actions relating to a certain place (Low & Altman, 1992). The emotions experienced by a person are further interdependent to aspects of the place, including geographical qualities, environmental aesthetics, and personal or group identity (Seamon, 2013). People are more attached to places with good environmental quality, including those that have natural elements and distinct physical features or urban design characteristics (Scannell & Gifford, 1992). The context and frequency in which we feel these emotions is also important to determining the connections we develop.

Everyday Places versus Ritualized or Special Places

A person's feelings of attachment are deeply rooted in their everyday life experiences, and can go unnoticed until something dramatically shifts, either for the person or the place (Seamon, 2013). For example, it isn't until we move to a new home in a new community, that we start to miss the peculiar and unique aspects of our previous community that we once took for granted. The scene at the end of the iconic 1946 Christmas film, *It's a Wonderful Life,* portrays this deep connection to our daily experiences and places. Having glimpsed what life would be like if he had never been born, George Bailey played by James Stewart, runs through the snowy street of his hometown Bedford Falls gushing with emotion as he greets all of the places that he cherishes (Dirks, 2019). Daily habits can be very important to how we connect with a place.

In contrast, ritual interactions with the physical environment are often ephemeral and can be periodic, setting them apart from ordinary behavior. Rituals are very meaningful and symbolic and may evoke feelings of nostalgia, sentimentality or inspiration (Lawrence, 1992). Pilgrimages, a spiritual or religious ritual within the landscape, can foster a sense of place attachment for the people participating. Illustrating a significant experience for nearly 15 million people who make the journey per year, is the Muslim Hajj pilgrimage to Mecca and Medina in Saudi Arabia. In efforts to retain the meaning of this journey and spiritual place, but also reduce the impact that the massive influx of people have on the environment, UK-based Muslims are leading efforts to manage the environmental impact (Bhattay, 2017). Although this new focus on sustainability may have been initiated through a top-down approach, it does suggest that through the pilgrimage experience, people have developed a sense of responsibility for the physical place. These emotional connections are important for designers to recognize and carefully consider, especially when proposing changes or introducing new developments. Even if the new design is seen as an improvement, the change or loss can be difficult to accept.

When that change is in conflict with heritage principles or values, conflict and limited place attachment can result. Consider, for example, the challenge of conserving, developing and managing the growth of holy cities in the Middle East. Architect Sami Angawi laments that many valued Islamic buildings and heritage sites have been destroyed by the fast pace of cookie-cutter urban development, 'turning the holy sanctuary into a machine, a city which has no identity, no heritage, no culture and no natural environment' (Angawi, cited in Wainwright, 2012). We see this when the traditional Islamic architectural element called *mashrabiya,* characterized by an oriel window and ventilating veils enclosed in carved wooden latticework and fixed with colored glass, is poorly reinterpreted in contemporary design. The traditional *mashrabiya* merges cultural, visual and technical considerations, providing local identity (*genius loci*), a cooling and sun-shading device against intense sunlight (sustainable and biophilic design), while the latticework offers the chance to see the environment, but to stay unseen (prospect-refuge) – combined into a single element that can represent and reinforce place attachment. Unfortunately, in contemporary practice, flawed imitations often do not open and instead of offering valued ventilation, are a 'meaningless applique' stuck on flimsy rows of concrete arches and timber trellis (Angawi, cited in Wainwright, 2012). As Saliba (2015) emphasizes in *Urban Design and the Arab World*, we must acknowledge that the forces of colonialism, postmodernity and globalism combine to shape, challenge and reform urban places, with unique and sometimes contested regional, political and cultural identities. As urban design practice changes our cities, we must pause and reflect on how to better design with place attachment theory in mind.

The gentrification of neighborhoods, which often garners intense social justice debates, is a prime example of a place-based phenomenon that can uncover deep-seated feelings of place attachment. Gentrification is the process of improving the physical qualities of a neighborhood, which can result in greater appeal to more affluent populations, and subsequently the displacement of lower socioeconomic people as they are no longer able to afford the area. Two issues related to place attachment can result. If new people have moved into a neighborhood but remain relatively anonymous, they will not develop attachments either with their neighbors or with their community spaces. Consequently they will be less likely to care for their home, or work with others to improve their community (Manzo & Perkins, 2006). Further, when a person or group has romantic notions of their neighborhood, which may be in contrast to those of new community members, developers or decision-makers, conflicts may arise. This can happen during the gentrification or development process. Proposed changes, especially if significant, can represent a threat to place attachment and identity, regardless of the perceived value or anticipated benefit of these changes (Manzo & Perkins, 2006). Urban designers and planners must consider this theoretical concept when proposing community change.

A study in the United States by the Knight Foundation investigating community attachment found that people with strong attachments to their communities have a greater sense of pride in them, have a positive outlook on their future, and have a sense that they are the perfect place for them. The study identified three main drivers that led to community attachment:

- **Social offerings** – including places to meet other people and participate in cultural and social events, as well as the presence of community members who care about each other.

- **Openness** – how welcoming the community is to diverse people, including families, ageing people, minorities, and college students.
- **Aesthetics** – the physical beauty of the community and whether it includes quality parks, playgrounds, and trails.

These aspects can be influenced by landscape architects, urban designers, planners, architects and policymakers. For example, city councils can initiate, approve, or fund social events that will foster community connections, while designers can create public spaces that accommodate those events. Using the other theories discussed in this book – affordance, personal space, sense of place, prospect-refuge, and biophilic design theories – spaces can be designed to be welcoming, functional, accessible, engaging, comfortable, safe, and enjoyable. When these theories are used to create great places, place attachment is more likely to be an outcome.

Place Attachment and Caring for the Environment

Gaining control over space or being able to manipulate it, mold it, decorate it, or change it in some way, can have an impact on a positive sense of self-identity, enabling a person to create a place where they feel comfortable (Cooper Marcus, 1992). Feelings of place attachment often reinforce actions and routines that represent environmental care, which then in turn encourages a greater sense of place attachment (Seamon, 2013). These concepts reflect this sense of ownership or territoriality that people might feel in relation to places. Similarly, research on significant life experiences suggests that when young people have memorable experiences in nature and are able to interact with it, they develop feelings of attachment and are therefore more likely to care for the environment or participate in environmental activism (Barrett Hacking et al., 2018).

The threat of losing a significant landscape due to a development proposal can often trigger an emotional response that leads to protests and petitions. Although arguments against the development may focus on environmental or cultural sensitivities, such as loss of wildlife habitat, the people involved often have personal attachments to that place and are passionate about conserving it. Place attachment bonds can be a motivator for engaging in pro-environmental activities such as volunteering for ecological conservation or renovation projects (Upham et al., 2018). Such behavior indicates that place attachment bonds are significant for sustainability and protecting environments under threat from climate change.

For many people, climate change may still represent a remote or ambiguous phenomenon. If they haven't personally experienced the negative impacts, such as flooding or drought, or witnessed environmental degradation, such as coral reef bleaching, they may not have a personal connection to the issues. With good reason, researchers have begun to investigate these connections in order to take advantage of them in the context of renewable energy initiatives (Upham et al., 2018). Global climate change is one of the key challenges to which designers can make a positive contribution, as we discuss in Chapter 10. Understanding place attachment theory and incorporating it into sustainable design practice, can potentially improve outcomes and lead to a better future for all.

Creating Places to Foster Social Connections

Positive social experiences can also generate feelings of attachment where the environmental setting becomes part of the narrative and is symbolic of that experience (Riley, 1992). In the earlier example, *It's a Wonderful Life*, it is predominately the social connections with people in his community that connected George Bailey to his hometown. Deep connections with family and friends are important, but so are the informal social ties you develop with the barista at your regular coffee shop, your mail carrier, or the owner of your favorite local restaurant. Designing places that afford opportunities for these connections is important for people to develop attachments.

Neighborhood settings are seen as important when friends are present, as they provide a sense of security and belonging for children and adults alike (Min & Lee, 2006). It is the social features of a place, such

Figure 5.2 International PARKing Day provides a day when community members can take over a parking spot to create a small parklet.

Sources: Andrew Merger (top); Brisbane City Council (lower left and right).

as community events, that afford opportunities to develop attachments (Scannell & Gifford, 1992). Providing space for social connections to be made, and programming our urban spaces to facilitate these opportunities can potentially lead to the development of place attachment. This also happens when design educators, practitioners and concerned citizens reclaim neglected everyday places in a process known as tactical or guerrilla urbanism. Whether it is through international PARK(ing) day, during which parking spaces are temporarily turned into green parklets, as shown in Figure 5.2, or smaller initiatives to turn urban footpaths into community gardens or placing outdoor furniture in an alley, revitalizing and reinventing left-over spaces helps foster place attachment, brings people together, and creates great places. Alley activism, as Fialko and Hampton (2011) argue, could significantly increase public space and positively change the way we engage with our city – fostering place attachment in the most unlikely of places.

Place Processes: How We Develop Place Attachment

The six different but intertwined processes that Seamon (2013) identifies as important for place attachment are presented below. He believed designers should understand these processes if they are to observe how designed urban environments are used, and are significant if designers are to understand how place attachment can be encouraged and facilitated through design.

1. Place **interaction** or 'a day in the life of a place' focuses on the actions and interactions people regularly have with a place (Seamon, 2013, p. 16). These interactions also illuminate ideas of place dependence, referring to how well the place meets the day-to-day functional needs of a person, including tourists to an area (Ram, Björk & Weidenfeld, 2016).
2. Place **identity** includes the process through which people, associated with a place, identify it as a significant part of their world.
3. Place **release** involves the unexpected encounters and events people experience in a place, and which can lead to feeling a deeper sense of 'release' into themselves (Seamon, 2013, p. 17).
4. Place **realization** refers to the palpable presence of a place that combines the physical qualities and the human activities. This realization can be described as the *genius loci* of the space, as discussed in Chapter 4.
5. Place **creation** expresses how planning, policy and design can be used to create or change a place.
6. Place **intensification** involves the mechanisms used to revive and strengthen place, enabling the physical environment to contribute to enhancing the character and quality of a place.

The last three processes, realization, creation, and intensification are easily connected with design processes. Designers can intensify, create, and realize the special qualities of a place through alterations to the physical environment. The first three of interaction, identity and release can be influenced by the physical qualities of a place, but are processes that occur over time and are more indirectly connected to design. They require activities to occur and for people to develop emotional connections to the physical space.

Place attachment often involves proximity, which can be expressed by people living in a place or visiting it repeatedly, such as annual vacations to the same beachside town (Scannell & Gifford, 1992). Attachments to places from the past that people visit less frequently, or places they have left completely, can be exhibited through the naming of places, using buildings in ways that reflect their home culture, or by adding cultural artifacts and symbolic imagery reminiscent of those places. People create these memories of place within their personal homes or workplaces, but this practice is evident in public spaces as well. Little Italy, Chinatown, Koreatown and other ethnic enclaves, as shown in Figure 5.3 commonly represent the physical manifestation of place attachment experienced by a group. These places are often associated with specific industries,

Figure 5.3 Ethnic enclaves in large cities, such as Little Italy, Chinatown, or Little Havana demonstrate deep place attachments.

Sources: Mike (Squeakymarmot), Flickr (Little Italy); Osbornb, Flickr (Chinatown); Prayitno, Flickr (Little Havana).

activities, or lifestyles. As Riley wrote, 'The tie between the culture of the people and their landscape is the key to understanding collective human activity' (Riley, 1992, p. 16).

Positive Benefits of Place Attachment for Health and Wellbeing

Attachments and connections to places can be important for our emotional wellbeing. The satisfaction of our core psychological needs which often include: belonging, freedom and control, self-esteem, and meaning, are affected by how we develop attachments with places (Scannell & Gifford, 2017). Visualizing a place you are attached to can also enhance a sense of belonging, self-esteem and meaningfulness. But visualization doesn't impact feelings of freedom or control over the environment. These psychological needs can also be supported or reinforced in the following ways:

- **A sense of belonging** is generated when we have a connection to past important places or cultures, social ties to a community, and having a place to call home (Scannell & Gifford, 2017). Significant places from the past can provide a 'psychic anchor' (Cooper Marcus, 1992).
- **Feelings of freedom and control** can be supported when we have a sense of ownership over a space and being a custodian of an environment.
- **Self-esteem** can be developed when we have a distinct place identity, and pride in a significant place with unique features or cultural meaning (Scannell & Gifford, 2017).
- **Meaning in life** can be reinforced by important places that ground us and provide a center through which the rest of the world becomes coherent (Scannell & Gifford, 2017). Places which align with a person's values and preferred lifestyle can support 'place-congruent continuity' (Scannell & Gifford, 2017, p. 363).

People can experience attachments to places that offer a 'safe haven' where they retreat and gain emotional or physical relief (Scannell & Gifford, 1992). When people are strongly attached to their neighborhoods or communities they are often perceived as safer. These feelings of safety, either real or perceived, can provide respite from daily stress, and as such contribute to quality of life and satisfaction. This sense of safety may also relate to places which enable a sense of privacy, and allow us to be ourselves, hidden from the rest of the world (Cooper Marcus, 1992). Spaces that are designed with clear affordances for respite, as well as prospect-refuge, and also embrace their sense of place, can enhance our psychological attachments. These design features are also what makes a place unique and memorable.

Making Places Memorable

Understanding why and how people develop attachments to places and using that knowledge during the design process, can aid in the creation of better places that people will use and enjoy, take ownership of, and thrive in. Places that are designed with respect to the *genius loci* are often those that stick in our minds. Whether we are attracted to these places (e.g. our local botanic garden), they leave us in awe (e.g. a grand skyscraper or suspension bridge), or they provide us with a valuable experience in our lives (e.g. our high school or summer camp), they become memorable to us, and we develop attachments. Although designers can't always predict which places will be memorable because of social connections, it is likely that boring and mundane spaces will not be memorable.

To record our experiences in memorable places, we often take a photo of the place. It is interesting to wonder how sharing these experiences on social media such as Facebook, Instagram, and Snapchat, impact our attachment to places. Does taking multiple photos just to get one that is Instagram-worthy, or posing numerous times to get the best selfie, impact our appreciation and experience of a place? We are reminded of a line in the 2018 Netflix movie *Ibiza* about three young women who are in Spain for a weekend. The film shows them sitting on the beach watching an incredible sunset over the water, when Nikki, played by Vanessa Bayer, is impressed that they are not taking selfies, remarking, 'Look at us being all in the moment.'

Does this phenomenon referred to as 'selfie-gaze' tourism or '#MeTourism' (Sigala, 2018) limit our actual connection with a place? Research suggests that for tourists 'their satisfaction does not depend on the quality of the destination and experience, but on how well they manage impressions and attract "likes" and positive comments' (Sigala, 2018, p. 1). In this sense, a person is relying on the approval and interest of someone else to determine how they experience a place. In addition, taking a selfie can actually be dangerous when combined with risky behaviors such as standing on the edge of a cliff or posing with dangerous animals (Chiu, 2018). Interestingly, in 2016, Mumbai designated 16 'no selfie zones' across the city in response to numerous selfie-related deaths (Chui, 2018, p. 1). As this phenomenon is more common among teenagers and young adults, it begs the question as to if and how place attachment is evolving and the impact this will have on our desire to care for the environment.

Young children, who are not yet part of the selfie crowd, require a different premise to develop attachments to places. Designers are guided to enhance access to nature and to afford opportunities for free exploration in their environment when creating places which are memorable for children (Chawla, 1992). A design repertoire must include small hideouts, forts, and small leftover spaces, as places that enable undisturbed privacy and some level of manipulation. And in fact, for children, it is the forts, club houses, hideaways, and dens that are evidence of the first acts of dwelling or claiming a territory (Cooper Marcus, 1992). These spaces can solicit endless adventures and wonderful childhood experiences and generate feelings of attachment.

Digging Deeper

Place attachment is often researched using *phenomenological methods* to gain a deep understanding of the experiences people have and how they contribute (or not) to the attachments people feel. This type of research can also determine to which environments people feel most connected (Seamon, 2013). Phenomenology research, however, is time-consuming and often not possible within the context of a design project. Developing partnerships between researchers trained in phenomenology processes and designers may be a viable option if the timeline of the project is not linked to the timeline of the research.

Autobiographical memory is often seen as the primary method to gain insight about connections that people have to past places, especially those places important to children (Chawla, 1992). Gathering memories from adults about places they were attached to as children enables researchers to better understand and find clues about the physical characteristics of a place that foster feelings of attachment. *Environmental autobiographies* are often used with students studying design to prompt them to reflect on significant environments in their past and determine how those experiences have impacted them over time (Cooper Marcus, 1992). These methods are commonly used for significant life experience research (Barratt Hacking et al., 2018).

Another method to better understand a child's place attachment is *favorite place analysis* (Chawla, 1992) where data is gathered using mapping techniques with aerial photos of neighborhoods or communities. Participants can identify and describe their significant places in order to understand where and why they have developed attachments. Other common techniques include child-led walking tours, drawing activities, and digital methods, such as photovoice or digital storytelling. These can be creative ways to gain rich qualitative information about place attachments which can provide designers with insights on what is important to stakeholders or even potential clients.

Designing with Place Attachment in Mind

Like many theories about people and place, place attachment can provide important clues about the impact of our environments on how we feel, think, and act. And like with most theories of this nature, understanding how this knowledge of place attachment informs design can be confusing. In fact, sometimes knowing that individuals have different attachments that are developed over long periods of time can often make design decisions more complex and difficult. Although, designing urban spaces for multiple stakeholders and population groups can be difficult, it is essential that we understand why and how people become attached to places. There is too much at stake if we ignore these connections. The next chapter discusses biophilia, which outlines people's inherent preference and need for nature.

References

Altman, I. & Low, S. (Eds.) (1992). *Place Attachment*. New York: Plenum Press.

Barrett Hacking, E., Cushing, D. & Barrett, R. (2018). Exploring the Significant Life Experiences of Childhood nature. In Cutter-Mackenzie, A., Malone, K. & Barratt Hacking (Eds). *Research Handbook on Childhoodnature*. Berlin: Springer, 1–18.

Bhattay, A. (2017). Hajj: How to Make this Three-Million Strong Muslim Pilgrimage Environmentally Friendly. *The Independent* (September 5). Retrieved from www.independent.co.uk/travel/asia/hajj-pilgrimage-green-guide-mecca-medina-muslims-environmental-friendly-travel-islam-sustainable-a7930676.html

Chawla, L. (1992). Childhood Place Attachments. In I. Altman & S. Low (Eds.), *Place Attachment*. New York: Plenum Press, 63–86.

Chiu, A. (2018). More than 250 People Have Died While Taking Selfies, Study Finds. *The Washington Post* (October 3). Retrieved from www.washington post.com/news/morning-mix/wp/2018/10/03/more-than-250-people-world wide-have-died-taking-selfies-study-finds/?utm_term=.9de1feaa0112

Cooper Marcus, C. (1992). Environmental Memories. In I. Altman & S. Low (Eds.), *Place Attachment*. New York: Plenum Press, 87–112.

Dirks, T. (2019). Filmsite Review: *It's a Wonderful Life* – 1946. Retrieved from www.filmsite.org/itsa.html (accessed February 7, 2019).

Fialko, M. & Hampton, J. (2011). *Seattle Integrated Alley Handbook: Activating Alleys for a Lively City*. UW Green Futures Lab, Scan Design Foundation & Gehl Architects. Seattle, WA: University of Washington.

Lawrence, D. (1992). Transcendence of Place. In I. Altman & S. Low (Eds.), *Place Attachment*. New York: Plenum Press, 211–230.

Low, S. (1992). Symbolic Ties that Bind. In I. Altman & S. Low (Eds.), *Place Attachment*. New York: Plenum Press, 165–185.

Low, S. & Altman, I. (1992). Place Attachment. In I. Altman & S. Low (Eds.), *Place Attachment*. New York: Plenum Press, 1–12.

Manzo, L. & Perkins, D. (2006). Finding Common Ground: The Importance of Place Attachment to Community Participation and Planning. *Journal of Planning Literature* 20(4): 335–350.

Min, B. & Lee, J. (2006). Children's Neighborhood Place as a Psychological and Behavioral Domain. *Journal of Environmental Psychology* 26(1): 51–71.

Ram, Y., Björk, P. & Weidenfeld, A. (2016). Authenticity and Place Attachment of Major Visitor Attractions. *Tourism Management* 52: 110–122.

Riley, R. (1992). Attachment to the Ordinary Landscape. In I. Altman & S. Low (Eds.), *Place Attachment*. New York: Plenum Press, 13–35.

Saliba, R. (2015). *Urban Design in the Arab World: Reconceptualizing Boundaries*. London: Routledge.

Scannell, L. & Gifford, R. (1992). Comparing the Theories of Interpersonal and Place Attachment. In I. Altman & S. Low (Eds.), *Place Attachment*. New York: Plenum Press, 24–36.

Scannell, L. & Gifford, R. (2017). Place Attachment Enhances Psychological Need Satisfaction. *Environment and Behavior* 49(4): 359–389.

Seamon, D. (2013). Place Attachment and Phenomenology: The synergistic dynamism of place. In L. Manzo & P. Devine-Wright (Eds.), *Place Attachment: Advances in Theory, Methods, and Applications*. Abingdon: Routledge, 11–22.

Sigala, M. (2018). #MeTourism: The Hidden Costs of Selfie Tourism. *The Conversation* (January 9, 2018). Retrieved from www.abc.net.au/news/2018-01-02/metourism-selfie-travel-instagram-facebook-holiday-snaps/9298140

Upham, P., Johansen, K., Bögel, P., Axon, S., Garard, J. & Carney, S. (2018) Harnessing Place Attachment for Local Climate Mitigation? Hypothesising Connections between Broadening Representations of Place and Readiness for Change. *Local Environment* 23(9): 912–919.

Wainwright, O. (2012). Mecca's Mega Architecture Casts Shadow over Hajj. *The Guardian* (October 23). Retrieved from www.theguardian.com/artanddesign/2012/oct/23/mecca-architecture-hajj1

6　Biophilic Design Theory
The Healing Power of Nature

Over 86,000 images of nature were shared on Instagram during the 30 Days Wild challenge in June 2018. The challenge was simple: *every day*, for the month of June, go outside and interact with nature. From a butterfly hunt, exploring a sensory garden, or simply pausing to engage with plants and insects on their daily work commute, more than 350,000 Britons made more time to experience nature during the Wildlife Trust's challenge. Mass engagement campaigns, such as 30 Days Wild, address a significant public health crisis: people spend nearly 80% of their time *indoors*, and are increasingly disconnected, both physically and psychologically, from nature. Biophilia is a conscious acknowledgment that people need contact with nature to thrive, and in this chapter we analyze the emerging movement of biophilic design, positioning nature as a central component in the design process.

Defining Biophilia

The theoretical concept of biophilia is the inherent desire humans have to connect with nature, and other forms of life. Bio means 'life or living things'; philia means 'love.' First defined by psychoanalyst Erich Fromm (1973) as 'the passionate love of life and of all that is alive,' the term biophilia was subsequently popularized by American botanist Edward Wilson in his 1984 book *Biophilia*, where he argued that our evolutionary past means humans are hard-wired to focus on, appreciate, and emotionally connect with nature and other living things, primarily animals. Historically, and for the vast majority of human history, we have lived in small family groups, in rural communities and in close contact with natural surroundings and animals. The sun provided warmth and light; large trees offered shade, building materials, and a place to sleep; animals and seasonal vegetation provided food; and herbs were used as medicine.

Our historically close connection to nature has been broken by rapid and unprecedented urbanization. In 1800, just 3% of the world's population

Figure 6.1 Biophilic Singapore.
Source: Victor Garcia (CC on Unsplash).

lived in cities. Two hundred years later, half of the world's population lives in densely populated urban areas. Thirty years from now, in 2050, 68% of humans will live in cities (United Nations, 2005). Yet, from an evolutionary perspective, we are not wired to live in buildings or urban settings. We have, at a very deep and unconscious level, a strong need to be close to and connected to nature. Whether it is biophilic design in high-density Singapore as in Figure 6.1, or using the stepping-stone crossing at Cheong-gyecheon stream in downtown Seoul in Figure 6.2, these designs are a good reminder that being in, viewing or having fun in nature, is enjoyable and makes us feel calmer and happier – especially in busy urban settings. And as Wilson explains, our desire to be in nature is why we naturally seek out national parks, green spaces, and rivers, and will frequently travel long distances to simply look at and walk beside the seashore.

The Therapeutic Value of People–Nature Interactions

A large and growing body of literature consistently demonstrates the therapeutic benefits of people–nature interactions. Contact with nature

Figure 6.2 Biophilic urban renewal in downtown Seoul, South Korea. Previously a highway, the 10.9 kilometre (6.8 mile) long Cheonggyecheon stream is now a popular public space.

Source: riNux (Flickr, CC BY SA-2.0).

is truly healing. Research on varying proximity, duration, scale, and sensory experience of people-nature interactions consistently concludes that nature is physically and psychologically restorative. Multiple qualitative, quantitative and experimental studies from a broad range of disciplines reveal that even a tiny dose of nature (e.g. a view from a window, a walk through a park, or simply looking at pictures of nature) has a positive impact on our health, happiness, and overall wellbeing. Contact with nature fosters child development, improves our immunity, reduces healing times after surgery, and increases our productivity and creativity. Specific benefits include reductions in depression, anxiety, blood pressure, heart disease, workplace stress, aggression, as well as reductions in rates of domestic violence, obesity, and diabetes. A comprehensive and up-to-date overview of this extensive body of research can be found in the *2018 Oxford Textbook of Nature and Public Health* (Van den Bosch & Bird, 2018).

The power of nature for healing was established by Roger Ulrich (1984), who in a study of surgical patients in a Pennsylvanian hospital revealed that (compared to matched patients with a view of an exterior brick wall) patients with a view of trees from their bed had statistically shorter hospitalization time, reduced pain medication, and fewer negative comments in nurses' notes. Ulrich also led the biophilic redesign of a windowless hospital emergency room which transformed the space from plain white walls and bland furniture into a biophilic-inspired space with a large mural of nature, large plants and furniture in naturalistic colors. These simple changes, which increased the *representation* and not the actual *contact* with nature, still resulted in significant reductions in aggressive behavior, stress and hostility (Kellert, 2018).

Other research consistently reports similar findings. A large UK-wide, cross-sectional study of 94,879 participants linked residential greenness with lower odds of depression, even when controlling for other physical, built and social environment variables (Sarkar, Webster & Gallacher, 2018). Research using brain scans concluded that a 90-minute nature walk reduced neural activity in the brain area linked to mental illness (Bratman, Hamilton, Hahn & Daily, 2015). In a hospital experiment, thirty elderly women were assessed at the same time for two days in two experimental areas: a hospital rooftop forest and, as a control, an outdoor parking lot. Despite only viewing each environment for 12 minutes, measurements of heart rate showed they entered a physiologically relaxed state when in the simulated rooftop forest environment (Matsunga et al., 2011). Most hospital patients only receive a few minutes of focused attention from doctors, nurses, and allied health staff, but are in their hospital room, bed or chair for hours. Ensuring people have views of and easy access to nature in hospitals, homes, and workplaces is a simple way to facilitate health and wellbeing. In fact, contact with nature is so healing that, alongside medical prescriptions, doctors in some countries have started issuing 'green prescriptions' – written advice that engaging in nature would help the person's physical and/or mental health (more on this in Chapter 7).

The positive society-wide benefits of incorporating nature in our urban spaces is well documented, particularly in terms of reducing rates of crime and violence. Seminal research by Kuo and Sullivan (2001a) documented the impact of greenery for residents of public housing developments in inner-urban Chicago. Compared to buildings with little or no vegetation, police records revealed that buildings with high levels of greenery reported half the amount of crime: 48% fewer property crimes and 56% fewer violent crimes. As well as reducing crime, the presence of greenery also reduced self-reported rates of domestic violence (Kuo & Sullivan, 2001b).

The presence of nature also reduces workplace absenteeism and enhances productivity in office settings, with experimental research reporting that the cognitive performance of workers in 'green' offices is double that of people working in conventional environments. One study systematically varied indoor environmental quality: compared to baseline data from a day in a conventional building, cognitive scores were after 61% higher spending a day in a green building and 101% higher after two days (Allen et al., 2015). A large body of building science research powerfully highlights the importance of sustainable green design features, such as ventilation, air quality, thermal comfort, noise, and day-lighting for wellbeing, health, and productivity, as discussed further in Chapter 10. Interactions with animals also support wellbeing; simply watching fish swimming in an aquarium fosters feelings of calmness, lowering both blood pressure and heart rate (Cracknell et al., 2016). In explaining the specific psychological mechanisms at play, most researchers point to attention restoration theory, which postulates that the constantly changing stimuli in nature (the wind, the grass, the leaves, sunlight and shadows, the birds and the bees) involuntarily grabs our attention and forces us to pause and relax – what Kaplan and Kaplan (1989) labelled the attention restoration hypothesis.

Designing with Biophilic Theory – the Emergence of Biophilic Design

Redesigning cities, spaces, and buildings so nature is incorporated is a design priority, given the public health benefits and cognitive, psychological and physiological wellbeing. And it is the theoretical concept of biophilia, biophilic urbanism and biophilic design that help make the experience of, and interactions with nature, a part of everyday urban life. By challenging the artificial separation of the built and natural environment, a biophilic city not only fosters health and wellbeing, it can also create a resilient city – beautiful, relaxing and exciting urban nature draws people away from technology and out of their homes, with informal social interactions fostering the development of social capital.

The biophilic design movement provides a framework for designing for, with, and from nature. This thoughtful, innovative and evidence-based design approach actively facilitates nature-human connections, ensuring nature is celebrated, not demolished or erased. As early proponents, Kellert and Wilson (1993) define biophilic design as the deliberate attempt to translate and apply an understanding of the human affinity to connect with natural systems and processes (biophilia) into the design of our built environments. Biophilic design explicitly acknowledges that, as a biological organism, (1) people need regular contact with nature to thrive, and (2) we must design our modern built environment to facilitate and support human-nature interactions. An extensive body of literature now documents the approach of biophilic urbanism and design, with biophilia an explicit guideline in some contemporary green building certification systems (see, for example, the Living Building Challenge described in Chapter 10). Biophilia helps reframe design practice, opening up a powerful new narrative and paradigm where nature is prioritized.

A biophilic city is much more than the visible physical design features of green infrastructure, urban wildlife and walkable environments (although they are, of course, critical; Beatley, 2010). A truly biophilic city requires a seismic shift in what we view as important – the emotional connection to, and curiosity about nature – which is reflected in policy and budget priorities. As we write this book, more than one million dead fish have been scooped from Australia's largest river system, the Darling River. January 2019 was Australia's hottest recorded month in more than 100 years. In conjunction with the ongoing drought, river pollution, and contested environmental policies on irrigation, the extreme heat resulted in this environmental disaster. Momentarily at least, this crisis has reminded disconnected city-dwellers about the interconnectivity of ecological systems in rural landscapes, as well as the potentially devastating impacts of climate change. In a similar fashion, engaging in biophilic design practice can reconnect urban dwellers with nature, and the hourly, daily, and seasonal variations of natural living systems.

The world's most revered buildings often demonstrate a strong affinity for the natural world and, in a process known as biomimicry, view nature as 'model, measure and mentor' – as Benyus (1997) explains, designers must look to and learn from nature, the 'wellspring of good ideas'. Think, for example how the close connection to the landscape in Frank Lloyd Wright's Fallingwater enchants viewers. Built in rural Pennsylvania in 1937, iconic Fallingwater (the top image in Figure 6.3) straddles a waterfall, with the building receding into the natural landscape thanks to the natural building materials, stone façade and long horizontal plane. Wright's innovative design, purposely situating the residence directly *above* the waterfall rather than merely *viewing* it, brings the embodied experience of nature, the presence, noise and movement of falling water, directly into the residents' everyday experience of the building. This thoughtful and experiential integration of nature into the built environment is the essence of biophilic design.

The bottom image in Figure 6.3 shows Bosco Verticale (Vertical Forest) in Milan, voted the best tall building in the world in 2015 and is a model for metropolitan reforestation that fosters urban biodiversity. Milanese architect Stefano Boeri tellingly described his vision for the building in biophilic terms, as 'a house for trees and birds, inhabited also by humans, in the Milan sky.' With over 20,000 trees and plants covering the twin high-rise residential towers, for every person living in the building, there are two trees, 10 shrubs and 40 herbaceous plants. The building attracts local wildlife, with many birds' nests on the roofs, including small hawks and swifts that had previously disappeared from the city. Bosco Verticale also clearly demonstrates how the contemporary vision of best practice architecture and urban design is radically biophilic. While the green roofs and living walls illustrated in Bosco Verticale are the most publicly visible example of biophilic design, this philosophy advocates an immersive sensory approach that integrates multiple natural elements into the built environment. Biophilic design requires repeated, sustained contact

Figure 6.3 Fallingwater, and the twin residential towers, Bosco Verticale.
Sources: Pixabey (Fallingwater); Chris Barbalis on Unsplash (Bosco Verticale).

with nature using the materials, patterns, textures, forms and features to engage all senses: vision (visual access to greenery and water, views, diversity of plants), sound (falling water, birds, butterflies, and insects), smell (scented plants), and touch (air, rain, mist, plants, sunlight). And by creatively responding to the unique local topography, climate and culture, biophilic design typically amplifies the local natural characteristics of the site and so fosters a unique sense of place, the *genius loci*, as presented in Chapter 4.

The nature-based solutions of biophilic design can also contribute to climate change adaptation and mitigation, when designers simultaneously engage with the principles of restorative and regenerative sustainability, as detailed in Chapter 10. Biophilic design features, such as trees, green roofs and walls, can also help cool the city, reducing the energy needs and impact of buildings and the urban heat island effect. Simple decisions, for example, to replace conventional asphalt or concrete parking lots with grass or permeable pavers, reduce stormwater runoff to mitigate the impact of flash floods. Despite originating from ancient practices and principles, biophilic design is positively disruptive. It boldly reimagines how nature might transform our built environment and actively seeks opportunities to repair, restore and creatively insert nature into urban settings, wherever possible.

Kellert, the first to identify key principles and practices, aided designers to integrate natural systems into their design process. He categorized biophilic design tools or strategies into three types: *direct experience with nature* (actual contact in the built environment with nature, including with natural landscapes, weather, sunlight, water, animals, air, plants); *indirect experience with natural forms* (patterns and processes of nature, images of nature, natural materials, botanical motifs, natural colors, naturalistic shapes and forms, biomimicry and artwork featuring nature); and *characteristics of space and place* (the spatial features of the natural environment, including connection to place and our preference for prospect-refuge). Kellert's Biophilic Design Framework identifies six elements and seventy attributes of biophilic design that promote positive interactions between people and the natural world (Kellert, Heerwagen & Mador, 2008; Kellert & Calabrese, 2015). Recognizing that such long lists were challenging for urban designers to put in practice, Browning, Ryan and Clancy (2014) recently consolidated these elements and attributes into 14 core patterns of biophilic design, grouped into three different contexts: *Nature in the Space, Natural Analogies* and *Nature of the Space.*

Browning and colleagues describe how each specific biophilic design feature supports stress reduction, cognitive performance, and emotion/mood enhancement. For example, water features help lower stress and blood pressure; breezes created by ventilation systems keep people alert; gardens and internal meandering paths inside buildings foster interactions. They also present one memorable experience for occupants of the

Table 6.1 Browning et al.'s fourteen core patterns of biophilic design.

Context	Pattern	Design features and examples
Nature in the space The 'direct, physical and ephemeral presence' of nature in the built environment, through movement, diversity, and multi-sensory interactions. Includes presence of plants, inside and out, green roofs and living walls, water features (fountains, aquariums), butterfly and courtyard gardens	1. Visual connection with nature	A view to elements of nature, natural processes and living systems. The internal birch tree and moss garden, centrally located at the entrance/exit to the *New York Times* building in New York City provides an oasis of calm in busy Times Square.
	2. Non-visual connection with nature	Often undervalued, non-visual design interactions stimulate our other senses (sound, touch, smell and taste; auditory, haptic, olfactory, or gustatory) to deliberately and positively remind us of our connection to nature. Obvious examples include the smells of fragrant herbs and flowers, and sounds of flowing water.
	3. Non-rhythmic sensory stimuli	This is the rich sensory non-rhythmic stimuli of nature, in consistent and unpredictable motion. Buildings located near natural habitats enable these ephemeral experiences for residents; leaves blow in a breeze, the water ripples and insects buzz. In Australia, Urban Arts Projects have created an ever-changing kinetic façade on the walls of Brisbane's Domestic Airport Terminal car park – which moves and ripples in the wind, and with the sunlight creating patterns of light and shade. This façade also addresses sustainability considerations, providing both ventilation and shade. The waterfront façade of the Bund Finance Center in Shanghai also moves with the wind.
	4. Thermal and airflow variability	Here buildings and spaces have subtle changes in airflow and surface temperature that mimic natural environments. Khoo Teck Puat Hospital in Singapore, described below, is a good example of how thoughtful design maximizes daylight, light/shade variability, fresh air and natural breezes to increase thermal comfort.
	5. Presence of water	Seeing, hearing or touching water is immediately calming. A water-filled channel runs down the central courtyard of Louis I. Kahn's 1965 Louis Kahn Salk Institute in California, towards the Pacific Ocean. The simple power and beauty of this space, where 'concrete meets calm' is immeasurable.
	6. Dynamic and diffuse light	Clever use of light and shadow displays the natural circadian processes occurring in nature, conveying movement, intrigue and calm. For example, the Paramit factory in Malaysia, built in 2017, receives diffused natural light from open glass walls and skylights, shaded by surrounding vegetation.

	7. Connection with natural systems	Being directly connected with natural systems raises awareness of nature's seasonality, and is often a relaxing or profound moment. Think, for example, how the use of natural materials, plants and sunlight bring the surrounding forest to life in E. Fay Jones's Thorncrown Chapel, or how the pedestrian bridges of Figure 6.4 directly connect users with water.
Natural analogues Use of organic, non-living and indirect evocations (patterns, materials) of nature	8. Biomorphic forms and patterns	Bringing the shapes and forms of nature indoors, this is the symbolic reference to contoured, patterned, textured or numerical arrangements as seen in nature. The biophilic patterns of the Kungsträdgården underground metro station in Stockholm are a clever example.
	9. Material connection with nature	Materials and elements from nature, with minimal processing, reflect the unique local ecology and create a distinct, authentic sense of place. For example, all materials for the ecologically sustainable development of Alila Villas Uluawtu (in Bali, Indonesia) designed by Singapore firm WOHA were sourced locally. Stones were from the site, only recycled bamboo and timber was used, and the terraced roof is made from Balinese volcanic pumice rock.
	10. Complexity and order	This pattern is seen when rich sensory information adheres to a similar spatial hierarchy as encountered in nature. Browning et al. list the cathedral-like Allen Lambert Galleria and Atrium at Brookfield Place in Toronto, Ontario as an example. Designed by Santiago Calatrava (1992), orderly columns form a canopy of complex tree-like forms shining diffused light and intriguing shadows onto the courtyard.
Nature of the space How humans respond, both psychologically and physiologically, to different spatial configurations	11. Prospect	Prospect, as discussed in Chapter 2, is when an unimpeded long view enables a sense of safety and control. The central plaza of the Salk Institute is often cited as an example, with the presence of balconies and open floor plans enabling prospect.
	12. Refuge	A refuge, as discussed in Chapter 2, is a protected place that provides concealment. Spaces with weather and climate protection, including seats with the sides covered, are common examples.
	13. Mystery	Mystery taps into that sense of discovery or anticipation offered by partially obscured views enticing people to explore. Browning et al. list the obscured views in Prospect Park in Brooklyn, New York, designed by Frederick Law Olmsted and Calvert Vaux, as exemplary examples.
	14. Risk/peril	A space with risk/peril feels a little dangerous, but has a reliable safeguard. An often-cited example is the public outdoor artwork Levitated Mass at Los Angeles County Museum of Art, where people walk directly underneath a large boulder.

COOKFOX Architects' New York office who witnessed a hawk killing a small bird, transforming perceptions of their green roof. No longer was the green roof simply a decorative garden; it was now seen as an important part of the urban ecosystem. Table 6.1 lists Browning et al.'s fourteen patterns, as well as practical design examples that show how these patterns often interconnect in design practice. And, as Kaplan, Kaplan and Ryan (1998) remind us, there is rarely one universal design solution: the 'correct' solution is locally-responsive to the site's unique characteristics.

Biophilic Design Theory in Practice

Our discussion of biophilic design now details three examples at very different scales: biophilic urbanism (Singapore, 'city in a garden'), innovative healthcare (hospitals and the Maggie's buildings), and bridges (the Moses bridge and Batbridge).

Singapore – Creating a 'City in a Garden' through Biophilic Urbanism

Figure 6.3 illustrates our first example, biophilic urbanism in Singapore. This compact island city-state in south-east Asia is the third most densely populated country in the world (7,909 people per square kilometer of land area) and has a strong vision to be a 'city in a garden'. In 1963, then-Singapore Prime Minister Lee Kuan Yew (dubbed Singapore's 'chief gardener') launched a greening scheme, planting a sapling at the Holland Circus traffic roundabout. More than two million trees have subsequently been planted, creating a lush green network of parks, gardens, nature reserves and greenspaces designed to purposely connect residents (and visitors) with nature. As well as improving urban biodiversity and visual amenity, the conscious integration of landscape design features (shade, shelter, air, views, vegetation) helps manage the tropical climate, reduces the heat island effect and ambient temperatures, and improves air and water quality.

Nature is central to Singapore's branding, as the project titled *Gardens in the Bay* illustrates. Built on reclaimed land, this iconic 101-hectare site is designed to bring people, nature and technology together, highlighting how natural systems work. These large metallic structures, 'Super Trees', are covered in plants and are climbable, as illustrated in the top images of Figure 6.3. A comparison of two satellite photos from 1986 and 2007 show that, with a 70% increase in population, the green canopy in Singapore has increased 20% (Newman, 2014). This story of biophilic Singapore has been made into a film, providing inspiration and guidelines to others (Films for Action, 2012).

A range of policies, financial incentives, seminars and award schemes support biophilic design practice. To increase vertical greenery, Singapore's

Skyrise Greenery Incentive Scheme funds up to 50% of installation costs of rooftop and vertical plantings, and celebrates innovative projects through annual awards. A 2017 winner was the fifth-story Eco-Community Garden at Our Tampines Hub. Managed by volunteers, this visible and lushly planted garden uses universal design principles to ensure there are specifically designed planters for older people and wheelchair users (for a discussion on age-friendly and inclusive design, see Chapter 9).

Singapore's National Parks Board also works to 'conserve, create, sustain and enhance the green infrastructure'. The Park Connectors Network converts otherwise neglected land (e.g., drainage swales, foreshore areas and road reserves) into green corridors that link major parks, as well as provide lighting, rain shelters and exercise stations. The transformation of a straight 3.2 km concrete stormwater collection and drainage ditch into a beautiful, naturally meandering stream is a wonderful example of turning underutilized space into a special biophilic-inspired place. Led by German landscape designer Herbert Dreiseitl, the development of Bishan-Ang Mo Kio park reconnected local residents in high rise apartments with the river and park, with the redesign of conventional grey infrastructure (concrete stormwater collection) into what has now become an exemplar of biophilic-inspired design and blue-green urbanism. Blue urbanism emphasizes the connecting of cities to their oceans, as well as nature, aka green urbanism (Beatley, 2014; Dreiseitl et al., 2015). This ecologically restored river has become an important part of the public realm, fostering social interactions, physical activity and engagement with nature.

Illustrating how good practice can become everyday practice, the work of Singapore-based WOHA, an architectural design team led by Wong Mun Summ and Richard Hassell (WOHA being a combination of their last names), is often recognized in these awards. WOHA designed *Kampung Admiralty*, winner of the 2017 Skyrise Greenery Outstanding Award and World Building of the Year at the 2018 World Architecture Festival. Kampung Admiralty is Singapore's first integrated public development, providing a mix of commercial, community, healthcare and medical services, as well as residential dwellings and senior living. This multi-purpose building has been described as a prototype that responds to an increasing ageing population. WOHA's biophilic design is a layered construction of spacious patios and greenery on a series of stratified levels. The amount of green space is greater than the building's overall footprint. Species that help with stormwater filtration have been purposely planted on the ground floor, with species that attract biodiversity and encourage habitat creation planted in the small farm plots that residents tend. These examples all illustrate how Singapore is taking purposeful steps toward a holistic vision of biophilic urbanism – one where people don't visit nature, but actually live in it. As Beatley argues, 'why should one have to walk to the park or visit the park – rather, shouldn't the city be situated in a park, that is, be the park?' (Beatley, 2016, p. 29).

Figure 6.4 Biophilic Singapore – Garden in the Bay, Bishan-Ang Mo Kio and Khoo Teck Puat hospital.

Sources: Chen Hu and Victor Garcia (Unsplash); You-Yong Sim (Flickr, CC BY SA-2.0) (Khoo Teck Puat hospital).

Biophilic Design in Healthcare

Our second example focuses on contemporary hospital design, which has become strongly biophilic. Once utilitarian, cold and clinical, healthcare spaces are increasingly designed to be comfortable, patient-centered and nature-inspired healing environments. Whether through installing internal gardens, bird feeders at windows, and vertical greening, or using technology to play soothing scenes and sounds from nature (see, for example, the tranquil ocean films from Mindsettle) contemporary hospitals are at the forefront of best practice innovative biophilic design (Totaforti, 2018). As Kellert explains, we are at the dawn of a revolutionary change in the design of healthcare facilities, with design 'that recognizes how much the human body, mind and spirit remain deeply contingent on the quality of the connections to a world beyond ourselves of which we remain a part' (Kellert, 2018, p. 251).

In Australia, the 2011 design of the 272-bed, one billion dollar Melbourne Royal Children's Hospital also had the vision to create 'a hospital in a park', winning over 30 awards including the 2012 World Architecture Festival 'World's Best Health Building'. The Bates Smart design team drew inspiration from the unique sense of place (see Chapter 4), specifically the natural textures, colors and forms of the surrounding bushland park, and integrated a 'soft fascination' of nature throughout the building. The exterior is covered in sunshade 'leaves', inspired from a tree canopy; inside, a spacious and naturally lit central atrium offers playgrounds, performance space and large scale artworks, as well as an aquarium and meerkat enclosure. The main hospital concourse has large scale artwork, shops and light-filled open spaces, centered around a two-story reef aquarium featuring 40 different fish species, two black tip reef sharks and one epaulette shark, all found on Australia's Great Barrier Reef. The design maximizes natural light and views of the neighboring parkland which features a large playground easily accessed from the hospital.

At a smaller-scale, nature can inspire design for creative and playful way-finding. London's Evelina Children's Hospital has a distinctive ecological theme for each level (for example, 'Ocean,' 'Arctic,' 'Forest' to 'Savannah,' 'Mountain,' 'Sky'), with different colors and creatures providing cues for way-finding. Whole creatures, such as butterflies, are found at the major arrival point, and become progressively dissected as you go further in – meaning a child might find a wing under a bed (Lawson, 2010).

Perhaps the most enlightening examples of biophilic-inspired healthcare designs are Maggie's Centres. Founded by the late Maggie Keswick Jencks and her husband, architecture theorist Charles Jencks, Maggie's Centres are beautifully designed, cozy sanctuaries for terminally ill patients, located across the UK and Hong Kong. Described as the 'architecture of hope', the expressively biophilic brief for Maggie's Centres, excerpt below, encourages the use of light, natural materials and contact with nature to raise 'your spirits when you walk into it' (Maggie's Centres, 2015, p. 10).

> The interplay between outside and inside space, the built and the 'natural' environment is an important one. Sheltered inside, it helps to be reminded by a seasonal and changing scene outside, that you are still part of a living world . . . Landscape gardeners will use their planting plans to incorporate scent as well as sight, to think about how their planting will behave in the rain as well as in the sun, to create areas which will have filtered privacy, to plant bulbs which will come up each year, trees and shrubs that bud and blossom and berry, plants that even 'die well' before returning next year. Sometimes, all that a person can bear, if they are in acute distress, is to look out of the window from a sheltered place, at the branch of a tree moving in the wind. We would like there to be as many opportunities as possible to look out from wherever you are in the building, even if it is to an internal planted courtyard.
>
> (Maggie's Centres, 2015, p. 5)

Whereas the institutionalized environments of hospital architecture are traditionally clinical and cold, architects for Maggie's Oldham purposefully uses the warmth of wood to express hope. Nature and daylight are powerfully brought into the interior via a large asymmetrical hole through which a tree grows. Similarly, Norman Foster's Manchester Maggie's Centre is a light-filled timber-framed space, designed to dissolve into the gardens. Large window walls offer nature views, angled cross-beams form zigzagging patterns, and triangular skylights filter light into the offices. Reflecting on Maggie's Centre London, one woman with cancer commented that the garden 'will allow people to be themselves and have their own space without having to speak to anyone and sometimes that's more valuable than any medicine: one can take courage from being in a good place, breathing in courage and breathing out fear' (Shackell & Walter, 2012, p. 8).

Biophilic Design in Unlikely Places

Biophilic design even extends to unlikely places, such as the pedestrian bridges in Figure 6.5. Several global design firms are turning the experience of walking across a bridge into a biophilic experience, for both people and local wildlife. In the Netherlands, RO&AD Architects created the Moses bridge; an invisible sunken pedestrian bridge that provides an access route to the 17th-century defense structure Fort de Roovere. This prize-winning bridge was 2011 Build of the Year by the Union of Dutch Architects, with its trench-like aesthetic inspired by the location. From afar, the bridge is non-existent; closer in, people experience walking through water – without getting wet (just as Moses did). This design is inherently biophilic, using predominantly natural materials (rot resistant wood lined with foil) to symbolize the immersion into the water.

Again in the Netherlands, Next Architects developed eco-friendly functional infrastructure that also serves nature: a bat friendly bridge, designed in collaboration with bat experts at the Dutch Mammal Society. Batbridge has a thick concrete core which warms the bats in winter, cooling them in summer, and provides crevices that facilitate springtime roosting. The wooden cladding is purposely spaced to fit the bats.

Moving toward a Greener Future

Of course, biophilic design is more than a stylistic aesthetic choice; it is a design philosophy that consciously integrates nature with the built environment, to elicit biophilic responses. These examples all demonstrate how best-practice biophilic design can afford a magical and deeply immersive experience, integrating the calming shapes, sounds, textures, and smells of nature into the design of buildings, parks, homes and office spaces. Across the globe, designers are using biophilic design principles in innovative ways.

Figure 6.5 Biophilic bridge design – the Moses bridge.
Sources: © RO&AD Architecten.

The examples shared in this chapter provide a strong evidence-base for biophila. Designers have a rare opportunity to positively re-design our built environment to foster physiological and psychological health. We must embrace, advocate for, and experiment with biophilic designs, to create an alternative nature-inspired vision for the future, in which our urban spaces are greener, not greyer.

References

Allen, J., MacNaughton, P., Satish, U., Santanam, S., Vallarino, J. & Spengler, J. (2015). Associations of Cognitive Function Scores with Carbon Dioxide, Ventilation, and Volatile Organic Compound Exposures in Office Workers: A Controlled Exposure Study of Green and Conventional Office Environments. *Environmental Health Perspectives* 124(6): 805–812.

Beatley, T. (2010). *Biophilic Cities*. Washington, DC: Island Press.

Beatley T. (2014). *Blue urbanism: Exploring Connections between Cities and Oceans*. Washington, DC: Island Press.

Beatley T. (2016). *Handbook of Biophilic City Planning and Design*. Washington, DC: Island Press.

Benyus, J. (1997). *Biomimicry: Innovation Inspired by Nature*. New York: HarperCollins.

Bratman, G., Hamilton, J., Hahn, K & Daily, G. (2015). Nature Experience Reduces Rumination and Subgenal Prefontal Cortex Activation. *PNAS* 112(28): 8567–8572.

Browning, W. D., Ryan, C. O. & Clancy, J. O. (2014). *14 Patterns of Biophilic Design*. New York: Terrapin Bright Green.

Cracknell, D., White, M., Pahl, S., Nichols, W. & Depledge, M. (2016). Marine Biota and Psychological Well-being: A Preliminary Examination of Dose–Response Effects in an Aquarium Setting. *Environment and Behavior* 48(10): 1242–1269.

Dreiseitl, H., Leonardsen, J. & Wanschura, B. (2015). Cost-Benefit Analysis of Bishan-Ang Mo Kio Park. National University of Singapore. Retrieved from https://ramboll.com/-/media/files/rnewmarkets/herbert-dreiseitl_part-1_final-report_22052015.pdf?la=en (accessed January 10, 2019).

Films for Action (2012) Singapore: Biophilic City. Retrieved from www.filmsforaction.org/watch/singapore-biophilic-city-2012

Fromm, E. (1973). *The Anatomy of Human Destructiveness*. New York: Holt, Rinehart & Winston.

Kaplan, R. & Kaplan, S. (1989). *The Experience of Nature: A Psychological Perspective*. New York: Cambridge University Press.

Kaplan, R., Kaplan, S. & Ryan, R. (1998). *With People in Mind: Design and Management of Everyday Nature*. Washington, DC: Island Press.

Kellert, S. (2018). Nature in Buildings and Health Design. In M. Van den Bosch & W. Bird (Eds.), *Oxford Textbook of Nature and Public Health: The Role of Nature in Improving the Health of a Population*. Oxford: Oxford University Press, 247–251.

Kellert, S & Calabrese, E. (2015). *The Practice of Biophilic Design*. Retrieved from www.biophilic-design.com (accessed September 13, 2018).

Kellert, S. R., Heerwagen, J. & Mador, M. (2008). *Biophilic Design: The Theory, Science, and Practice of Bringing Buildings to Life.* Hoboken, NJ: John Wiley.

Kellert, S. & Wilson, E. O. (1993). *The Biophilia Hypothesis.* Washington, DC: Island Press.

Kuo, F. & Sullivan, W. (2001a). Environment and Crime in the Inner City: Does Vegetation Reduce Crime? *Environment and Behavior* 33(3): 343–367.

Kuo, F. & Sullivan, W. (2001b). Aggression and Violence in the Inner City. *Environment and Behavior* 33(4): 543–571.

Lawson, B. (2010). Healing Architecture. *Arts & Health*, 2(2): 95–108.

Maggie's Centres (2015). Maggie's Architecture and Landscape Brief. Retrieved from www.maggiescentres.org/media/uploads/publications/other-publications/Maggies_architecturalbrief_2015.pdf (accessed December 1, 2018).

Matsunaga, K., Park, B., Kobayashi, H. & Miyaazaki, Y. (2011). Physiologically Relaxing Effect of a Hospital Rooftop Forest on Older Women Requiring Care. *Journal of the American Geriatrics Society* 59(11): 2162–2163.

Newman, P. (2014). Biophilic Urbanism: A Case Study on Singapore. *Australian Planner* 51(1): 47–65.

Sarkar, C., Webster, C. & Gallacher, J. (2018). Residential Greenness and Prevalence of Major Depressive Disorders: A Cross-sectional, Observational, Associational Study of 94,879 Adult UK Biobank Participants. *The Lancet Planetary Health* 2(4): e162–e173.

Shackell, A. & Walter, R. (2012). *Green Space Design for Health and Well-Being.* Edinburgh: Forestry Commission.

Totaforti, S. (2018). Applying the Benefits of Biophilic Theory to Hospital Design. *City, Territory and Architecture* 5(1): 1–9.

Ulrich, R. (1984). View Through a Window May Influence Recovery from Surgery. *Science* 224: 420–421.

United Nations (2015). *World Urbanization Prospects. The 2014 revision.* New York: United Nations. Retrieved from https://esa.un.org/unpd/wup (accessed January 12, 2019).

Van den Bosch, M. & Bird, W. (2018). *Oxford Textbook of Nature and Public Health: The Role of Nature in Improving the Health of a Population.* Oxford: Oxford University Press

Wilson, E. (1984). *Biophilia.* Cambridge, MA: Harvard University Press.

Part II

Applying Design Theory to Global Priorities

In Part II, we discuss how engaging with the design theories from Part I might help foster more thoughtful, innovative and creative urban design responses to four key global priorities: salutogenic, child-friendly, age-friendly and inclusive, and sustainable design.

Our argument is simple: applying the lens of theory – through theory-storming – and consciously putting on the *'affordances'* design theory hat, the *'genius loci'* design theory hat, the *'biophilic'* design theory hat and so forth – is an explicit strategy designed to improve practice, enable generative thinking and facilitate the creation of great places. As well as describing the origins and rationale of each global priority, Part II presents a range of different evidence-based design considerations, ideas and possibilities using one common scenario as an example for each. The age-friendly and inclusive design chapter, for example, explores what a bus shelter designed from the lens of prospect-refuge, affordance, personal space, place attachment, and biophilic design might look like.

We urge you to critically reflect on these scenarios, relating them to your own experiences and community, and if relevant, your design practice, and to ponder the potential impact of explicitly designing with theory. Could adopting a *theory-storming* approach positively transform your design practice?

7 Salutogenic Design
Promoting Healthy Living

Salutogenic design creates environments that are health promoting by including preventative measures that address the whole person, rather than only focusing on treating disease. It is about designing great places that afford healthy activities and lifestyles for all people on a daily basis.

Today we have a global health crisis. It seems you cannot read the newspaper or listen to a morning talk show without hearing a story about obesity, heart disease, depression, cancer, or diabetes. It can be overwhelming. And it has become increasingly evident that we need to find ways to enable all people to lead healthy lives. This chapter argues that salutogenic design can create better places, places that can reduce stress, encourage physical activity, and afford opportunities for socializing, in order to enhance our daily health and wellbeing.

In the late 1980s my high school had an actual smoking room. As a non-smoker, I never went in there, but I was definitely curious about it. It was next to the cafeteria and if I walked by when a student or teacher happened to come out, I got more than a whiff of cigarette smoke. Thankfully, this room would be banned today as we have convincing evidence that links smoking with lung cancer and a host of other health problems. These consequences affect not only the smoker, but anyone exposed to the second-hand smoke, making it a serious public health issue. Many cities, businesses and institutions are taking steps to discourage and ultimately prevent smoking in public or communal places. This is a good step. Yet, other unhealthy behaviors are still enabled within our urban environments.

Unhealthy eating is a prime example. We know that fast food is not good for you, especially when eaten regularly. It is usually high in saturated fat, sugar and salt, which is part of why we crave it. Morgan Spurlock's social experiment, portrayed in his 2004 documentary *Supersize Me*, showed convincing evidence of the negative effects of eating too much fast food. Though he took this to the extreme by eating at McDonalds daily, we can't ignore the general population obesity statistics. Worldwide, about 39% of adults 18 and over were overweight, and 13% were obese in 2016 (WHO, 2018). The numbers vary for specific countries and age

Figure 7.1 A wide walking path along the Brisbane River provides an ideal environment for being active, getting fresh air, and socializing.

Source: Debra Cushing.

categories. But regardless, the numbers are astounding. Fast food within our urban environments is convenient and readily available at all hours. People who work longer hours tend to eat more fast food, regardless of their job or socio-economic status (Zagorsky & Smith, 2017). With such a widespread and dangerous situation, we cannot chalk this up to individual motivation and self-control. On some level, our urban environment must be altered in order to address unhealthy eating. Easy access to healthy food options facilitates healthier eating habits, and may lower a person's risk of being overweight and obese (Hilmers et al., 2012). If designers, planners and policymakers make it easier, or even required, for food venders to offer convenient, healthy options, then healthy choices are more likely to become the norm. It is salutogenic urban design that embraces these progressive ideas so as to have a positive impact on our health and wellbeing, both now and into the future.

As well as discussing the importance of salutogenic design practice, the second half of this chapter documents the value of explicitly engaging with theory – through theory-storming – in the design process. Later in this chapter, Table 7.2 illustrates some theoretical considerations for salutogenic design, focusing on one common design example: a multi-use trail. Before discussing these design considerations, however, we first outline the origins, impact, and value of a proactive salutogenic approach to design practice.

Theoretical Origins of Salutogenesis

Salutogenic design uses the salutogenesis model to create places that enable people to establish a balance between mind and body for overall health and wellness. The resulting places are innovative, supportive and exciting – rather than degrading or stigmatizing. The focus is often on affording daily opportunities for physical activity, balanced nutrition, access to nature, clean air, safe places, and social interactions. Affording these lifestyle choices from the outset – through thoughtful design – can help address and possibly prevent global health challenges including obesity, dementia, mental health issues, loneliness and social isolation.

Medical sociologist Aaron Antonovsky is credited with the theory of salutogenesis, which translates as 'health origins' (Antonovsky, 1996; Mazuch, 2017). The salutogenic model considers a person as a complex human being, without identifying them by their pathology, disability or particular characteristics. Salutogenic design uses a systems thinking approach to view an individual within a context, recognizing that the two are interconnected (Eriksson, 2017). The model requires 'studying the strengths and the weaknesses of promotive, preventive, curative, and rehabilitative ideas and practices' and advocates the presence of factors which *actively* support health and wellbeing (Antonovsky, 1996, p. 13). We emphasize the word '*actively*' here, recognizing that environments which might not necessarily cause sickness or ill health, do not necessarily enable people to be healthy either. Being neutral is no longer good enough. We need to create great places which are proactive in the pursuit of good health for all people.

It is logical to position a salutogenic model, which is inherently proactive, as the opposite of a pathogenic model, which is inherently reactive. A pathogenic approach starts with the disease, to then determine how the person can 'avoid, manage, and/or eliminate' that disease (Becker et al., 2010, p. 2). In contrast, the salutogenic model first considers health, to determine how a person can 'create, enhance, and improve physical, mental, and social well-being' (p. 2). As Becker et al. note, 'Together these strategies will work to create an environment that nurtures, supports, facilitates optimal well-being' (p. 5). We certainly need both models in today's urbanized society if we are to successfully promote and achieve optimal health.

This holistic approach is seen in the World Health Organization's (WHO) definition of health as 'a state of complete physical, mental and social well-being and not merely the absence of disease or infirmity' (WHO, 2019a). This well-used definition reiterates that a pathogenic approach is not enough. Designers, planners and policymakers often feel pressure to use a reactive approach to fix existing problems. This approach is, of course, critical to manage many current scenarios. But it is also important to consider how to maintain and promote health *before* the situation becomes dire. Designers must not only address a problem or issue through a creative solution but also find ways to mitigate and prevent this problem for the future.

Like most environmental and behavioral concepts we present in this book, there is an interaction between the designed environment and people. Designers can't simply focus on changing the environment, without understanding the human psychology of interacting with that environment. Likewise, health professionals and others interested in changing people's behavior to improve their health cannot simply ignore how the design of the built environment in which people live, work and play impacts our daily choices and resulting health outcomes. Both sides need to be part of the conversation. The salutogenic design framework contributes to this conversation and relies on an individual's sense of coherence to understand how they might react to, interact with, or alter the built environment.

Using the Sense of Coherence Construct

The six key elements of the salutogenic model include: complexity, conflict, chaos, coherence, coercion, and civility (Eriksson, 2017), all of which are experienced by a person or group within a context. The sense of coherence essentially describes the ability for people to confront a source of stress with: the motivation to cope with it (meaningfulness); the belief that they understand it (comprehensibility); and the resources to deal with it (manageability) (Antonovsky, 1996). Within this construct, health is seen as a process. If people have a sense of coherence, they have the ability to comprehend a stressful or negative situation, be motivated to engage in an activity to counteract or deal with it, and have the capacity and resources to be successful (Eriksson, 2017). Translating these elements and experiences into the realm of design, shifts the focus to the opportunities provided within the environment, rather than the resources of each individual.

A sense of coherence is considered a life orientation that involves a person's ability to rely on, and benefit from their internal resources, as well as the external resources at their disposal (Eriksson, 2017). It is a way to deal with chaos in the world. These resources have been termed generalized resistance resources and can be physical (e.g. being strong), artefactual (e.g. having money), cognitive (e.g. being educated), social (e.g. having supportive friends), and macrosocial (e.g. having strong cultural beliefs) (Griffiths et al., 2011). The challenge for us all is to create great urban places that afford opportunities for people to develop personal resistance resources and take advantage of what the environment has to offer.

Researchers have identified three factors that help people develop a strong sense of coherence: having relative consistency rather than constant change and unknowns; a balance of stress and relaxation; and the opportunity to participate in decision-making which affects their situation (Eriksson, 2017). Each of these factors is influenced by the built environment and explicit design theories. For example, appropriate affordances and cues ensure people have opportunities to release stress but are not bored, to develop a sense of agency through meaningful participation in decision-making, and to develop place attachment through community engagement.

This design challenge is not easy. Take, for example, daylight. The availability of light is associated with levels of serotonin, influencing our circadian rhythms and inflammation (Golembiewski, 2012). When we are constantly in environments that lack sufficient daylight, our serotonin levels may be lowered, may disrupt our sleeping patterns, or may increase the inflammation we experience. It is partly for these reasons why light therapy is used to treat seasonal affective disorder and depression (Golden et al., 2005). If we design buildings and spaces that have access to natural light, we could potentially pre-empt these disorders. But there is a flip side. If there is too much sunlight and not enough shade, especially in warm climates that have high rates of skin cancer, people could also be deterred from walking or spending time outside. We need to understand all of the contextual factors in order to find a balance. Table 7.1 presents some of these health-promoting contextual factors and resources within the built environment that align with behavioral outcomes (adapted from Stokols, 1992, p. 9).

Good health requires the interplay between the resources provided within the environment and a person's sense of coherence. Someone with a stronger sense of coherence may be better able to engage in health promoting activities, even in a resource-poor environment. However, it will be much more challenging for someone with a low sense of coherence within a resource-poor environment to engage in healthy activities. It is therefore an equitable approach that relies on universal design and social justice principles. This just makes sense.

Creating Healthy Cities

Although creating a healthy city is a complex task that needs the support and input of multiple decision-makers and professionals, designers have a critical role. At multiple scales, built environment professions need to be involved in rethinking how we design our urban environments to ensure they are more conducive to health promotion. At a global level, the WHO reminds us that healthy places are complex systems, noting that, 'action to create supportive environments has many dimensions: physical, social, spiritual, economic and political. Each of these dimensions is inextricably linked to the others in a dynamic interaction. Action must be coordinated

Table 7.1 Facets of healthfulness and environmental resources.

Facets of healthfulness	Environmental resources	Behavioral and psychological outcomes
Physical health	Injury-resistant and ergonomically sound design; non-toxic and non-pathogenic environments	Physiological health; absence of illness and injury; perceived comfort; genetic and reproductive health
Mental and emotional wellbeing	Environmental controllability and predictability; environmental novelty and challenge; low distraction; aesthetic qualities; symbolic and spiritual elements	Sense of personal competence, challenge and fulfillment; developmental growth; minimal experience of emotional distress; strong sense of personal identity and creativity; feelings of attachment to one's physical and social milieu
Social cohesion at organizational and community levels	Social support networks; participatory design and management processes; organizational responsiveness; economic stability; low intergroup conflict; health-promotive media and programming.	High levels of social contact and cooperation; commitment to and satisfaction with organization and community; productivity and innovation at organizational & community levels; high levels of perceived quality of life; prevalence of health-promotive, injury preventative and environmentally protective behavior

Source: Adapted from Stokols (1992).

at local, regional, national and global levels to achieve solutions that are truly sustainable' (WHO, 1991).

The WHO Healthy Cities initiative focuses on the city as a whole and integrates key people and place concepts, including *urban form, transport and accessibility, green spaces, recreation and physical activity, infrastructure, environmental quality*, and *politics* (Maass et al., 2016). Created in 1986 and now including more than 1000 cities worldwide in efforts to implement strategies to improve population health, the WHO Healthy Cities programs have resulted in a new understanding of the link between the environment and health outcomes, as well as creating intersectoral partnerships (WHO, 2019b). Designers and planners are further guided by the WHO definition of a health city as:

one that is continually creating and improving those physical and social environments and expanding those community resources which enable people to mutually support each other in performing all the functions of life and developing to their maximum potential.

(WHO, 2019b)

City-wide and multi-city initiatives are growing. And we are seeing more research about the contextual factors that enable people to lead healthier lifestyles. Although the findings are sometimes conflicting and are not easily translated into design and planning practice, it is important to identify what we, as design educators, researchers and practitioners, can do to make a difference. The Center for Disease Control in the United States has developed the *Healthy Community Design Checklist Tool* to focus on health districts that are livable, walkable neighborhoods with at least one health facility (Cooper Marcus & Sachs, 2014). This tool provides residents with an easy list of health-promoting amenities they can look for in their community, such as farmers markets, sidewalks and street lighting. Context-specific strategies that incorporate community participation, local knowledge, and reliable data need to be prioritized as we move forward. And, as we have argued in this book, engaging with design theories – especially the place-orientated theories of *genius loci* and place attachment – provide a good starting place for this process.

Placemaking Strategies to Promote Health and Wellbeing

Salutogenic design is also about creating stimulating places that capture people's attention and interest, making them want to spend time being active and healthy. Danish architect and urban designer Jan Gehl suggests that a good city street should provide something interesting to see every five seconds for the average person walking five kilometers per hour (Ellard, 2015). A common walkability distance is 500 meters, which may be an acceptable and manageable walking distance in many contexts; it depends on the quality of the route, if the area is interesting and the walking surface is in good condition (Gehl, 2010). Anyone who has spent time in hot, humid climates will also tell you that the amount of shade and hills will impact whether 500 meters is an acceptable distance. The context matters.

Creating places that are not boring, but are stimulating, interesting, unique, and fun can increase our health and wellbeing. Boring or monotonous situations can be detrimental to our health. The term '*going postal*' was coined in the United States in the early 1990s to refer to a demonstration of uncontrollable anger or outburst that resulted from working in a repetitive, boring or stressful work environment, such as a post office. Next time you go to your local post office, hospital, or municipal building, look around. Is it designed in a way that makes you feel happy or calm? Or is it boring and dull, perhaps making you feel anxious or impatient?

Lively and enjoyable places can make us feel good. By combining the restorative benefits of plants and green space, as well as daylight, and even the use of color, we can create places where we enjoy participating in daily activities. Just think about how different those dull buildings might feel if they were designed with plants and green walls (biophilic design), windows that open allowing in fresh air and sunlight, attractive paint colors and local artwork on the walls (*genius loci*), comfortable, well-placed seating (affordance and personal space theories), and pleasant music playing. Shouldn't we create places inherently associated with stress, such as a dentist's office, using design principles that are known to make us feel better? Imagine the experience if your local healthcare facility was designed with biophilic design principles at the forefront, and featured views of natural landscapes, vertical green walls and a wall size aquarium to engage with nature.

These design principles and theories also work in public settings, such as the street. One that has shade, sidewalks, bike lanes, benches, and interesting building facades is often considered more walkable than a street devoid of those elements. Research has shown that streets with a focal point for visual interest, and ground floor windows (which often indicate retail shops or restaurants), were more likely to be perceived as walkable, as was the presence of other people (Oreskovic et al., 2014). Although it is important that buildings offer something of interest at the street level, overall building heights did not have an impact on the perceived walkability of a street. So whether it is the financial district in a large city, or the main street in a small town, as Figure 7.2 shows, there is no excuse for it not to be walkable.

Taking inspiration from Figure 7.2, take a moment to reflect on how you might apply an evidence-based theory-storming approach to design a walkable street in your own community. Designing through the lens of *genius loci* and place attachment theory means emphasizing a unique and valued characteristic of the site. One popular idea is graffiti murals or art walks, such as Bee Gees Way near Brisbane, Australia. The commemorative 70-meter walkway features photographs, album covers and interesting facts about former local residents the Gibb brothers, who formed the Bee Gees in the late 1960s. A gamification approach might include basketball hoops in laneways, or technology-enabled messages that share the average speed of the last runner, or an interactive musical stairway such as the 'piano stairs' seen in various subways and suburban shopping centers. Designing streetscapes through the lens of personal space theory would mean ensuring there were multiple spaces for a range of individual and social activities. Affordance theory would

Figure 7.2 Examples of walkable streets often include wide sidewalks with street
trees and could include a separated path along a busy road.

Source: Debra Cushing.

emphasize well-lit and wide footpaths, legible signage (with clear graph-
ics and widely recognized symbols), and street furniture for resting, sitting, observing and interacting with others. These elements would thus
create a great place that welcomes all users – and better meets the needs
of elderly people, those with limited mobility, and children. Prospect-
refuge and biophilic design would maximize views and interactions with
nature, being both more salutogenic and aesthetically pleasing. Thinking with and through the lens of theory is a powerful design strategy for
placemaking.

The Health Benefits of Nature

As we discuss in Chapter 6, biophilia describes our inherent predisposition to nature and using this knowledge to design great places is an important component of the salutogenic philosophy. A large body of research is now available to show how 'nearby nature' and accessing natural areas for physical activity can improve our physical and emotional wellbeing when we suffer from sickness or ill-health (Cooper Marcus & Sachs, 2014). Taking a more proactive approach means ensuring people have access to nature *before* they get sick.

Healthcare professionals and organizations are encouraging people to exercise in parks and open space. Young people in particular can benefit from spending time in nature, with those diagnosed with attention deficit hyperactivity disorder (ADHD) responding better and presenting fewer symptoms when playing in nature as opposed to other areas. Children with ADHD actually concentrated better after a 20 minute walk in the park as compared to a 20 minute walk in a downtown area (Kuo & Taylor, 2004; Taylor & Kuo, 2009). These findings suggest that although physical activity is important for a host of conditions, it is nature that is important for improving concentration and reducing stress.

Research that supports contact with nature as a health promotion intervention is also available, with Maller and colleagues (2006) providing a systematic review confirming the benefits of viewing natural scenes, being immersed in natural environments, and having nearby nature. The review concluded that 'natural areas can be seen as one of our most vital health resources. In the context of the growing worldwide mental illness burden of disease, contact with nature may offer an affordable, accessible and equitable choice in tackling the imminent epidemic, within both preventative and restorative public health strategies' (Maller et al., 2006, p. 52). This sentiment is put into practice by the rise of 'green prescriptions' across the globe; instead of medicine, doctors prescribe outdoor exercise or time spent in nature to patients. Of course, as we discuss below, the design of our built environment sometimes makes exercising difficult.

Affordances for Physical Activity and Active Transport

Regular physical activity is another key component of health and wellbeing, with adults generally advised to aim for 150 minutes of moderate to vigorous physical activity each week and children and teenagers 60 minutes each day. This activity doesn't have to occur at the gym, and ideally the affordances of the built environment would support active lifestyles. As Vaandrager and Kennedy (2018) remind us, resources for healthy living must be available *and* people need to recognize and access these resources. Ponder, for example, the growing numbers of gyms for adults in parks. Is there one near you, and have you ever used one? Why or why not? Too often, these are designed generically, without a sense of the local context (*genius loci*) or affordances for intergenerational activities, such that parents or caregivers can use the equipment while watching their children play nearby.

On the other hand, New York City's Fit City initiative and associated annual conference is a good example of transdisciplinary collaborations to foster health and wellbeing. The New York City Department of Health and Mental Hygiene, Department of Design and Construction, Department of Transportation, and Department of City Planning combined efforts to produce evidenced-based *Active Design Guidelines* (Center for Active Design, 2010) for creating environments conducive to physical activity, complementing efforts to address sustainability and universal accessibility (Lee, 2012). In dense urban areas like New York City, walking, cycling and other active modes of travel are a critical component of an active lifestyle and equally critical for people to get exercise during their busy days. To accommodate active travel within the urban realm, the *Guidelines* reference the five 'D' variables of *density, diversity, design, destination accessibility* and *distance to transit*. Too many cities do the opposite and present barriers to active travel with: a lack of sidewalks, crosswalks, and bikeways; a lack of connectivity of pedestrian and bicycle infrastructure; actual and perceived dangers of walking and cycling; and a poor supply of public transportation (Buehler et al., 2016). We must, in our return brief to clients, explicitly require active and enjoyable transportation modes – and ground our arguments in evidence-based practice and design theory.

Theory-Driven Salutogenic Design Considerations

As we have argued throughout this book, effective design practice must be supported by research evidence and grounded in theory. Well-designed salutogenic spaces should ideally involve a layered approach to placemaking, and address most, if not all, of the theories highlighted in section one of this book. An example of this comprehensive approach can be seen in the 2014 Selwyn Goldsmith Award-winning Tumbling Bay Playground and Timber Lodge cafe and community center. Located within the north section of the Queen Elizabeth Olympic Park in east London, and originally built for the 2012 Olympic Games, the playground and adjacent lodge connects interior and exterior spaces incorporating universal design features of step-free access, hard-standing surfaces, accessible toilets, induction loops and audio assistive systems; a succession garden for sensory exploration of plants and natural systems; a play area designed with sand and water, a large climbing net, rubber swings, tree houses, a bridge, accessible slide, and musical instruments; a multi-faith prayer room for quiet reflection; wide pathways throughout the site for walking

Table 7.2 Theory-storming to inform salutogenic design – a multi-use trail scenario.

Key theories	Considerations for salutogenic design	A multi-use trail scenario through a theoretical lens
Prospect-refuge	People need to feel and protected from harm (refuge) in the urban environment. Views are important in terms of how we understand and comprehend the physical and social setting and can deal with things that occur. This understanding aligns with a sense of coherence.	A multi-use trail should: provide benches or platforms for people to safely sit on the side to watch others or simply rest; incorporate good sight lines at corners and intersections; provide adequate cover or refuge from intense sun and inclement weather; and be positioned to take advantage of quality views of the surrounding landscape.
Affordance	Affordances for health-promoting daily activities need to be provided throughout the environment, and the cues to those opportunities need to be clear and easily understood. Affordances for unhealthy behaviors need to be minimized, especially for vulnerable or marginalized populations who may experience particular barriers.	A trail should be sufficiently wide to afford multiple activities such as cycling, scooting, inline skating, running, pushing a baby stroller or wheelchair, and walking. Trail surfaces should also be appropriate for the intended uses. Highly visible signage on or along the trail needs to indicate any restricted uses, and incorporate universal symbols or simple language to convey important rules or safety issues.
Personal space	Consideration for personal space is important for people to feel comfortable, avoid the spread of germs, and better avoid unwanted contact with strangers. Accommodating large numbers of people in urban spaces must consider comfortable levels of personal space that the desired or anticipated number of people will require.	A multi-use trail must be wide enough to accommodate at least two people to walk beside each other, such as a parent and a child. People on bicycles and scooters often require greater personal space bubbles because they are going faster and need to balance. This is also a factor in the required distances to walls or other vertical elements next to a trail.
Sense of place/ genius loci	Engaging, uplifting, and unique places can prevent boredom and anxiety, and reduce the chances of depression. Places that embrace their genius loci and provide interesting streetscapes will be more walkable, and accommodate greater levels of physical activity.	The design should incorporate local materials for paving surfaces, seating, retaining walls, plantings, fences and railings, signage and sculptures. The unique sense of place should also be reinforced through framed views of the surroundings, references to the historic and contemporary cultural context, and design themes

Place attachment	People who feel attached to a specific park, playground, gym or exercise facility are more likely to go frequently which can lead to more regular exercise. Social bonds are an important factor in place attachment, which can help foster social capital and personal/community resilience.	When located appropriately, trails can provide convenient access for regular use which will in turn help local people feel attached to it. Cafes, parks, schools, and other facilities which people may feel territorial about should be located adjacent to trail systems to accommodate socializing and intergenerational use.
Biophilic design	Nearby nature, views of nature, and being in natural areas within urban settings are important for mental health and wellbeing. Incorporating places such as community gardens can provide access to healthy fruits, vegetables, and herbs.	Trails that are located either adjacent to or within natural areas offer people the chance to also benefit from nature and will often be preferred. Trees and shrubs along the trail can provide valuable shade and serve as a buffer from roads, or other incompatible land-uses.

Figure 7.3 A well-designed salutogenic multi-use trail will provide enough personal space for cyclists and pedestrians, amenities such as mileage markers and drinking water, and well-placed benches that offer prospect and refuge.

Sources: Debra Cushing (top and bottom left); La Citta Vita on Flickr, CC (bottom right).

and running; and artwork that recognizes the local character. The space is inherently biophilic in design with plant life-cycle stories told through play. Affordances for nature play and spaces that offer prospect-refuge helped imaginatively engage children with nature and provides people of all ages and abilities a place to be active and healthy, and have fun.

To design more places like this, and move forward with salutogenic design as a model, we need to recognize and understand how it is informed by the underpinning theories. Table 7.2 discusses the six key theories in relation to salutogenic design. We have used a multi-use trail, an amenity common in urban areas, as an example, shown in Figure 7.3.

Where Do We Go from Here?

The statistics show there is a global health problem to be addressed. And bad places that promote unhealthy behaviors are all around us. Being proactive instead of reactive in the context of urban design means understanding how humans interact with and are impacted by their environments. Although it can be a challenge to retrofit cities and urban spaces in order to facilitate positive behaviors and healthy living, it is not impossible. What we must do, however, is ensure that our design responses are grounded in evidence-based theory.

Antonovsky's suggestion that we need to focus on successes and find out why people are doing well means we can develop and test hypotheses to explain positive health outcomes (Becker et al., 2010). Using this evidence, we can then create salutogenic environments that provide a balance of opportunities. Going forward, we need to focus on designing environments that provide healthy options that are easy and preferred over unhealthy options. And these need to be equitably available to all people, regardless of socio-economic status, gender, age, and ability. Thinking with theory, and engaging with evidence-based practice helps us create great, salutogenic places.

References

Antonovsky, A. (1996). The Salutogenic Model as a Theory to Guide Health Promotion. *Health Promotion International* 11(1): 11–18.

Becker, C., Glascoff, M. A., Felts, M. (2010). Salutogenesis 30 Years Later: Where Do We Go from Here? *International Electronic Journal of Health Education* 13: 25–32.

Buehler, R., Götschi, T., Winters, M. (2016). *Moving toward Active Transportation: How Policies Can Encourage Walking and Bicycling.* Retrieved from https://activelivingresearch.org/sites/activelivingresearch.org/files/ALR_Review_ActiveTransport_January2016.pdf (accessed February 19, 2019).

Center for Active Design. (2010). *Active Design Guidelines: Promoting Physical Activity and Health in Design.* Retrieved from https://centerforactivedesign.org/dl/guidelines.pdf

Cooper Marcus, C. & Sachs, N. (2014). The Salutogenic City. *World Health Design* 7(4): 18–25.

Ellard, C. (2015). Streets with No Game. Retrieved from https://aeon.co/magazine/culture/why-boring-cities-make-for-stressed-citizens

Eriksson, M. (2017). The Sense of Coherence in the Salutogenic Model of Health. In M. B. Mittelmark et al. (Eds.), *The Handbook of Salutogenesis*. Berlin: Springer, 91–96.

Gehl, J. (2010). *Cities for People*. Washington, DC: Island Press.

Golden, R. N., Gaynes, B. N., Ekstrom, R. D., et al. (2005). The Efficacy of Light Therapy in the Treatment of Mood Disorders: A Review and Meta-analysis of the Evidence. *American Journal of Psychiatry* 162: 656–662.

Golembiewski, J. (2012). Salutogenic Design: The Neural Basis for Health Promoting Environments. *World Health Design Scientific Review* 5(4): 62–68.

Griffiths, C., Ryan, P., Foster, J. (2011). Thematic Analysis of Antonovsky's Sense of Coherence Theory. *Scandinavian Journal of Psychology* 52: 168–173.

Hilmers, A., Hilmers, D. C. & Dave, J. (2012). Neighborhood Disparities in Access to Healthy Foods and Their Effects on Environmental Justice. *American Journal of Public Health* 102(9): 1644–1654.

Kuo, F. E. & Taylor, A. F. (2004). A Potential Natural Treatment for Attention-Deficit/Hyperactivity Disorder: Evidence from a National Study. *American Journal of Public Health* 94(9): 1580–1586.

Lee, K. (2012). Developing and Implementing the Active Design Guidelines in New York City. *Health and Place* 18(1): 5–7.

Maass, R. Lillefjell, M. Espnes, A. (2016). The Application of Salutogenesis in Cities and Towns. In M. B. Mittelmark et al. (Eds.), *The Handbook of Salutogenesis*. Berlin: Springer, 171–180.

Maller, C., Townsend, M., Pryor, A., Brown, P., St Leger, L. (2006). Healthy Nature Healthy People: 'Contact with Nature' as an Upstream Health Promotion Intervention for Populations. *Health Promotion International* 21(1): 45–54.

Mazuch, R. (2017). *Salutogenic and Biophilic Design as Therapeutic Approaches to Sustainable Architecture*. Chichester: John Wiley.

Oreskovic, N. M., Charles, P. R., Shepherd, D. T., Nelson, K. P. & Bar, M. (2014). Attributes of Form in the Built Environment that Influence Perceived Walkability. *Journal of Architectural and Planning Research* 31(3): 218–232.

Stokols, D. (1992). Establishing and Maintaining Healthy Environments: Toward a Social Ecology of Health Promotion. *American Psychologist* 47(1): 6–22.

Taylor, A. F. & Kuo, F. E. (2009). Children With Attention Deficits Concentrate Better After Walk in the Park. *Journal of Attention Disorders* 12(5): 402–409.

Vaandrager, L. & Kennedy, L. (2018). The Application of Salutogenesis in Communities and Neighborhoods. In M. B. Mittelmark et al. (Eds.), *The Handbook of Salutogenesis*. Berlin: Springer, 159–170.

WHO. (1991). Sundsvall Statement on Supportive Environments for Health, 15 June 1991, Sweden. Retrieved from www.who.int/healthpromotion/conferences/previous/sundsvall/en/index1.html (accessed February 23, 2019).

WHO (2018). Obesity and Overweight. Retrieved from www.who.int/newsroom/fact-sheets/detail/obesity-and-overweight (accessed February 18, 2019).

WHO (2019a). Constution of WHO Principles. Retrieved from www.who.int/about/mission/en (accessed February 10, 2019).

WHO (2019b). Healthy Settings. Retrieved from www.who.int/healthy_settings/ types/cities/en (accessed February 18, 2019).

Zagorsky, J. L. & Smith, P. (2017). Do Poor People Eat More Junk Food than Wealthier Americans? Retrieved from https://theconversation.com/ do-poor-people-eat-more-junk-food-than-wealthier-americans-79154

8   Child-Friendly Design
Where Young People Thrive

Child-friendly design addresses the developmental needs of young people, while also respecting their human rights. By focusing on young people and their families, child-friendly design creates places where they are able to grow up being supported, have their needs and wants met, and have their opinions integrated into policies and practices. Most importantly, it is a design priority that allows kids to be kids, use their imaginations and have fun as they learn about the world and their unique role in it.

Have you heard of the mosquito device? If you have, you may not have actually *heard* it. That is because it is an anti-loitering sound device, also called an ultrasonic teenage deterrent, that emits a high-pitched, high-frequency sound only audible to young people. The manufacturers website claims that it works by 'being UNBELIEVABLY annoying to the point where kids CANNOT stay in the area being covered by the mosquito sound' (from www.compoundsecurity.co.uk; emphasis original).

The inherent discriminatory nature of this device, and the fact that it was originally designed for prisons, suggests it is not something to include in a child- and youth-friendly environment. One issue is that it can discriminate against all young people within a localized area (a 35–40-meter maximum range), not just those who may be potentially causing trouble. Many believe the device breaches rights of young people who are protected by the United Nations Convention on the Rights of the Child (UNCRC) (Kirk, 2017). The device is a band-aid for perceived anti-social behavior. And forcing teenagers out of a specific area if they actually are up to no good, will do nothing to change the situation or give them the support, guidance or opportunity for positive, healthy, fun activities they might need.

The mosquito device may seem extreme, but we use this example to show how important it is to consider *all* people within the design and planning of a city, especially those who may be marginalized. A child-friendly city (CFC) is more than just a place where young people can play and go to school. It supports them as whole people, both now and into the future, as they grow into adults. Urban spaces are especially significant

Figure 8.1 A child expresses her delight on a slide artfully integrated into a rock embankment in Tear Drop Park in New York City, designed by Michael van Valkenburgh Associates.

Source: Debra Cushing.

for young people, and must be designed appropriately and with attention to theory and best-practice evidence-based research findings. If not, there can be underlying discrimination within design solutions that we don't perceive, particularly if we are not marginalized ourselves (a topic further discussed in Chapter 9, in the context of disability and ageing). The needs and specific considerations of young people in an urban space must be considered from the start of any design process and involving young people directly is often the best way to understand these issues.

This chapter has two core purposes. In addition to outlining the origins, rationale and design opportunities within CFCs, we use the common scenario of designing an urban park to demonstrate the value of actively integrating evidence-based research and theory-storming into the design process. Examples throughout the chapter also illustrate how thinking through the unique lens of design theory, from affordance to place attachment, helps foster creative, generative thinking and innovative design practice. As design practice occurs within a local and global policy context, we start by exploring how the CFC initiative is positively changing design practice – and the implications and opportunities for educators, practitioners and researchers.

Policy Origins of Child-Friendly Cities

Communities are focusing more on the needs of children, youth and families, and the UNCRC policy ratified in 1989, recognizes their right to have a healthy environment in which to live, play and work. The UNCRC is the most widely and rapidly ratified treaty in history, stating that all children (18 and under) have basic human rights. South Sudan and Somalia recently ratified it, leaving the United States as the last of the 197 member nations to have signed but not ratified this significant policy (OHCHR, 2019). The UNICEF Child-Friendly City Secretariat in Florence, Italy, developed a framework for defining and creating a CFC and to address a range of childhood needs (Schulze & Moneti, 2007). The framework addresses multiple childhood dimensions and aspects that can be impacted by the urban environment and the policies and practices within that environment. This UNICEF CFC initiative promotes places that ensure all children:

- are protected from exploitation, violence and abuse;
- have a good start in life and grow up healthy and cared for;
- have access to quality social services;
- experience quality, inclusive and participatory education and skills development;
- express their opinions and influence decisions that affect them;
- participate in family, cultural, community and social life;
- live in a safe, secure and clean environment with access to green spaces;
- meet friends and have places to play and enjoy themselves; and
- have a fair chance in life regardless of their ethnic origin, religion, income, gender or ability (UNICEF, undated).

Many of these goals are dependent on social policy and government decisions. And as we acknowledged in section one of this book, the physical environment is just as important for realizing these goals. Kevin Lynch, a well-known American urban planner, initiated the UNESCO Growing Up in Cities program in the 1970s, which was later reprised by environmental psychologist Louise Chawla. This international project uses an engaging approach – often participatory methods such as action research, child-led interviews and walking tours, community and neighborhood mapping, photovoice, and digital storytelling – to hear directly from young people what is important to them, and their needs and wants for their community.

These global initiatives are supported by a significant body of research that supports CFCs in terms of the design of the physical environment, planning of public spaces, improving independent mobility, enhancing access to the natural environment, and providing opportunities for life chances more generally (see for example Derr et al., 2018; Derr et al., 2013; Chawla et al., 2012; Chawla 2002; Gleeson & Sipe, 2006). For example, a key area of CFC design is safety, so well-designed walking and bicycle paths that effectively and efficiently connect residential areas to places that children need to access, such as parks, public spaces, schools, local shops, and community facilities are critical. Providing access to their community and affording opportunities to move around independently and play safely outside are also critical for young people's health and well-being.

The Importance of Independent Mobility

Young people as a population generally do not drive or have a large disposable income to spend on taxis or Ubers. They must rely on adults to get to places in their community. Prioritizing urban design that affords independent mobility is a critical aspect of a child-friendly environment. Cities that provide opportunities for youth to walk, bike, or take public transit on their own can help limit their isolation, and enable them to rely less on adults for transportation. As with most affordances, opportunities for independent mobility must not only be safe, accessible, affordable and efficient, they must also be perceived as such (both by young people and their parents or caregivers). Age-appropriate distances or ranges within which children can independently go places, enable them to develop a sense of agency and confidence, and increase their knowledge and skill at making their way through their neighborhood (Kyttä, 2004). These affordances are actually important for adults as well, as our increasing reliance on GPS and digital wayfinding devices can make us less aware of how to get places (Ishikawa et al., 2008).

One interesting child-friendly design solution can be seen in the mid-size city of Pontevedra in Spain, population 80,000. Most street parking has been removed and streets have been closed to cars within the downtown area, both actions to address independent mobility and make things easier for parents (Velazquez, 2018; Burgen, 2018). Although cars are not strictly banned, and people who live within the inner city or are making deliveries are still allowed, car use in the inner city has decreased 77%. CO_2 emissions have dropped by 66% and the crime rate has also decreased. The area is much more pedestrian-oriented and child-friendly. Eighty percent of children aged 6 to 12 years walk alone to school every morning. In fact, you can walk across the entire city in about 25 minutes (Burgen, 2018). Previously traffic-dominated streets and urban plazas, once extremely unsafe for pedestrians, are now safe places for children to play in.

With estimates that 500 children die each day in road crashes in cities across the globe, initiatives such as CFC, 8–80 Cities and Streets for

Kids prompt action. The simple motto of the Global Designing Cities Initiative, launched in 2014 is 'change streets, change the world.' As well as outlining examples of international best practice in their free online *Global Street Design Guide*, their website also depicts several short films highlighting the different space, speed and sensory experience of streets in cities, from Fortaleza in Brazil to Bandung in Indonesia or Milan in Italy (see https://globaldesigningcities.org).

Creating Great Places and Fostering Health and Wellbeing through Shared Streets

Other interesting ways to provide young people with safe spaces to get around include the home zones concept in the UK and the *woonerf* in the Netherlands. Home zones, first introduced in the UK in the late 1990s, consisted of residential streets specifically designed to allow residents to walk and cycle, and for children to play within a shared zone with automobiles (Gill, 2006). The concept was initiated by road-safety advocates and specifically focused on children's safety. Home zones were inspired by the Dutch concept, the *woonerf*, a shared street in which the pedestrian is given equal or perhaps higher importance than the car, with a focus on integrating rather than separating the uses. Research suggests that these unique designs can reduce traffic accidents, increase social interaction and play, and lead to higher resident satisfaction (Ben-Joseph, 1995). Design elements of a *woonerf* include: visible entrances, physical barriers, shared and paved spaces, landscaping and street furniture. Figure 8.2 shows examples of streets designed as shared spaces.

Even when public transportation, cycling and walking are feasible options, safety, distance, and cost are other considerations that young people have to negotiate. Urbanization can impact these options. Children living in urban areas of South Australia had a more restricted range of independent travel, for example, than those living in rural areas (Mac-Dougall et al., 2009). Children in rural communities indicated there were few places they could not go, but they often had to rely on buses or adults with cars to access activities. Similarly, research about children and their travel around the fast developing city of Bandung, Indonesia (two-hours from the capitol Jakarta), found children are highly dependent on automobile travel, especially for the school commute which significantly increased morning traffic volumes (Drianda et al., 2015). Imagine, for a moment, a participatory design charrette and theory-storming approach that tackled this issue to re-design the streets outside schools to support independent mobility, and the health and wellbeing of youth. An affordances approach might integrate technology chargers with seating, while biophilic, personal space and prospect-refuge theories would prioritize

Figure 8.2 Home zones and *woonerfs* prioritize pedestrians within a shared
      space with vehicles.

Sources: Eric Fischer, Flickr (top); La Citta Vita, Flickr (bottom).

interactions with nature, wide lanes and a variety of seating that offers
opportunities for both calming respite and social connections. Understanding research evidence and using theory-storming is a good way to
approach the policy and design challenge of creating CFCs and shared
streets, helping foster creative, generative thinking and innovative design
responses that are strongly situated in their local context – the essence of
genius loci and place attachment theory.

Personal Health and Safety

Children's health is important for their quality of life, now and as they grow up. Generally speaking, children are smaller than adults and do not have the same level of agility or physical strength. Because their internal systems and immunity are not as fully developed, they are more susceptible to the dangers of environmental toxins and pollution. The presence of toxins is compounded by the fact that children like to touch things, put stuff in their mouth, and crawl or roll around in the grass, all actions that increase their risk of ingesting toxic chemicals from harmful substances. Pesticides and herbicides are often sprayed in public parks and can be invisible, and so pose a dangerous threat to the health and safety of children. Though we are slowly becoming more aware of these specific dangers, little is known about the long-term impacts of other less potent substances used in urban environments. And as children are more susceptible to these dangers than adults, it is critical that we are careful about the materials we use and introduce, a topic covered briefly in the chapters on biophilic and sustainable design.

Children's susceptibility also impacts their levels of safety within unknown and potentially risky situations. Personal safety is often considered one of the most important concerns for young people in urban areas. They are still developing their cognitive and social awareness, which makes them wonderfully inquisitive and trusting, but also puts them more at risk of being manipulated or unaware of potential dangers. Again, it is the perceived safety that is often as important as the actual risk. In developed countries like the United States, some of these risks are exacerbated by the media. 'Stranger-danger' for example, is not any more of an issue now than 50 years ago, and in some places, kidnapping rates are going down (Keohane, 2010). For good or bad, the more we read about and see instances when children have been abducted or manipulated in some way, it puts their safety and susceptibility at the forefront of our minds, and triggers a protective response. Such a fear can cause parents and caregivers to limit independent mobility.

Personal safety and security are legitimate concerns in particular countries and specific urban centers. Research on CFCs in South Africa found that safety was the most prominent concern, a reflection of the high levels of crime and violence that significantly impact children's wellbeing (Adams et al., 2018). In response to both real and perceived dangers, many small urban playgrounds, in New York City for example, now have designated 'exclusive children's playgrounds' with signs restricting entrance to allow only those adults who are accompanying children aged 12 years and under (Kozlowski, 2015, p. 1). Although this action could prevent child abduction or deviant behavior, it also prevents intergenerational engagement that is often harmless, and could in fact build an understanding between different people. Ironically, we have moved beyond blatant segregation based on race or gender (in most countries), but still allow segregation based on age. Rethinking design practices, though the lens of personal space theory, for example, or prospect-refuge might enable the development of more appropriate responses. Given rapid population ageing, discussed in the next chapter, there is much interest in intergenerational park design. Drawing on place attachment to guide memory creation activities that bring together grandchildren and grandparents, is one very tangible example of how thinking with theory might inform and enhance the design of CFCs.

Supporting Healthy Child Development through Urban Design

Depending on their age and specific needs, young people are developing physically, socially, and cognitively as they experience their everyday environments. Much of their time is spent within private or institutionalized places such as school, childcare, and home, places seen by adults as well-controlled, focusing on developmental needs (de Visscher & Bouverne-de Bie, 2008). Urban public space, however, is typically not controlled in a similar fashion, or seen as a place to provide important opportunities for exploration, independence, and developing skills (Arlinkasari & Cushing, 2018). These opportunities for development are critical, with the UNICEF (2009) promoting children's healthy development as an indicator of a CFC.

Urban spaces can be designed in playful and engaging ways that encourage young people to physically explore their surroundings, and this is especially significant for younger children. Urban design strategies should recognize that young people have size and strength capabilities that may differ from adults. Spaces designed for all ages, and especially for young people, should therefore provide visual interest and seating at a lower height, avoiding elements that can block children's view. They need fun elements that encourage jumping, climbing, balancing, swinging, and other movements to help develop agility and motor skills. When provided with large blocks arranged on the ground, children naturally tended to jump from block to block, and engage in vigorous physical activity, indicating a sense of enjoyment and liveliness (Prieske et al., 2015). Adults might actually enjoy and benefit from these affordances too, if the popularity of outdoor yoga, boot camp, and parkour is any indication.

Through a process of theory-storming, designers can and should create places that support opportunities for creative play, physical activity, social connections and cognitive development. Recall, for example, the giant outdoor chess board shown in the Introduction. Providing such spaces, that educate either formally or informally by simply providing opportunities to play, explore and engage with a space, can help teach children about the world and their community. Learning about plants, animals and natural systems and having significant experiences in nature, all precipitate pro-environmental behavior. And in the face of major climate change impacts (discussed in Chapter 10), we desperately need young people to embrace the environment and understand why and how to protect it, now more than ever.

Figure 8.3 Children playing traditional games in Jakarta, Indonesia.

Source: Fitri Arlinkasari.

Young people develop their social skills and learn how to live in a community with other people. In urban public spaces, it is important they feel included and comfortable, and at the same time, safe. They can learn about different cultures and people by seeing and interacting with them. Designing multi-cultural spaces that recognize and celebrate people from different backgrounds can prompt questions and lead to new ways of looking at the world. Opportunities for social engagement in places like farmers markets, festivals, and popular urban plazas and parks can all encourage young people to make friends and meet other people who may be similar or different from them. These opportunities enable young people to learn about social norms, and develop social skills that are important to being productive and contributing members of a community.

Incorporating play into the built environment may also afford opportunities for young people to learn about their own cultural heritage or a communities' history. As part of their CFC initiative, the Indonesian government established a series of Child-Friendly Integrated Public Spaces (RPTRA) in 2015 that serve as community parks or centers (Caninski & Arlinkasari, 2017). Using traditional games played long before technological devices were around, managers and play workers in these centers encourage local children to learn the traditional games that focus on cooperative play, learning social skills while also having fun, as seen in Figure 8.3.

The Importance of Play

Play is an important part of being young. Children learn and grow through play within their environment, be it imaginative make-believe, sports and physical games such as hide-and-seek, and educational games such as puzzles and scavenger hunts. Urban environments often afford play through designated playgrounds or play spaces. These outdoor places for play are often mentioned by young people as critically important settings within high-density urban neighborhoods, including both general play areas and parks or green space (Min & Lee, 2006). Research in South Africa found that natural spaces were overwhelmingly children's favorite places (Adams et al., 2018). Similarly, the natural area next to a school in Indonesia afforded valuable opportunities to play outdoors, be active, and develop social skills (Drianda et al., 2015).

All too often, play is considered the work of children. Yet, new research suggests that play is also important for adult health and wellbeing. The World Health Organization (WHO) promotes play as a way to afford physical activity and increase health for all (Donoff & Bridgman, 2017; WHO, 2014). Play, because it incorporates an element of fun and enjoyment, can be more appealing than simply doing push-ups or going to the gym. If designers provide clear opportunities to do so, play can be beneficial for getting all people active and socially connected. A growing body of research, policy and design initiatives have emphasized the value of creating a 'playable city' which activates and invigorates urban spaces for all ages, often using technology (such as *Pokémon Go*) to gamify exercise and place-based activities.

Risky play is also experiencing a revival of sorts, partly in response to overly protective parents and the so-called 'bubble-wrap generation' (Malone, 2007, p.513). Young people need opportunities to test their abilities and develop a personal awareness of their strengths and limitations. The importance of providing 'safe' opportunities for them to do so in a public park, while building their strength, agility, and spatial awareness, is becoming more widely recognized by designers and local governments.

Adventure playgrounds are one option for this. Found in places like the UK, they provide opportunities for youth to freely create, build, explore, and even destroy things using found objects, discarded materials, and tools (Kozlovsky, 2007). Danish landscape architect Carl Theodor Sørensen developed the first 'junk playground' in conjunction with schoolteacher Hans Dragehjelm who observed that children were not playing with the adult designated playgrounds. Instead they preferred the construction zones and left over sites available after World War II. The innovative and somewhat controversial spaces enabled children to 'become architects and masters of their own play destinies' (Adventureplay.org.uk), a concept seen as a critique of the conventional playground with manufactured play equipment (Kozlovsky, 2007). The spaces enable young people to test their limits and challenge themselves in order to learn and grow. Play workers assist as needed in order to provide a certain level of safety and instruction, likely as much to reassure the parents or caregivers as to benefit the children.

Another example of risky play can be seen in play spaces that incorporate heights, hard surfaces, edges, and other elements that provide a physical challenge or slight risk. Providing such challenges for different motor skills is supported by research that suggests children are attracted to actions they know they can definitely accomplish, but also to those with more risk on occasion (Prieske et al., 2015), as Figure 8.4 illustrates with the recently built, and somewhat controversial Frew Park in Brisbane, Australia. This award-winning park affords 'risky' play by including multiple tall climbing structures and slides. By providing options in urban spaces, young people are ideally able to play according to their developmental stage and slowly push themselves to grow and build confidence about what they can do.

Play should not be limited to specific purpose-built areas. A playful city needs to afford opportunities within multiple situations and not just designated zones. Adrian Voce (2018) suggests ten approaches to create

Figure 8.4 Playgrounds such as Frew Park in Brisbane, Australia, provide elements of 'risk' that enable children to test their abilities in a safe space, while also having fun.

Source: Brisbane City Council, Flickr, CC.

a playful city that appeals to young people and supports their positive physical, social/emotional, and cognitive development:

1. create city streets that are not dominated by cars;
2. prioritize open space within housing developments and embed playful affordances;
3. create public playgrounds that are integrated throughout a liveable, intergenerational landscape, rather than ones that are always fenced with safety surfaces and equipment;
4. allow unplanned spaces to evolve as communities use them;
5. build traditional adventure playgrounds;
6. create parks for everyone, including teenagers;
7. make childcare services truly child-friendly by staffing them with qualified play workers, rather than teaching assistants;
8. welcome children into public space by banning anti-loitering sound devices and reviewing how anti-social behavior is defined and addressed;
9. open up school grounds for neighborhood play; and
10. develop safe routes to schools, parks, and play areas to enable independent mobility.

Designing to Stimulate the Senses

We use our senses to understand our environments and when our senses are stimulated, our experience and our appreciation for physical surroundings is enhanced (Clements-Croome, 2011). This sensory stimulation is especially true for children, who are experiencing things for the first time on a regular basis. Designing rich urban environments that offer multi-sensory experiences encourage development and learning, and afford opportunities to explore through auditory, taste, smell, and touch, not simply visual attributes of a place. Sensory design can spark curiosity and wonder.

Organizations such as the 7 Senses Foundation (www.7senses.org.au) in Australia promote unique urban design solutions that are not only engaging and fun, but also use sensory design to accommodate and embrace the different abilities and needs of diverse young people, as shown in Figure 8.5. In addition to the traditional five senses, the foundation addresses the vestibular sense which contributes to our balance, posture, and orientation, as well as proprioception, how we perceive the position and movement of our body parts. The inclusion of movement in sensory design is important as it recognizes the complexity of how we perceive space and our interactions with material environments (Degen & Rose, 2012). Note how many of the design decisions evident in Figure 8.5 signal a strong awareness of design theory, for example affordances for different ages and abilities.

Figure 8.5 Designing creative places for children, their parents and grandparents to enjoy together.

Source: www.7senses.org.au.

Urban spaces that stimulate our senses can also trigger memories and attachments to place. Whenever I am in a large city and smell steaming concrete just after a summer rain shower, I am brought back to the summer I spent in Manhattan when I was 19. The smell is strong and distinct and immediately conjures images of the places I walked and my experiences of that summer. Smells, as well as tastes and sounds, can remind us of past experiences that have meaning to us. Perfumes, flowers, foods cooking, and other pleasant smells can add another layer of interest in the environment and provide a way to understand the complexities of the urban realm. Western societies often have a tendency to dilute or remove smells perceived as unpleasant, using air fresheners, deodorants, and incense to mask smells in both interior and exterior environments (Xiao et al., 2018). But if smells and other sensory attributes of a place are critical to our experience and enable us to develop feelings of connectedness, then creating great places for children means affording opportunities for layered sensory engagement within urban spaces. For example, the smells of cities were collected using a 'urban smellscape aroma wheel,' to create 'city smell maps' through which good and bad smells were recorded and mapped (Swanson, 2015). The next evolution of this could include a smell-walk that draws on place attachment theory and smells that trigger significant memories, and on affordance theory which could focus on the activities associated with different urban aromas.

Using Theory to Inform the Design of Child-Friendly Cities

As a key purpose of this book is to identify how theory and research findings can and should be used to inform meaningful design, Table 8.1 describes how the six theories from section one are important to consider in child-friendly design. Using the case of an urban park (see Figure 8.6), we outline how engaging with these theories can inform the creation of an effective and well-considered design.

Moving Forward with Child-Friendly Design

Creating child-friendly cities is a complex and multi-faceted task. Like any design process, it needs to include multiple stakeholders from multiple disciplines and organizations, and multiple voices, including those of children, parents, grandparents, and caregivers. Looking through a theoretical lens informed by research documenting the diverse needs and wants of all stakeholders will enable the creation of better places for young people. And most importantly, designers should take their cues from children to create great places that spark imagination, privilege curiosity and exploration, and foster excitement and joy about the world around us. Let's use evidence and theory to create great places that enable young people to thrive.

Table 8.1 Using design theory to create child-friendly spaces – an urban park scenario.

Key theories	Considerations for child-friendly design	An urban park scenario through a theoretical lens
Affordance	Cues to affordances need to address the specific characteristics of young people in terms of their height/size and cognitive ability. Developmental affordances are critical for young people as they are still developing physically, emotionally/socially, and cognitively.	Park signage should use simple language and symbols to communicate the rules to young people. Access to natural areas can afford engaging opportunities to learn about and explore native plants and local wildlife. Providing affordances for multiple generations to participate in activities together, within parks, can help build social bonds and make park trips special.
Prospect-refuge	Parents and caregivers need to be able to visually watch their young children in public places (good prospect) and see approaching people or potential hazards, such as bicycles and scooters. Young children like to create forts or small enclosed spaces (refuge) where they can be hidden from view (or have the perception of being hidden) but also able to peek out.	Constructed or naturally occurring hills can enable parents/caregivers to look out over their children playing. Climbing towers and treehouses can give children the chance to feel protected while having a view out over a certain area.
Personal space	Personal space is different for different cultures and is a learned concept. Children need to understand this concept so they can respect the personal space of others. Young children have small personal space bubbles as they are often held or carried. It is important they have spaces they feel comfortable in and can interact with people close up.	A cozy space or small table where children can sit close to other children allows them to enjoy smaller personal space bubbles. Parks can provide spaces designed specifically for children, including cubby houses, tents, huts, caves, hobbit holes, teepees and other intimate spaces where they can go to be separated from adults but remain safe.
Sense of place/genius loci	Embracing the special qualities and unique culture of places give children an opportunity to learn about the world and their place in it. Places that look the same are uninspiring, and can lead to boredom and a lack of engagement.	Parks designed with special themes can make learning about the particular history and culture fun and engaging. It can also make a place memorable, leading to greater visitation.

(Continued)

Table 8.1 (Continued)

Key theories	Considerations for child-friendly design	An urban park scenario through a theoretical lens
Place attachment	Young people develop special bonds with places through social connections. Place attachment often leads to a desire to care and protect a place which in turn can help maintain important landscapes.	Fostering children's place attachment to a park can encourage frequent use, enabling them to spend more time outside being physically active. And when children feel a special attachment to a place, they may be more inclined to care for it and protect it.
Biophilic design	Children, especially those with Attention Deficit Hyperactivity Disorder, can better deal with stress and anxiety by being in natural spaces. Plants and wildlife habitat can enhance the sensory aspects of a place through shade, color, smells, tastes, sounds, textures, and forms.	A grove of trees in a park can provide an ideal spot to play hide and seek, climb, pick fruit, sit in the shade to have a picnic, look at insects, listen to birds chirping, or discover a nest of eggs. Exploring nature in an urban park setting is a safe, accessible way to learn about the natural world by spending time in it.

Figure 8.6 Child-friendly urban parks should embrace the *genius loci*, afford opportunities to test skills, provide parents and caregivers an ideal vantage point to watch their children, and for kids to simply have fun and play.

Sources (clockwise from top): Glenda Caldwell; Cecilia (Flickr); Debra Cushing; Debra Cushing; Randy Wick (Flickr).

References

Adams, S., Savahl, S., Florence, M. & Jackson, K. (2018). Considering the Natural Environment in the Creation of Child-Friendly Cities: Implications for Children's Subjective Well-being. *Child Indicators Research* 12(2): 545–567.

Arlinkasari, F. & Cushing, D. F. (2018). Developmental-Affordances: An Approach to Designing Child-Friendly Environments. Paper presented at Annual Conference on Social Sciences and Humanities (ANCOSH 2018), Malang, Indonesia, April 24.

Ben-Joseph, E. (1995). Changing the Residential Street Scene: Adapting the Shared Street (Woonerf) Concept to the Suburban Environment. *Journal of the American Planning Association* 61(4): 504–515.

Birch, J., Parnell, R., Patsarika, M. & Sorn, M. (2017). Participating Together: Dialogic Space for Children and Architects in the Design Process. *Journal of Children's Geographies* 15(2): 224–236.

Burgen, S. (2018). 'For Me, This is Paradise': Life in the Spanish City that Banned Cars. *The Guardian* (September 18, 2018). Retrieved from www.theguardian.com/cities/2018/sep/18/paradise-life-spanish-city-banned-cars-pontevedra

Caninsti, R. & Arlinkasari, F. (2017). Children Talk About City Park: Qualitative Study of Children's Place Attachment to City Park in Jakarta. In *The First Southeast Asia Regional Conference of Psychology: Human Well-being and Sustainable Development*. Hanoi: Vietnam National University Publisher, 428–438.

Chawla, L. (2002). *Growing Up in an Urbanising World*. London: Earthscan.

Chawla, L., Cushing, D. F., Malinin, L., Pevec, I., van Vliet, W. & Zuniga, K. D. (2012). *Children and the Environment*. Oxford: Oxford University Press.

Clements-Croome, D. (2011). The Interaction between the Physical Environment and People. In S. A. Abdul-Wahab (Ed.), *Sick Building Syndrome*. Berlin: Springer, 239–259.

Degen, M. & Rose, G. (2012). The Sensory Experiencing of Urban Design: The Role of Walking and Perceptual Memory. *Urban Studies* 49(15): 3271–3287.

De Visscher, S. & Bouverne-de Bie, M. (2008). Recognizing Urban Public Space as a Co-Educator: Children's Socialization in Ghent. *International Journal of Urban and Regional Research* 32(3): 604–616.

Derr, V., Chawla, L. Mintzer, M. Cushing, D. F. & van Vliet, W. (2013). A City for all Citizens: Integrating Children and Youth from Marginalised Populations into City Planning. *Buildings* 3(3): 482–505.

Derr, V., Chawla, L. & Mintzer, M. (2018). *Placemaking with Children and Youth: Participatory Practices for Planning with Children and Youth*. New York: New Village Press.

Donoff, G. & Bridgman, R. (2017). The Playful City: Constructing a Typology for Urban Design Interventions. *International Journal of Play* 6(3): 294–307.

Drianda, R., Kinoshita, I. & Said, I. (2015). The Impact of Bandung City's Rapid Development on Children's Independent Mobility and Access to Friendly Play Environments. *Children & Society*, 29: 637–650.

Gill, T. (2006). Home Zones in the UK: History, Policy and Impact on Children and Youth. *Children, Youth and Environments* 16(1): 90–103.

Gleeson, B. & Sipe, N. (2006). *Creating Child Friendly Cities: Reinstating Kids in the City*. New York: Routledge.

Ishikawa, T., Fujiiwara, H., Imai, O. & Okabe, A. (2008). Wayfinding with a GPS-Based Mobile Navigation System: A Comparison with Maps and Direct Experience. *Journal of Environmental Psychology* 28(1): 74–82.

Keohane, J. (2010). Joe Keohane: The Crime Wave in Our Heads. Retrieved from www.dallasnews.com/opinion/commentary/2010/03/26/Joe-Keohane-The-crime-wave-762

Kirk, T. (2017). The Use of sonic 'Anti-Loitering' Devices is Breaching Teenagers' Human Rights. Retrieved from https://theconversation.com/the-use-of-sonic-anti-loitering-devices-is-breaching-teenagers-human-rights-81965

Kozlovsky, R. (2007). Adventure Playgrounds and Postwar Reconstruction. In M. Gutman & N. de Coninck-Smith (Eds.), *Designing Modern Childhoods: History, Space, and the Material Culture of Children; An International Reader.* New Brunswick, NJ: Rutgers University Press, 171–190.

Kozlowski, J. (2015). Park Playground Ban on Adults Unaccompanied by Children. Retrieved from www.nrpa.org/parks-recreation-magazine/2015/march/park-playground-ban-on-adults-unaccompanied-by-children (accessed February 8, 2019).

Kyttä, M. (2004). The Extent of Children's Independent Mobility and the Number of Actualized Affordances as Criteria for Child-Friendly Environments. *Journal of Environmental Psychology* 24(2): 179–198.

MacDougall, C., Schiller, W. & Darbyshire, P. (2009). What Are Our Boundaries and Where Can We Play? Perspectives from Eight-to Ten-Year-Old Australian Metropolitan and Rural Children. *Early Child Development and Care* 179(2): 189–204.

Malone, K. (2007) The Bubble-Wrap Generation: Children Growing Up in Walled Gardens, *Environmental Education Research* 13(4): 513–527.

Min, B. & Lee, J. (2006). Children's Neighborhood Place as a Psychological and Behavioral Domain. *Journal of Envrionmental Psychology* 26(1): 51–71.

OHCHR. (2019). Status of Ratification Interactive Dashboard. Retrieved from http://indicators.ohchr.org (accessed February 8, 2019).

Prieske, B., Withagen, R., Smith, J. & Zaal, F. (2015). Affordances in a Simple Playscape: Are Children Attracted to Challenging Affordances? *Journal of Environmental Psychology* 41: 101–111.

Schulze, S. & Moneti, F. (2007). The Child-Friendly Cities Initiative. *Proceedings of the Institution of Civil Engineers – Municipal Engineers* 160(2): 77–81.

UNICEF. (undated). What is a Child-Friendly City? Retrieved from https://childfriendlycities.org/what-is-a-child-friendly-city

UNICEF. (2009). Child Friendly Cities Promoted by UNICEF National Committees and Country Offices. Retrieved from www.unicef.de/blob/23350/110a3c40ae4874fd9cc452653821ff58/fact-sheet—child-friendly-cities—data.pdf on 17 Feb, 2019.

Velazquez, J. (2018). What Happens to Kid Culture When You Close the Streets to Cars. Retrieved from www.citylab.com/design/2018/11/car-free-pedestrianization-made-pontevedra-spain-kid-friendly/576268/

Voce, A. (2018). 10 Features of the Playful City. Retrieved from www.childinthecity.org/2018/01/17/10-features-of-the-playful-city

WHO. (2014). Physical Activity and Older Adults: Global Strategy on Diet, Physical Activity and Health. Retrieved from www.who.int/dietphysicalactivity/factsheet_olderadults/en

Xiao, J., Tair, M. & Kang, J. (2018). A Perceptual Model of Smellscape Pleasantness. *Cities* 76: 105–115.

9 Age-Friendly and Inclusive Design

Designing for Everyone

Age-friendly and inclusive design is a process of thinking and designing for a diverse population. Described variously as Universal Design or Design for All, the aim of age-friendly and inclusive design is to create spaces, buildings, services, products and environments that can be accessed, understood and used to the greatest extent possible by all people, regardless of their age, size, culture, ability or disability.

This chapter documents the importance and value of age-friendly and inclusive design practice, to create better places for everyone. The World Health Organization (WHO) estimates over one billion people – approximately 15% of the world's population – have some form of disability. The definition and spectrum is broad, ranging from functional limitations in mobility, vision, cognition, or hearing, to sensory-processing difficulties, mental illness and acquired brain injury, as well as arthritis, stroke or dementia. Disabilities can be permanent or temporary, due to accidents, illness, pregnancy, or other changes in circumstances.

Stereotypical views of disability often focus primarily on wheelchair users, and blind or deaf people; yet, people with disabilities are diverse and heterogeneous, ranging in disability type, age, ethnicity, gender, sexuality and socio-economic status. Disability is a universal experience, and is *not* something that happens to only a minority of people. Disability encompasses the child born with cerebral palsy, the teenager paralyzed after a car crash, the young soldier who loses her leg to a land mine, the doctor with autism, and the older man with severe arthritis. At some point in life, as seen in Figure 9.3, almost everyone will experience temporary or permanent disability. And it is our society, with our socio-cultural beliefs, systems, structures and physical environments, that disables more than any specific physical characteristic:

> If I lived in a society where being in a wheelchair was no more remarkable than wearing glasses, and if the community was completely accepting and accessible, my disability would be an inconvenience and not much more than that. It is society which handicaps me, far more seriously and completely than the fact that I have Spina Bifida.
>
> (NPDCC, 2009, p. 12)

Figure 9.1 Sitting in a garden, with her walking cane nearby, an older woman sends a text.

Source: Andrea Popa on Unsplash (CC BY 2.0).

Disability and human rights activists have challenged the traditional 'medical model' of disability (where it is positioned as a tragedy or medical problem), arguing for the 'social model' of disability – where people are viewed as being disabled by society, rather than by their bodies or minds. Jackson (2018) explains this approach purposefully shifts the onus of responsibility, 'away from the individual (to be cured) to society (to dismantle barriers that construct disability).' It is not the inability to walk that keeps a person from entering a building independently, but inaccessible stairs. It is not having dementia or autism spectrum disorder that stops people from doing their grocery shopping, it is the poor signage, confusing store layouts, and the lack of quiet, calm sensory-free spaces for respite. It is not being vision impaired that makes navigating busy urban streets challenging, it is the lack of a Braille trail. The social model of disability seeks to change the surroundings, not the person. As Lois Keith explains:

> Doing disability all day long can be an exhausting process. I don't mean having an impairment, in my own case not being able to walk. Like most disabled people I can deal with this. I mean having to spend a significant part of each day dealing with a physical world which is historically designed to exclude me and, even more tiring, dealing with other people's preconceptions and misconceptions about me.
>
> (Keith, 1996, p. 71)

As well as highlighting the importance of universal design practice, this chapter illustrates how applying each of the six core design theories supports the creation of great age-friendly and inclusive places. Drawing on the hypothetical design of a bus shelter, Table 9.1 at the end of this chapter shows how systematically engaging with theory (the process we term theory-storming) reframes the conversation and amplifies consideration of different and creative age-friendly and inclusive design ideas. First, however, we document why embracing an age-friendly and inclusive design mindset is a priority, outlining global policy and design initiatives, as well as the lived experience of older people or those with disabilities.

From SHUT OUT to Inclusive Design

The voices of people with disabilities continually remind us that the power to create a built environment that enables, rather than disables, lies in the hands of policymakers and designers. Read, for example, the submissions to a recent Australian Government review on disability. Almost a third of submissions to this adeptly titled 'SHUT OUT' review emphasized how poor design excluded people with disabilities from experiences many take for granted –not being able to attend their child's end-of-year ballet concert or meet friends for dinner because the venue is not accessible. The lack of accessible bathrooms, lifts without Braille signage, narrow doorways, uneven surfaces, and unclear signage all combine to make the day-to-day experience of life exhausting, frustrating and isolating. One submission noted, 'I do not expect to get access to the pyramids or Uluru but I do want to get into all of the library and all of the community centre.'

Just how inaccessible our world can be is illustrated in Figure 9.2. The first two photographs highlight environmental enablers and disablers to participation, taken by people with spinal cord injuries living in

Table 9.1 Integrating theory into age-friendly and inclusive design – a bus shelter scenario.

Theories	Considerations for age-friendly and inclusive design	A bus shelter scenario
Affordance	Adopting an affordance mindset helps challenge existing conventional practice and reframes utilitarian features as opportunities for inclusive, creative placemaking. Health and wellbeing-enhancing affordances, including invitations for action, are especially valuable for socially-isolated older and disabled people.	Low walls and ledges become informal seating. Flip seats are creatively added to light-poles, along with built-in chargers, push-button fans and heat lamps. Transform bus stops into places for collaborative digital art, creative writing and games, perhaps chess or scrabble. Use gamification to integrate hearing, vision, exercise and mental health games, or a water fountain to assess and prompt water intake. Smart lights integrate motion sensors, automatically extend pedestrian crossing times, provide beacon navigation for blind people and blink for an arriving bus.
Prospect-refuge	Older and disabled people benefit from places to observe and safely rest; in other words, opportunities for prospect and refuge foster mobility and social inclusion. Adopt an urban acupuncture approach and think about how to inject creative 'pinpricks' of prospect and refuge throughout our public realm.	Protected overhead and from behind (refuge) and offer long-range view, so a person can watch for an approaching bus – a visually safe environment (prospect). Consider prospect and ensure pillars do not block a seated view of an arriving bus and integrate recesses, so rubbish skips do not block the path of travel. Refuge can be enhanced for older people through thoughtful bench design (arm rests and higher seats), while digital visual displays of arrival/departure times benefits people with hearing impairments, dementia or autism sensory disorders.
Personal space	Explicitly considering personal space theory and boundaries helps support the spectrum of space preferences and diverse uses. Creating places that offer a range of opportunities for individual, personal and social experiences are especially important for more isolated members of our community.	Handrails and places to rest, as well as helping users to maintain their balance, provide a sense of personal space and safety in busy shared public walkways. Widening footpaths, and building entrances and circulation spaces with ramps and clear passages enables universal access, and make urban mobility easier for all. Quiet seating, rest pods or quiet retreat spaces respects personal space boundaries.

(Continued)

Table 9.1 (Continued)

Theories	Considerations for age-friendly and inclusive design	A bus shelter scenario
Sense of place/genius loci	Genius loci is a powerful tool to amplify local character and distinctiveness. As towns and cities become more similar in their design and architecture, this 'cookie-cutter' aesthetic can disorientate and confuse vulnerable users. For older people, especially those with dementia, distinctive places that provide a sense of orientation and assist with way-finding are extremely important – and can support older people to age in place for longer	The bus shelter design reflects and celebrates the unique distinctiveness of the place, honoring important memories and moments. Shelters near the beach could feature roofs and seats made from surf boards (see Figure 4.3 in Chapter 4), or integrate historical or cultural symbols into the façade. The walk to the transit stop might become a history trail, with significant markers at each location and local residents encouraged to share memories at designated benches. Identifiable, memorable character makes it easier for older people and those with neuro-diversity to navigate their neighborhoods.
Place attachment	Everyone, but especially the vulnerable and marginalized, has an innate desire to belong and feel connected to our local community. Thinking in terms of place attachment means respecting and preserving memory in urban places. This is particularly important for older people, who often have a lifetime temporal relationship to a place that is rapidly changing.	Designing with and around valued built or natural heritage can have a powerful positive impact on how connected older residents feel to their community. Consider a bus shelter designed around a much valued century-old tree or one that integrates into the design a view of ancient relics or historical documents. A bus shelter opposite a school could feature names, school photographs and achievements of past graduates, or build in technology to show photographs of local events.

| Biophilia | Biophilia draws attention to and celebrates nature and all living things. Take a moment to reflect on how enjoyable it would be if the walk to your local transit stop was strongly biophilic?

Imagine pausing to watch fish jump out of a stream, sitting for a peaceful moment underneath a waterfall, or picking and eating a strawberry from the living garden growing across your bus stop, which also provides much-needed shade. That is biophilic design | The sculptural qualities of nature should be reflected in materials, patterns and form, but in a disability- and age-friendly way.

Often biophilic designs are purposely integrated into the surrounding landscape, which may make them more difficult for people with dementia to locate. Supportive wayfinding and distinctive signage are key, as is ensuring accessibility. For example, leaving a space for a wheelchair seating and ensuring people in wheelchairs can easily access any features or viewing platforms. |

Figure 9.2 The built environment – enabler and disabler.

Sources: Susan Newman (USA); Evonne Miller (Brisbane).

Charleston, South Carolina, USA (Newman & SCI Photovoice Partici-pants, 2010). The second two photographs were taken by the informal caregivers of frail older family members in Brisbane, Australia (Miller, 2019). Both identify steps as a barrier, restricting access to meals with friends, and preventing a frail 92-year-old using a walker from easily using support services. Accessible large public bathrooms were valued, yet in the home context it is often expensive to retrofit for disability. A family carer explained how stiff arthritic hands meant her mother-in-law could not easily turn a doorknob, and until they could afford to replace it, they temporarily added a rubber band to provide extra grip. Although from different countries, these images highlight a universal story: despite decades of awareness, laws and advocacy, we are not yet a disability-inclusive society. As one American participant explained:

> These just aren't any steps. At the top of these steps sits a local bar/ restaurant and all-around local hangout favored by many of my cow-orkers. Why am I showing them to you? I mean, I know you've seen steps, and while they are really nice brick steps, they don't appear to be anything special. But they are! These steps provide access to much of the social interaction between my friends at work. These steps

hold the insight to private jokes and conversations of people whose company I enjoy. These steps lead to the way for me to interact with friends. These steps stop me in my tracks. There is no ramp. These steps are my enemy.

(Newman & SCI Photovoice Participants, 2010)

Much of our contemporary urban form remains inaccessible and non-inclusive for disabled people,[1] despite many years of disability activism, national building codes, and global policy initiatives including the United Nations Habitat III and the New Urban Agenda. These initiatives emphasize that while an accessible environment does enable people with disabilities, it also has broader benefits for a wide range of people. Curb cutouts benefit parents pushing baby strollers and older people with walkers for example; information in plain language assists people with less education, children, and speakers of a foreign language; announcements at each stop on public transit aids both visitors unfamiliar with the route and people with visual impairments. Quite simply, inclusive and universal design practice is good user-centered design practice. We must, as Jos Boys argues in her 2014 book *Doing Disability Differently*, stop treating disability as an afterthought and make disability and disabled bodies central, rather than peripheral, to the design process. It is only by rethinking disability that we will create radical opportunities for truly innovative and inclusive places.

Fostering Inclusive Design through Design Tools, Principles and Processes

A number of design tools, principles and processes help designers create more inclusive and accessible communities, and design differently, for all abilities. A good starting place is the *Seven Principles of Universal Design*. Listed below, these principles guide designers to consider and evaluate whether their designs can be used by as many people as possible. Architect Ronald Mace (1941–1998) from North Carolina State University coined the phrase universal design, which emerged from concepts such as barrier-free design, the accessibility movement, and adaptive/assistive technology. Instead of providing alterations or special features to cater for the unique needs of various segments of the population, universal design is an inclusive approach that makes buildings, products and environments inherently accessible and better for everyone – for people with and without disabilities. A classic urban design example is the dropped curb; curb cutouts are essential for people in wheelchairs and are now a ubiquitous feature of our built environment that benefits everyone. The dropped curb was created by Selwyn Goldsmith, a pioneer of the concept of free access for disabled people and author of the ground-breaking book *Designing for the Disabled* (1963). Another example of universal design is building entrances with automated doors, which enable all customers to enter the same way; more recently, some have also argued for slowing the speed at which automatic sliding doors close, 'to make the pace of places more inclusive' for people with mental health or sensory processing conditions (Söderström, 2017, p. 70).

- **Principle 1 – Equitable use:** Design that is useful and marketable to persons with diverse abilities.
- **Principle 2 – Flexibility in use:** Design that accommodates a wide range of individual preferences and abilities.
- **Principle 3 – Simple and intuitive use:** Design that is easy to understand, regardless of individual experience, knowledge, language skills, or concentration level.
- **Principle 4 – Perceptible information:** Design that communicates necessary information effectively, regardless of ambient conditions or an individual's sensory abilities.
- **Principle 5 – Tolerance for error:** Design that minimizes hazards and the adverse consequences of accidental or unintended actions.
- **Principle 6 – Low physical effort:** Design that can be used efficiently and comfortably and with a minimum of fatigue.
- **Principle 7 – Size and space for approach and use:** Design that provides appropriate size and space for approach, reach, manipulation, and use regardless of an individual's body size, posture, or mobility

While a range of building codes, rules and accessibility regulations guide current practice, inclusive design practice is best understood as a mindset shift. Design has traditionally accommodated the mythical average user, an elusive human archetype originating in the Renaissance ideal of Vitruvius's proportional and perfectly built man. In contrast, an inclusive design mindset means accommodating a wide variety of real people within real life scenarios. As universal design has sometimes been criticized for focusing more on ambulatory disability than the broad range of cognitive and sensory impairments, the series of personas represented in Figure 9.3 serve as a good reminder to design for all abilities. Developed by the team at New Zealand's Auckland Design Manual, in conjunction with the Universal Design Forum (a group of dedicated universal design advocates from a range of disability organizations), these personas highlight how affordances and the cues to those affordances can have a significant impact on how people are able to use urban space.

We also see the power of place in Figure 9.4, showing photographs taken by people with spinal cord injuries living in India. Because the road is often damaged, mobility is limited. Reaching the train platform requires a tense negotiation across tracks, with the ever-present worry about what to do if a wheel gets stuck in the rail lines. As one participant laments: 'even a ramp can't help me to step down – now I need wings' (Newman,

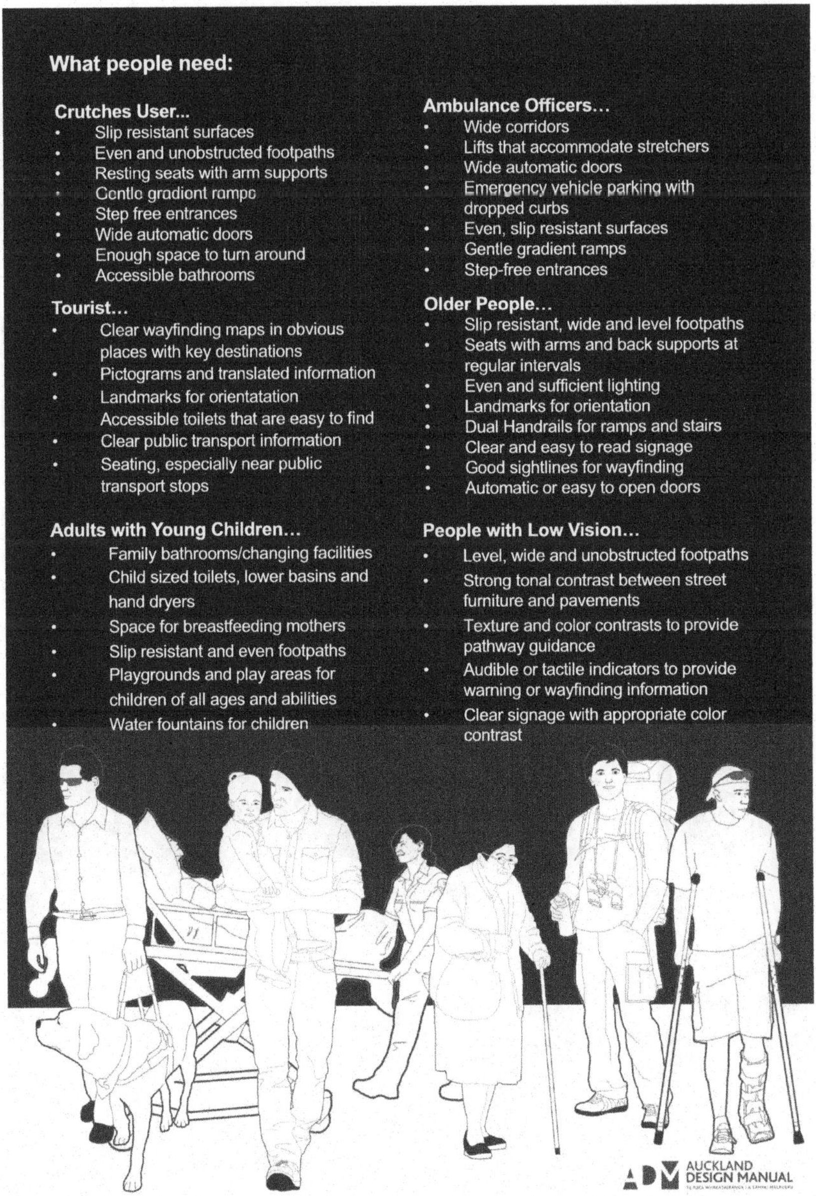

What people need:

Crutches User...
- Slip resistant surfaces
- Even and unobstructed footpaths
- Resting seats with arm supports
- Gentle gradient ramps
- Step free entrances
- Wide automatic doors
- Enough space to turn around
- Accessible bathrooms

Tourist...
- Clear wayfinding maps in obvious places with key destinations
- Pictograms and translated information
- Landmarks for orientatation
  Accessible toilets that are easy to find
- Clear public transport information
- Seating, especially near public transport stops

Adults with Young Children...
- Family bathrooms/changing facilities
- Child sized toilets, lower basins and hand dryers
- Space for breastfeeding mothers
- Slip resistant and even footpaths
- Playgrounds and play areas for children of all ages and abilities
- Water fountains for children

Ambulance Officers...
- Wide corridors
- Lifts that accommodate stretchers
- Wide automatic doors
- Emergency vehicle parking with dropped curbs
- Even, slip resistant surfaces
- Gentle gradient ramps
- Step-free entrances

Older People...
- Slip resistant, wide and level footpaths
- Seats with arms and back supports at regular intervals
- Even and sufficient lighting
- Landmarks for orientation
- Dual Handrails for ramps and stairs
- Clear and easy to read signage
- Good sightlines for wayfinding
- Automatic or easy to open doors

People with Low Vision...
- Level, wide and unobstructed footpaths
- Strong tonal contrast between street furniture and pavements
- Texture and color contrasts to provide pathway guidance
- Audible or tactile indicators to provide warning or wayfinding information
- Clear signage with appropriate color contrast

AUCKLAND DESIGN MANUAL

Figure 9.3 How universal, inclusive design benefits everybody.

Source: Debra Cushing, adapted from Auckland Universal Design Manual.

Figure 9.4 Living with spinal cord injury in India.
Source: Newman, Qanungo & Singh (2018).

Qanungo & Singh, 2018). All too often, as many design researchers have powerfully argued, contemporary urban design practice is not disability or age friendly, universally designed, 'sensory-sensitive' or radically inclusive. There are frequent 'problematic encounters between people's bodily capabilities and the built form' (Imrie & Kullman, 2017, p. 7), with design rarely taught or practiced from a caring perspective (Fry, 2010). And, as we argue throughout this book, evidence-based design theory must be more strongly embedded in design practice.

Why We Must Design for an Ageing Population

An ageing population means that the number of people experiencing disability is also expected to increase. For the first time in human history, older people will outnumber children in 2020. By 2050, older people will make up 15.6% of the global population, whereas young children (under 5) will comprise 7.2%. Data from the United Nations predicts that the number of older persons (which they define as 60 years and older) will double by 2050 (to 2.1 billion) and triple by 2100 (to 3.1 billion). The magnitude of this demographic change is powerfully communicated with Commonwealth citizens, who when they turn 100 years of age, can receive a congratulatory birthday card from Queen Elizabeth II. In Australia, there are currently 2,500 centenarians; by 2050, nearly 20,000 Australian centenarians will receive a congratulatory birthday card, every year. In the United Kingdom, more than 14,000 Britons are currently aged 100 years or older. This is an increase of 350% in the last thirty years, with the Queen's 'birthday card' team growing in size from one person to seven.

Our built environment must respond to this changing demographic, as how we plan, design and re-design our urban form has a significant impact on older people's mobility, independence, inclusion and quality of life. Considered a global responsibility, the WHO (2007) has identified eight key and interrelated domains of an age-friendly city: outdoor spaces and buildings, transportation, housing, social participation, respect and social inclusion, civic participation and employment, communication and information, and community support and health services. The WHO has 84 helpful recommendations on how to foster an age-friendly city, which they define as:

> An age-friendly city encourages active ageing by optimizing opportunities for health, participation and security in order to enhance quality of life as people age. In practical terms, an age-friendly city adapts its structures and services to be accessible to and inclusive of older people with varying needs and capacities.
>
> (WHO, 2007, p. 1)

As universal and inclusive design is in practice good design, so too is age-friendly design. What benefits older people generally benefits everybody, regardless of age or abilities. This rationale underpins the 8–80 Cities movement, whose motto is: 'if everything we do in our cities is great for an 8 year old and an 80 year old, then it will be great for all people.' This rationale is perhaps best exemplified in intergenerational playground design, as discussed briefly in Chapter 8; instead of adults passively sitting on a bench and watching their child or grandchild play, these spaces increasingly include activities for people of all ages and abilities. In practice, however, contemporary urban environments are generally not designed with older people in mind, who all too often are 'in the public imagination at least, marginal to urban life – conceptually and often quite literally less visible' (Handler, 2014, p. 12). Such a practice is problematic, because ageing amplifies the impact of ordinary micro-environmental features of our urban space (Peace, Holland & Kellaher, 2006).

Consider, for a moment, the common urban experience of crossing busy roads. To cross a street within a pedestrian crosswalk, people must typically walk at a speed of 1.2 meters per second. Less than 20% of those aged 65+ years walk this fast. And the impact of tripping, perhaps over a curb or a broken or poorly laid tile, is significant. Falls account for nearly half of all injury-related hospital admissions and deaths in older people, with a fear of falling potentially stopping older people from engaging in community life (Nyman et al., 2013; Webb et al., 2017). And design features that support one user group might disable another. Tactile paving tiles, for example, are an enabling and supportive fixture for those with visual impairments but a trip hazard for older people. For older people with dementia, experiencing difficulties in memory, thinking and attention, navigating a fast-paced urban environment is often stressful. Despite a large body of research documenting best-practice dementia design principles for long-term aged care facilities, hospitals, private homes, and sensory gardens (Fleming & Purandare, 2010), much less research has explored how to design dementia-friendly public space. Since the preferred option of *ageing in place* also means *ageing in public place*, this gap is a concern. Simple design features, such as age-appropriate affordances and cues, logical sequencing, legible street signs, appropriate levels of stimulation, and quiet spaces that offer prospect and refuge, all help make public urban space more accessible for people with dementia – and easier to navigate for everybody (Burton & Mitchell, 2006; Mitchell et al., 2003; Barrett et al., 2019).

As we redesign our urban environment to be more age-friendly and inclusive, a range of projects, policies and products provide inspiration – as do the design theories in Section 1. In Singapore, the Green Man+ scheme gives older or disabled people a special pass to tap for extra time at pedestrian crossings. Australia's National Toilet Map project's interactive app provides accessibility information on 19,000+ publicly available toilets across Australia, enabling people with incontinence issues, as well as families and tourists, to better plan toilet stops when travelling. Technology is a life-changer for people with disabilities. Over a million sighted volunteers across the globe have downloaded the free *Be My Eyes* app, which connects them in real-time to help solve daily challenges experienced by blind and low-vision people (for example, distinguishing food labels, putting outfits together, navigating through a busy street and determining the next bus departure time). Other apps are designed to foster empathy and understanding, by providing a brief immersive glimpse at the experience of disability – notable examples include the Alzheimer's Research UK virtual reality app *A Walk Though Dementia* and the interactive online game *Auti-sim*, which aims to educate users about what it might be like to be a child experiencing sensory overload at a busy playground. While any simulation will never fully convey the true lived experience of disability, such apps do help challenge assumptions and provide designers with the empathetic insight needed to make user-centered age-friendly and inclusive design practices more common.

Great Places are Age-Friendly and Inclusive – and Informed by Design Theory

The following practical examples illustrate how the criteria by which buildings and spaces are judged as being 'great' is changing. No longer is it enough for a place to be architecturally innovative or aesthetically beautiful – great places are now also inclusive and age-friendly, a criteria most evident in the winners of the United Kingdom's Civic Trust Selwyn Goldsmith Award for Universal Design for projects demonstrating 'excellence in providing a scheme which is accessible for all users, from people with decreased mobility, to parents with small children, to people with sensory impairments and everything in-between'. Inclusively designed great places also frequently demonstrate evidence of thoughtful engagement with theory.

The 2015 winner of the Selwyn Goldsmith Award was the Library of Birmingham, Europe's largest public library with ten thousand visitors a day. Libraries are an important third space, enabling people to meet one another as fellow citizens regardless of age, mobility, ability or socio-economic status. This public building is welcoming and accessible for all ages and backgrounds, with travellators, a cylindrical lift to the Secret Garden and a Changing Places toilet facility featuring a height adjustable changing bench and hoist. The Birmingham Access Committee guided the design team, Dutch studio Mecanoo, to ensure the space was accessible. From level access entry and lower counters at information points, to the easily identifiable blue lobby walls near the lifts, removable seats for wheelchair access in the theatre, braille and embossed signs, and induction loops for people with hearing aids, an array of design features support users of all abilities.

Alongside principles of universal design, *genius loci* and biophilic design theories are demonstrated, as Figure 9.5 illustrates. The circular delicate filigree skin façade features interlinking aluminum rings of various sizes,

Figure 9.5 Rooftop garden at the Library of Birmingham.

Source: Teresa Grau Ros on Flickr (CC BY 2.0).

with the circle motif inspired by the artisan jewelry-making tradition of this once industrial city – an example of designing from a strong sense of place or *genius loci*. Eight circular spaces within the building provide natural daylight and ventilation throughout, with the repeating circles generating shadows and reflections from changing weather in the natural world – an element of biophilic design, alongside vegetated grounds, roof-top garden terraces, and a lively streetscape. A commitment to sustainability is reflected through a BREEAM excellent rating, with the temporary construction hoarding a five-meter-high green living wall. Some have criticized the circular façade for its ornamentation and visual predictability; Keedwell (2017) unfavorably compares the library's façade with Gaudi's Casa Batlló building in Barcelona, where the varied original, dissimilar and unpredictable proportions and textures offer much more visual interest to surprise and delight the viewer. Overall, however, the library is a good example of a vibrant, memorable and award-winning inclusively designed space – with several examples of design theory in practice.

Sensory Gardens Provide Refuge for All

As well as larger-scale buildings, a frequently cited exemplar of universal age-friendly design practice is therapeutic, sensory gardens. Great places include sensory gardens as refuge for people with dementia and autism, and for everybody, as the gardens in Figures 9.1 and 9.5 illustrate. Traditional display gardens were designed to be passively observed from a distance; in contrast, sensory gardens actively encourage people to use all their senses, to touch, smell and experience a beautiful garden. The first sensory gardens were often small spaces within public parks, designed specifically as 'gardens for the blind' and, given their therapeutic benefits, frequently attached to hospitals and aged care facilities (Cooper-Marcus & Sachs, 2013).

The Oizumi Ryokuchi Park in Osaka Japan is identified by the Centre for Universal Design as an exemplar of universal design principles in practice. This Yoshisuke Miyake designed sensory garden is successful because it also engages with the design theories of affordance, biophilia, personal space and prospect-refuge. Designed in 1997, multiple cues within the garden assist with orientation and wayfinding. Information is clearly presented using words, signs, a push-button audio system and Braille. Explicit affordances include prominent ornamental pillars marking the entrance, with the main route – a single wide path – clearly defined for sighted, physically and visually impaired visitors with pillars and a metal guide rail. Bench seats are comfortable and wide, and thoughtfully spaced so wheelchairs, walkers and strollers/prams fit in-between.

Too often, edging and loose materials on the surface of paths (such as gravel) make greenspaces inaccessible to people using walkers or wheelchairs. That is not the case in Miyake's Sensory Garden, where multiple features – including sculptures, planting beds and a pond – are purposefully placed at waist-height, meaning people in wheelchairs, children, those with less flexibility or who 'see' with their hands, have multiple opportunities to interact with plants and water without needing to kneel, stretch, bend, or stoop. Thoughtful zoning means this sensory space provides a place of refuge from the stresses of everyday life.

Principles of personal space and prospect-refuge theories are evident in the clearly defined spaces for different activities where there are multiple opportunities to sit in groups or alone, quietly and safely enjoying different views of the colorful sights, textures, shapes, and scents of flowers, as well as the birds, and fish in the flowing water. Miyake also designed another healing garden in Osaka, the Kansai Rosai Hospital Garden, which researchers have recently praised as an exemplar of designing *care* into urban spaces (Bates, Imrie & Kullman, 2017).

Good universal design can ensure that every person positively experiences a place. Take, for example, wayfinding. While everybody benefits from directional markers that inform, direct and identify key features, good signage is especially beneficial for people with dementia and sensory processing disorders. Uncomfortable with unpredictability and change, these user groups benefit from the opportunity to retreat into cocoon-like spaces. In their practical book *Designing for Autism Spectrum Disorders*, Gaines and colleagues (2016) discuss how severely autistic adults living in a residential group home experienced enhanced mobility, increased independent activity and less frantic movement patterns with the installation of sensitively designed therapeutic gardens. Unlike many sensory gardens, the plants here were selected to purposely minimize sensory input and avoid perceptually demanding features such as bright colors, strong fragrances and intense contrasts. The affordances of clearly defined pathways enhanced independent wayfinding, with different zones for social activities and individual respite that respect people's innate need for privacy, personal and social space.

Sensory challenges, as Davidson and Henderson (2017) explain, are not predictable, but ASD-friendly urban design emphasizes the value of retreat spaces, wide circulation, low noise and natural daylighting over the flickering/buzzing fluorescent lights that dominate public and institutional spaces. A similar desire for refuge was also expressed by young Swiss people with psychotic troubles, who described an ambivalent relationship with the urban environment – simultaneously seeking excitement and anonymity of urban spaces but also trying to 'avoid the hyper-stimulation it generates, its complexity and chaos' (Söderström, 2017, p. 63).

Exemplar therapeutic outdoor spaces respect the *genius loci* of the site, as well as the unique attachments and memories of users and their need for prospect-refuge and personal space, in a way that deeply reaches, comforts and refreshes the soul and spirit. For example, beyond the expected waist-height vegetable plots, some dementia care gardens feature old antique cars that residents enjoy washing and polishing. Other gardens respect a rural heritage by including farm sheds with tractors, workbenches and farm animals, and encourage meaningful, salutogenic activity with residents encouraged to sweep paths, water plants and hang out washing on clotheslines. One rural aged care facility even has a small working dairy farm.

Given the global ageing population, the design of age-friendly communities must form a greater part of design curriculum and discourse (Brittain et al., 2010; Shannon & Bail, 2019). The institutional and strongly age-segregated design of aged care facilities has clearly created an 'otherness' that has disconnected and isolated older people from their local environment. In contrast, some contemporary facilities are residential in character and connected to the local community, and as such foster social activity through the co-location of childcare centers, community and wellness centers, cinemas, pools, libraries and men's sheds (Regnier, 2018; Farrelly & Deans, 2014). Some dementia care facilities have replaced the standard beige doors leading to residents' bedrooms with larger external entry doors that vary in color, style and motif. As well as assisting with orientation and wayfinding, a comfortable and distinctive design fosters a sense of belonging and attachment. Further, the provision of bench seating half way up the stairs (in a small balcony overlooking the atrium below) gives residents a reason to choose the stairs over the elevator, fostering both daily exercise and social interactions (Regnier, 2018).

Pragmatic considerations about the location of parking which can make visiting easy (or not) for older or disabled visitors, and the provision of outdoor gardens, benches and walking routes motivating aged care residents to engage in outdoor activities are all examples of prospect-refuge and biophilic theory in practice (Miller et al., 2019a). Simple design decisions can also be restrictive, with residents in one Australian retirement village explaining that – without an outdoor tap – they struggled to continue gardening or easily water plants on their balcony (Miller et al., 2019b). Some facilities purposely co-locate residents according to their different life histories, interests and hobbies, an example of how great places reflect and embody the identity of the people who live within and the places they are attached to (in other words, place attachment theory). When informed by evidence-based design theories, these design decisions can lead to the creation of great places for all.

Using Design Theories to Create Inclusive, Age-Friendly Places – a Bus Shelter Scenario

Explicitly engaging with design theories that are supported by evidence is a way for urban planners, designers and built environment

Figure 9.6 From whimsical painting and musical instruments that foster play-ful engagement, to biophilic inspired shelters with trees, to an air-conditioned shelter in hot climates, we must creatively re-think the design of public seating and transit shelters so they connect people and accommodate all needs.

professionals to create great places that are inclusive, accessible, and foster health and wellbeing of all users. Table 9.1 uses one universal example – a bus shelter – to illustrate how consciously engaging with each design theory is a strategy that will improve design practice. All too often, bus shelters are ugly, neglected and – worst of all – challenging for older and disabled people to navigate. Paths to access public transit are frequently narrow, poorly maintained, poorly lit and often dangerous after dark. Bus benches face the wrong direction, and are not sheltered, so users must wait in the pouring rain or hot sun. And, too often, there is inadequate maneuvering space for wheelchairs or walkers, with route and schedule information inaccessible for deaf and vision-impaired people.

Take a moment now to think about the standard design of your city's bus shelters. How do people use them? What is missing? Are they disability- or age-friendly? And, most importantly, how would *you* creatively re-design them to be a more enjoyable, inclusive and great places for people of all ages and abilities? Systematically engaging with the six theories described in Part I, Table 9.1 forces a deep consideration of different perspectives, and triggers a wide range of creative design possibilities, ideas and directions. Some examples of bus shelters which creatively rethink the typical model are shown in Figure 9.6.

Next Steps

Designing inclusive age-friendly communities is about creating inviting, accessible and calming spaces that benefit people of all ages, mobility levels, and abilities. For too long, the urban world has not been designed with disability in mind. Too often, every interaction reminds disabled people that they and their bodies are 'misfits', with street furniture impeding vision-impaired people and steps preventing ease of movement for wheelchair users (Boys, 2014; Bates, Kullman & Imrie, 2017). The explicit use of theory-storming and evidence-based approaches helps foster considered, inclusive, best-practice design innovation. Designers must challenge the implicit ageist and ableist bias, leading the charge toward 'a more inclusive society in which every citizen, regardless of impairment, has the right to access public spaces in dignity' (Kitchin & Law, 2001, p. 225). Only then will we create truly great places for everyone.

Note

1. We acknowledge the power of language. Some disability scholars prefer the phrase 'people with disabilities,' as this positions the person first. Others argue for 'disabled people,' as it is a signifier of the social model of disability (i.e. that disabled people are disabled by society). It is a contentious issue, with differing opinions, and we use both phrasings.

References

Auckland Design Manual. (undated). Universal Design Personas. Retrieved from http://content.aucklanddesignmanual.co.nz/designsubjects/universal_design/Documents/Universal%20Design%20Personas.pdf.

Barrett, P., Sharma, M. & Zeisel, J. (2019): Optimal Spaces for Those Living with Dementia: Principles and Evidence. *Building Research & Information* 47: 734–746.

Bates, C. Imrie, R. & Kullman, K. (Eds.). (2017). *Care and Design: Bodies, Buildings, Cities.* Chichester: Wiley Blackwell.

Bates, C., Kullman, K. & Imrie, R. (2017). Configuring the Caring City: Ownership, Healing, Openness. In C. Bates, R. Imrie & K. Kullman (Eds.), *Care and Design: Bodies, Buildings, Cities.* Chichester: Wiley Blackwell, 95–115.

Boys, J. (2014). *Doing Disability Differently: An Alternative Handbook on Architecture, Dis/Ability and Designing for Everyday Life.* New York: Routledge.

Brittain, K., Corner, L., Robinson, L. & Bond, J. (2010). Ageing in Place and Technologies of Place: The Lived Experience of People with Dementia in Changing Social, Physical and Technological Environments. *Sociology of Health & Illness* 32(2), 1–16.

Burton, E. & Mitchell, L. (2006). *Inclusive Urban Design:. Streets for Life.* Oxford: Architectural Press.

Cooper-Marcus, C. & Sachs, N. A. (2013). *Therapeutic Landscapes: An Evidence-Based Approach to Designing Healing Gardens and Restorative Outdoor Spaces.* New York: John Wiley.

Davidson, J. & Henderson, V. (2017). The Sensory City: Autism, Design and Care. In C. Bates, R. Imrie & K. Kullman (Eds.), *Care and Design: Bodies, Buildings, Cities.* Chichester: Wiley Blackwell, 74–94.

Farrelly, L. & Deans, I. (2014). *Designing for the Third Age: Architecture Redefined for a Generation of 'Active Agers.'* New York: John Wiley & Sons.

Fleming, R. & Purandare, N. (2010). Long-Term Care for People with Dementia: Environmental Design Guidelines. *International Psychogeriatrics* 22(7): 1084–1096.

Fry, T. (2010) *Design as Politics.* London: Berg.

Gaines, K., Bourne, A., Pearson, M. & Kleibrink, M. (2016). *Designing for Autism Spectrum Disorders.* New York: Routledge.

Goldsmith, S. (1963). *Designing for the Disabled: The New Paradigm.* New York: Routledge.

Handler, S. (2014). *An Alternative Age-Friendly Handbook (for the Socially Engaged Urban Practitioner).* Manchester: University of Manchester Library.

Imrie, R. & Kullman, K. (2017). Designing with Care and Caring with Design. In C. Bates, R. Imrie & K. Kullman (Eds.), *Care and Design: Bodies, Buildings, Cities.* Chichester: Wiley Blackwell, 1–15.

Jackson, M. (2018). Models of Disability and Human Rights: Informing the Improvement of Built Environment Accessibility for People with Disability at Neighborhood Scale? *Laws* 7(1): 10.

Keedwell, P. (2017). *Headspace: The Psychology of City Living.* London: Aururm Press.

Keith, L. (1996). Encounters with Strangers: The Public's Responses to Disabled Women and How this Affects our Sense of Self. In J. Morris (Ed.), *Encounters With Strangers: Feminism and Disability,* London: Women's Press, 69–88.

Kitchin, R. & Law, R. (2001). The Socio-spatial Construction of (In)accessible Public Toilets. *Urban Studies* 38(2): 287–298.

Miller, E. (2019). Co-designing Care – a Digital Exhibition. Retrieved from https://ourcarejourney.wordpress.com

Miller, E., Buys, L, & Donoghue G. (2019a). Photovoice in aged care: What do residents value? *Australasian Journal of Ageing* 38(3): e93–e97.

Miller, E., Donoghue, G., Sullivan, D. & Buys, L. (2019b). Later Life Gardening in a Retirement Community: Sites of Identity, Resilience and Creativity. In A. Goulding, B. Davenport & A. Newman (Eds.), *Resilience and Ageing: Creativity and Resilience in Older People*. Bristol: Policy Press, 247–264.

Mitchell, L., Burton, E. & Raman, S. (2004). Dementia-Friendly Cities: Designing Intelligible Neighbourhoods for Life. *Journal of Urban Design* 9(1): 89–101.

Newman, S. & SCI Photovoice Participants. (2010). Evidence-Based Advocacy: Using Photovoice to Identify Barriers and Facilitators to Community Participation after Spinal Cord Injury. *Rehabilitation Nursing* 35(2): 47–59.

Newman, S. D., Qanungo, S. & Singh, R. E. (2018) '*All Were Looking for Freedom': A Photovoice Investigation of Assets and Challenges Affecting Health and Participation after Spinal Cord Injury in Delhi, India*. Charleston, SC: Medical University of South Carolina, Center for Global Health.

NPDCC. (2009). *Shut Out: The Experience of People with Disabilities and their Families in Australia*. Canberra: Department of Social Services,

Nyman, S., Ballinger, C., Phillips, J. & Newton, R. (2013). Characteristics of Outdoor Falls among Older People: A Qualitative Study. *BMC Geriatrics* 13: 125.

Peace S., Holland, C. & Kellaher, L. (2006). *Environment and Identity in Later Life: Growing Older*. Maidenhead: Open University Press.

Regnier, V. (2018). *Housing Design for an Increasingly Older Population: Redefining Assisted Living for the Mentally and Physically Frail*. Hoboken, NJ: John Wiley & Sons.

Shannon, K. & Bail, K. (2019). Dementia-Friendly Community Initiatives: An Integrative Review. *Journal of Clinical Nursing* 28(11–12): 2035–2045.

Söderström, O. (2017). 'I Don't Care About Places': The Whereabouts of Design in Mental Health Care. In C. Bates, R. Imrie & K. Kullman (Eds.), *Care and Design: Bodies, Buildings, Cities*. Chichester: Wiley Blackwell, 56–73.

Webb, E., Bell, S, Lacey, R. & Abell, J. (2017). Crossing the Road in Time: Inequalities in Older People's Walking Speeds. *Journal of Transport and Health* 5: 77–83.

WHO. (2007). *Global Age-Friendly Cities: A Guide*. Geneva: World Health Organization.

10 Sustainable Design
Radically Redesigning Our Built Environment

Sustainable design, variously known as environmentally sustainable design, environmentally conscious design, eco-design, green, net zero, circular, or net positive design, is the philosophy of thoughtfully designing physical objects and the environments to reduce and ideally eliminate negative environmental impacts.

The United Nations World Commission on Environment and Development published the landmark Brundtland report, *Our Common Future*, over three decades ago. Chaired by Gro Harlem Brundtland, Norway's first woman prime minister, the Brundtland report placed environmental issues at the forefront of the global political agenda, defining sustainable development as 'development that meets the needs of the present without compromising the ability of future generations to meet their own needs' (WCED, 1987, p. 43). Three fundamental pillars were identified: economic growth, environmental protection, and social inclusion, the so-called 'three P's' of *profit*, *planet* and *people*.

John Elkington subsequently popularized the concept of the *triple bottom line* (3BL) in 1994, which argued that organizations had a corporate social responsibility to account for the environmental (planet) and social (people) consequences of their activity, just as they would typically report their economic impact (profit). More recently in 2013, a group of global political and business leaders, including Gro Harlem Brundtland, Virgin Founder Sir Richard Branson and the CEO of Unilever, Paul Polman, launched the B Team initiative. This initiative argues that businesses must adopt Plan B and become a driving force for social, environmental and economic benefit, rather than opting for Plan A, in which profit is the primary motive. And on the global stage in 2015, world leaders adopted the United Nations 2030 Agenda for Sustainable Development and its 17 Sustainable Development Goals – designed to transform our world and create a better, more sustainable future for all. Later in this chapter, Figure 10.3 will outline some of these goals, which include 'good health and wellbeing,' 'responsible production and consumption' and 'climate action.'

Despite this raft of global environmental policy initiatives, progress toward sustainability has been, as former UN Secretary-General Ban

Figure 10.1 A green roof above housing in Stockholm Sweden.

Source: Design for Health, Flickr CC BY 2.0.

Ki-moon acknowledged in 2013, 'uneven and insufficient.' In 2018, the current Secretary-General António Guterres further noted that climate change is still 'running faster than we are,' explaining there is no more time to waste and 'every day we fail to act is a day that we step a little closer towards a fate that none of us wants – a fate that will resonate through generations in the damage done to humankind and life on earth.' His full speech is in Box 10.1.

Box 10.1   United Nations Secretary-General's Remarks on Climate Change

Climate change is the defining issue of our time – and we are at a defining moment.

Many times journalists ask me what are my priorities. I always say we have many priorities in the UN – peace and security, human rights and development, but I would say that *this is the absolute priority . . .*

Climate change is indeed running faster than we are, *and we have the risk to see irreversible damage that will not be possible to recover if we don't act very, very quickly . . .*

The effects of climate change are already upon us, with disastrous consequences for people and all the natural systems that sustain life in the planet.

Just last year the economic costs of climate-related disasters hit a record: US$320 billion.

We know what we need to do. We have the resources and technologies at our disposal.

Climate action makes moral sense, it makes business sense, and it is the keystone in our efforts to achieve sustainable development that leaves no one behind.

So why is climate change faster than we are?

The only possible answer is that we still lack strong leadership to take the bold decisions we need to put out economies and societies on the path of low-carbon growth and climate-resilience . . .

The time is long gone when we could afford delay.

Each day brings further evidence of the mounting existential threat of climate change to the planet.

Every day that we fail to act is a day that we step a little closer towards a fate that none of us wants – a fate that will resonate through generations in the damage done to humankind and to life on Earth.

Our fate is in our hands.

Let us finally commit – together – to rise to the challenge before it is too late.

Source: Guterres (2018); emphasis added.

The damage to humankind and life on earth includes global greenhouse gas emissions, which continue to increase, as do average global temperatures and bio-diversity loss: in the 40 years since the Brundtland Report, 60% of all natural life (mammals, birds, fish, reptiles) on the planet has been lost. Global emissions of carbon dioxide (CO_2) have increased by almost 50% since 1990, with the Intergovernmental Panel on Climate Change (a global group of 1,300 independent scientific experts) concluding that human activities, especially increased fossil fuel consumption, over the past 50 years have warmed our planet. Significantly, renowned naturalist and filmmaker Sir David Attenborough soberly joined Secretary-General Guterres in his opening address at the 2018 United Nations climate change summit in Poland to remind the world that time is running out. Decisive collective action is needed to tackle this unprecedented manmade disaster of global scale: *we must change how we live and save our planet.*

Designers must rise to the challenge of climate change, and become part of the solution – not the problem. As John Thackara, author of *How to Thrive in the Next Economy: Designing Tomorrow's World Today*, notes design practitioners, educators, activists, and researchers must make a choice: to be part of the problem, cringing and ignoring the impact of design decisions on the planet, or actively become part of the solution:

> Are designers guilty of killing the planet? Eighty percent of the environmental impact of products and buildings that surround us is determined at the design stage, after all . . . There are three ways for designers to respond to the charge they are personally responsible for trashing the biosphere: argue the toss; cringe with guilt; or become part of the solution . . . Someone has to redesign the structures, institutions and processes that drive the economy along. Someone has to transform the material, energy and resource flows that, unchecked, will finish us.
>
> (Thackara, 2007, p. xvi)

Radical, innovative and disruptive design approaches are 'shifting the needle' on climate change. It is design inspired concepts, including systems thinking, product life-cycle, and circular design, that are challenging the current linear 'take-make-dump' mentality. This shift is illustrated in Figure 10.2. In a linear economy, a product is designed, manufactured and sold to a consumer, with little concern of how people use or dispose of this product. In a recycling economy, most materials eventually end up in landfills, though some are disassembled and reassembled. For example, eco-friendly products made from recycled waste include: sunglasses, skateboards, and carpets from abandoned plastic fishing nets;

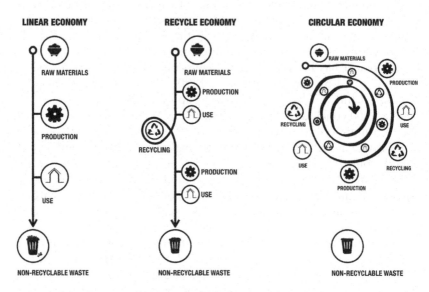

Figure 10.2 The value of transitioning from a linear to a circular economy.
Source: Ama Hayyu Marzuki, adapted from Circular Design Guide.

glass bowls from smartphone screens; decking, fencing and benches from recycled soft plastics; and rubberized paving made from shredded tires. It is in a circular economy however, where waste is designed out through a closed loop approach. Here, the entire industrial system is intentionally restorative or regenerative, with products continually cycling in our economy – creating a circular, closed loop economy where nothing is sent to landfill. The freely available Circular Design Guide, launched at the 2017 World Economic Forum by the Ellen MacArthur Foundation and IDEO, provides a set of tools, propositions and case studies to help business and designers think innovatively and design differently – to develop products, projects, and places that help, not hurt, our planet.

Creating Green, Sustainable, Restorative and Regenerative Buildings

The commitment to rise to the challenge of climate change can start with designers and architects creating green, sustainable, restorative, and regenerative buildings and spaces. Traditionally, buildings are resource-heavy, with their construction, demolition, and operational energy requirements accounting for approximately 40% of global greenhouse gas emissions. The design response is to make buildings more sustainable. As founding president of the US Green Building Council Rick Fedrizza explains:

[The] green building movement is driven by a simple, yet revolutionary idea; that the buildings in which we live our lives can nurture instead of harm, can restore instead of consume, and can inspire instead of constrain . . . at its core, green building is about making the world a better place to live.

(Fedrizza, 2013, p. xiii)

The following sections outline some of the key concepts, emerging trends, and high-profile or innovative projects, buildings, places, and products that exemplify best-practice sustainable design, as well as highlighting the value of consciously drawing on design theories. Acknowledging the enormity of the climate change challenge, and the wealth of rapidly growing literature documenting sustainable design, construction, materials and processes, this chapter focuses on designers, and why and how designers should integrate sustainability considerations into their practice.

While policy-makers debate the best course of action and citizens question climate science or the impact of local actions on a global challenge, a significant number of designers have already embraced the opportunity and challenge of sustainable design. These designers are guided by numerous global certification systems that explicitly quantify the environmental performance of buildings; for example, the Leadership in Energy and Environmental Design [LEED] and the SITES certification for sustainable landscapes in the United States, the United Kingdom's Building Research Establishment Environmental Assessment Method [BREEAM] for green building certification, and Australia's Green Star rating system.

These certification systems provide a stringent structure of checklists and credits, which quantify various aspects of the building and site's environmental impact at global (emissions, site, land), local (water, energy, transport, neighborhood development) and building scale (indoor performance, interior design, materials, suppliers, management, occupant health and performance) (Gou & Xie, 2017). Arguing that our changing climate means we must reshape the way we make green buildings the center of our lives, the World Green Building Council (WGBG), a global network of Green Building Councils, launched their Net Zero Carbon Buildings Commitment in September 2018, challenging businesses, organizations, cities, states, and regions to reach net zero carbon operating emissions within their portfolios by 2030. Significantly, as Figure 10.3 illustrates, the WGBC see accelerating the uptake of green buildings as a means to achieve many of the United Nations Sustainable Development goals.

Designing buildings to be resource-efficient and environmentally friendly, with net zero energy, net zero water, and net zero waste is a critical first step towards sustainability. But is it enough? While better than 'business as usual,' current sustainability building assessment systems rarely consider social impact or the holistic local context. Many designers believe the performance benchmarks are relatively conservative, and

Figure 10.3 Green buildings contribute to the UN's Sustainable Development goals.
Source: World Building Council.

the rigid adherence to checklists actually constricts creative design innovation. Yet, in the last decade there has been a significant paradigm shift towards restorative sustainability. This restorative approach interestingly takes many forms – away from creating '*less bad*' buildings (with a narrow focus on building energy performance) to fostering a broader '*more good*' approach to proactively reverse the damage we have caused, and with the aim to create a *positive* (not neutral or negative) environmental footprint for future generations.

Emerging Trends in Sustainable Design

Many contemporary design theorists believe tackling climate change will require disruptive, radical change in how we design cities. Critical work, from authors such as William McDonough, Janis Birkeland, Martin Brown, and Dominique Hes together argue we must move beyond *reducing* the environmental impact of a building, product or place to actively put back more than is taken in construction and operation of the building or space. The sustainability discourse has moved from business as usual to green, net-zero and now net-positive, restorative, and regenerative. As the European Union's RESTORE (**RE**thinking Sustainability **TO**wards a Regenerative Economy) project, and many other initiatives argue, we no longer have the luxury of being less bad and must do more good. Space restricts a deep discussion of this literature, but green and regenerative design is now an essential part of current practice – with attention turning to thorny unresolved issues such as how to retrofit the existing built environment for sustainability and fully engage built environment, development and design professionals, as well as the broader community, with the sustainability imperative (Dixon, Connaughton & Green, 2018; Miller & Buys, 2008; Miller, 2018). From the 2008 Clinton Climate Change Initiative 'Energy Efficiency Building Retrofit Program' to Dezeen's series 'Good Design for a Bad World,' sustainably minded designers, policymakers and consumers are advocating for positive change in our built environment.

Best-practice contemporary places, products and spaces actively restore the environment (for example, producing more energy than they use), and also contribute socially to their occupants and local communities, often using the healthy salutogenic design principles discussed in Chapter 7. The Living Building Challenge (LBC) (International Living Future Institute, 2014), for example, prompts designers to create living buildings that 'give more than they take.' LBC is the built environment's most rigorous performance standard, with an end goal of creating a regenerative built environment that has a positive impact on the natural and human systems with which it interacts. Using the metaphor and image of a flower, the LBC has seven performance areas called petals (site; water; energy; health and happiness; materials; equity; and beauty), and an inspiring mission to 'lead and support the transformation toward communities that are socially just, culturally rich and ecologically restorative.'

The LBC equity petal, for example, has a democracy and social justice imperative that aims to 'transform developments to foster a true, inclusive sense of community that is just and equitable regardless of an individual's background, age, class, race, gender or sexual orientation.' Whether it is through the provision of an edible community garden, space for community meetings, a men's shed, green space for exercise, facilities for outdoor community movies, interactive signs about water recycling, or simply incorporating local history and memories into the design, restorative design has a broader 'social good' objective. As the Plan B Team posits 'business can't thrive in workplaces and communities that are failing—just as it can't succeed on a planet that is failing.' Similarly, it is no longer enough to design a sustainable building that is environmentally friendly, but operates in isolation from its local context. It must be connected, in a more positive way, to its site and surroundings.

Take, for example, Skygarden, London's highest public garden, located at 20 Fenchurch Street. While an environmentally sustainable building, critics argue this distinctive 'Walkie-Talkie' building has no meaningful relationship with its surroundings. The provision of a 'public park' was a key rationale for allowing this commercial skyscraper to be built on the edge of a conservation area. To access this public park, people must book online at least three days beforehand, queue for airport-style security checks with photographic identification and then ride crowded lifts to a slightly underwhelming three-level garden – albeit with wonderful views. Like Wilding (2015), who labels the Skygarden a symbol of inequality, we also question the true accessibility for marginalized and vulnerable communities. The online booking process restricts the most marginalized people in our community, those without internet access. And visiting is challenging for larger families, with a maximum of three children per adult and no outside food or drink allowed. This place is not, as the extract below from architecture critic Rowan Moore emphasizes, a park. And, while the building has been awarded BREEAM accreditation for its sustainability credentials, we doubt it would be awarded an LBC equity petal. As Wilding suggests, it is actually a place that keeps people apart:

> As to being a park, this is not a place where adults or children could walk a dog, jog, have picnics, paddle in ponds, play on swings, kick a ball, build snowmen, or sunbathe. It has 9,000 square feet of green space – the same sort of area as a very generous house, but not a park.
>
> (Moore, 2015)

Designing for restorative and regenerative sustainability means collectively adopting a triple bottom line, living systems-thinking, and circular design perspective, all grounded in biomimicry, a cradle-to-cradle, and a broader social impact perspective. What this means in practice is that the best climate-aware designs also incorporate elements of evidenced-based design theory, as we clearly see in the examples below.

Sustainable Design through the Lens of Theory

Table 10.1 outlines the value of explicitly considering design theory in design practice – focusing on the example of green roofs, with one pictured in Figure 10.1. Green roofs are an interesting example, with the best having strong environmentally sustainable credentials while also fostering social justice. And, as Table 10.1 illustrates, explicitly adopting a 'theory' thinking hat is a strategy that encourages creative, divergent thinking in the design process – whether it is designing a building, a landscape or a green roof.

The Intersection of Biophilic Design Theory and Sustainable, Regenerative Design

Adopting a sustainable design mindset, as Table 10.1 and Figure 10.4 illustrate, is about thinking differently. Take, for example, traditional construction hoardings and scaffolding used during construction – these could easily be replaced with educational or green wall hoardings. As well as keeping people safe from the work site, these can feature educational historic info-graphics or become the site of a temporary green living wall. Featuring grasses, flowers and fruits, green scaffolding improves visual amenity, helps prevent vandalism and graffiti, and may reduce noise and air pollution. As Figure 10.4 illustrates, thinking with personal space and prospect-refuge theories will see the creation of beautiful places (such as the teepees on a rooftop bar in Singapore) as well as general biophilic design used in many Singapore buildings.

When it comes to designing for sustainability, the theoretical concept of biophilia (designing with nature, see Chapter 6) is frequently evoked in the green, sustainable, and regenerative building toolkit. The Health Petal of the Living Building Challenge, for example, explicitly requires the 'biophilia imperative.' This is exemplified in Pittsburgh's Phipps Conservatory and Botanical Gardens, which have challenged and re-conceptualized learning spaces by designing modular classrooms with non-toxic materials, net-positive energy, and net-zero waste. Their LBC certified Nature Lab is an inspirational place. There is natural light, ventilation, furniture from reclaimed wood and a large plant wall, while the native rain garden provides food and habitat for wildlife. The rainwater tank is inside the classroom so students can hear the rainwater being captured and open the tank to monitor water levels. A ladybug house introduces children to integrated pest management, while an observational beehive in the classroom allows kids safe access to bees. These close and

Table 10.1 Integrating design theory into sustainable, regenerative design – a green roof scenario.

Key theories	Considerations for sustainable design	A green roof scenario
Affordance	Affordances for sustainability can fully integrate sustainable behaviors into daily activities. Clear sustainability cues can help maximize the positive impact of a building or place, meaning that sustainable features and decisions also have wider social or ethical benefits.	Making a green roof as a public space, perhaps as a community garden, commercial or recreational space, is longer-term affordance thinking – as well as mitigating the heat island effect, the green roof can build community and foster physical activity (salutogenic design) and social interactions, thus helping tackle social isolation.
Prospect-refuge	Approaching sustainable design with a prospect-refuge mindset means ensuring the provision of good quality spaces, where people can easily oversee an area of activity and thus feel safe and in control.	On green roofs, design practices such as views, general spaciousness and natural light all enable prospect. Refuge means providing comforting and nurturing spaces for retreat, which might mean cozy alcoves and corners that provide comfortable spaces to safely observe others.
Personal space	Preserving personal space boundaries, alongside providing space for social interactions, is frequently an explicit consideration in sustainable design.	Use outdoor furniture, and visual and acoustic partitioning to support a need for both personal and social spaces across the green roof. Clear zoning, separating social activities (such as gardening or mini-golf) from personal spaces for solace, retreat and relaxation, is needed.
Sense of place/*genius loci*	*Genius loci* typically fosters sustainability, as it encourages vernacular architecture – design strongly grounded in the local context and responsive to the unique history, topography, climate, building materials, customs and values of local people. *Genius loci* in sustainable design practice often means embracing local construction methods and materials. The choice of plantings should also be appropriate for the region and setting.	Local resources native to the region are typically a more sustainable option, thus reducing embodied energy from transporting goods longer distances, with the style also often better aligned to the cultural design aesthetic. Think also about the local setting; is there a need for a playground or a men's shed for the ageing population? The best green roof would respond to the unique sense of place, in terms of historical, geographic and socio-cultural characteristics.

Place attachment	Thoughtful design choices can help engage people and foster place attachment. As attachment to place usually develops over time, the best sustainable designs reflect local values, culture and memories – thus readily evoking and cementing connections. Place attachment is not often an explicit common design consideration in sustainability, but would help better engage the broader public.	Local residents could be encouraged to embrace 'collaborative consumption,' for example, by providing a community garden or a community hub (to hold community meetings, offer a shared tool library or book-swapping). Interactive information and signage could also communicate key elements of the site's history, as well as activities and progress on any sustainability goals.
Biophilia	Principles of biophilia theory feature heavily throughout sustainable design. Vertical walls and gardens can create a visually striking aesthetic, with contemporary practice emphasizing tactile design that directly connects people with soothing experiences of nature.	Maximize biophilia connections by including views of and interactions with animals and nature (for example, ensuring birds, insects, fish and animals are visible from walkways and windows), and focusing on natural light, vegetation, living walls, natural textures, and materials.

Figure 10.4 Alongside sustainable and biophilic considerations, green roofs should incorporate opportunities for playful social interaction, including outdoor chess, basketball and gardening, as well as places for peaceful retreat.

Source: Clockwise from top: Thea Blackler (teepee tents, rooftop bar, Singapore); Matt Brown on Unspash, CC (rooftop chess); Evonne Miller (gardening, rooftop bar Singapore); Design for Health, Flickr CC (green roof above housing in Sweden).

rare interactions, the designers argue, 'mesmerize and inspire' and create a space that fosters 'inspiration, education and beauty.'

In Vancouver, the VanDusen Botanical Garden Visitor Centre has been designed to be one of the most sustainable buildings in Canada. A LEED-NC Platinum-certified project, the Visitor Centre was the first Canadian building to apply for and receive LBC Petal, and was named the 2014 World Architecture News Most Sustainable Building of the Year. The Visitor Centre uses on-site, renewable sources, including geothermal boreholes, solar photovoltaics and solar hot water tubes to manage heating requirements and achieve net-zero energy. Rainwater is collected off the building, filtered and used as greywater, with other products chosen according to their carbon footprint, ability to be recycled and their individual life cycle. Beyond its sustainability credentials, it is the biophilic design that makes this building outstanding.

In 2018, it won the second annual International Living Future Institute Kellert Biophilic Design Award, which celebrates biophilic buildings that amplify the human/nature connection and perform like nature. The jury citation below confirms the value of using biophilic theory to create a sustainable, regenerative design. The visual perspective, experience and form is inspired by and references an indigenous British Columbia orchid. Drawing on natural systems and organic forms, the building is primarily constructed out of wood and has 'undulating green roof "petals" that float above rammed earth and concrete walls,' with a petal-like floor plan. The roof 'petals' converge at the central operable glazed skylight oculus, the design of which was inspired by biomimicry and the natural climate control mechanisms used in termite mounds. The oculus provides the atrium space with natural light and cools the building, serving as a solar chimney and assisting with natural ventilation. The building's green roofs purposely attract and support native fauna, and are linked to the ground, enabling creatures – from butterflies to coyotes – to access the roof ecosystem:

> The building is overwhelmingly multi-sensory, from the natural updraft in the central 'oculus' to the tactile qualities of the materials, the sparkle of sunshine and gentle diffusion of daylight, to soothing aromas and sounds of nature. The architecture embraces rainwater capture, stores passive solar energies for heating, and induces natural ventilation, just as nature would have done.
>
> Delighting the senses with natural patterns and processes that are abundant through the architectural settings, the success of the Van Duesn Botanical Garden Visitor Centre is most evident in the Evolved Human Nature Relationships that have been created – the order and complexity, the spaces for prospect and refuge, and the tripling of new visitors to a Canadian national treasure with reverence and spirituality.

Genius Loci and Sustainable, Regenerative Design

Complementing the process of sustainable restorative and regenerative thinking is sense of place theory, or *genius loci*. In essence, sense of place theory reminds us that a key first step in designing great places is to respect and celebrate the unique characteristics of the individual site. Take, for example, the recent expansion and re-design of the Oslo Airport, strategically shaped to leverage passive solar energy, using recycled wood and steel throughout, as well as low-carbon technologies including natural thermal energy. Perhaps the most unusual site-specific feature is that snow is stored onsite in a storage depot to be used as a coolant in the summer. The problem of lots of snow has been turned into an asset and defining design feature. These design innovations together have reduced energy use by 50%, making Oslo Airport the first airport ever to earn a BREEAM Excellent rating for sustainability. Construction too was sustainable, with 91% of all waste reused. The design, by the Nordic – Office of Architecture, won the 2017 World Architecture Network Sustainable Buildings Award. Though a clever layout, the walking distance from check-in to departure gate is only 500m, a design feature that supports families, older people, those with disabilities, and tired business travelers. A greater consideration of users' needs, however, might have taken the re-design to the next level. For example, in 2017, Shannon Airport opened the first European sensory room (dim lighting, calming visuals, comfy cushions) to provide a soothing respite place (away from the activity of a busy airport) for kids with autism and sensory processing disorders.

While Oslo Airport innovatively used the natural resource of snow, the Walumba Elders Centre in Western Australia responded to the local place – hot climate – and local culture – the indigenous heritage. After a flood displaced 300 people in the community, Iredale Pedersen Hook Architects worked with care home staff and local aboriginal elders, the Giga people, to co-design an aged care facility. Winner of the World Architecture Festival Health category and Best of the Best award 2015 Sustainability Award in Australia, the jury citation below emphasizes the value of authentic design that respects and dialogues with the sense of place, more than just the environmental and economic considerations. The thoughtful design acknowledges important cultural considerations including gender separation, access to public and private outdoor spaces, the ability to hold ceremonies that may involve fire and smoke, and the purposeful planting of bush medicine and smoking ceremony plants. The colors and form embraced the unique sense of place –the *genius loci* of the physical typology, the hill and river landscape – and respected place attachment and broader historical and socio-cultural considerations. The aged care facility was purposely located close to the school, to ensure elders could easily maintain regular contact with youth and enable the cultural transmission of knowledge:

Here is a building which does all of the important things really well and is the epitome of sustainability. Not only does it sit comfortably in its environment with a very appropriate climatic design response, it is clearly responsive to the often complex cultural requirements of its users. An innate understanding of both people and place by the designers resulted in a building that reacted to, rather than imposed upon, its landscape and culture. The elevated floors are more than just flood-proofing – they provide areas of deep cool at ground level in the hot months where people of   all ages can gather, sit and 'do community'. And when it rains, the water is celebrated and featured rather than considered a problem and just piped away.

(Architecture and Design, 2015)

When sense of place theory interacts with sustainability we witness the Microlibrary initiative in Indonesia, winner of the 2018 'The Influencer' Indi-Pacific INDIE award. The mission of the Microlibrary is to use beautiful architecture to foster literacy, rekindle interest in books, and provide a dedicated local space for reading. In 2016, two Microlibraries were built in Bandung, each uniquely designed to fit the potential of the site, the tropical climate and programmatic demands of its community, but with a low budget and construction cost. One microlibrary was constructed from 2000 ice cream buckets, a facade that facilitates lighting, ventilation and visibility. Using a binary code, the ice cream buckets can be adjusted to read '*buku adalah jendela dunia*' (translated to 'books are the windows to the world'). This message repeatedly spirals down around the perimeter. A passive climate strategy, adopted through external shading and cross ventilation that expels moisture, provides sufficient daylight so artificial lighting is not needed during the day. While this small-scale project is unlikely to meet the stringent criteria required for larger sustainability awards, it is a powerful exemplar of grassroots design activism. The message now is very simple: be it the design of multi-million-dollar exemplar projects or smaller local initiatives, consideration of design theory – for example, biophilia or *genius loci*, alongside the sustainability imperative, needs to be standard practice.

Radically Redesigning the Built Environment

Sustainable design is not an optional extra. It must be a core guiding principle. From using a triple bottom line, cradle to cradle, circular design, or net-positive approach, a wide array of tools, principles and guidelines exist to lead innovative, eco-friendly design decisions. And increasing numbers of inspirational designers are creatively embracing sustainable design philosophies and pushing traditional boundaries. Transitioning to a sustainable world demands designers continually and radically re-think the design and use of products, buildings, spaces and places. If every single thing we create, design, build and manufacture serves (rather than screws) our planet, then our world and our future will look radically different. Design, through thoughtful and innovative decisions, and using relevant theory, can be a powerful force for positive action on climate change. As designers, we must embrace, raise awareness of, and advocate for a circular economy, net positive and regenerative design approaches. Our future depends on it.

References

Architecture and Design (2015). Walumba Elders Centre by Iredale Pedersen Hook Architects Wins 2015 Sustainability Awards – Multi-Density Residential Prize. Retrieved from www.architectureanddesign.com.au/projects/multi-residential/walumba-elders-centre-by-iredale-pedersen-hook-arc

Dixon, T., Connaughton, J. & Green, S. (2018). Understanding and Shaping Sustainable Futures in the Built Environment to 2010. In T. Dixon, J. Connaughton & S. Green (Eds.), *Sustainable Futures in the Built Environment to 2050: A Foresight Approach to Construction and Development*. Hoboken NJ: Wiley Blackwell, 339–364.

Fedrizza, R. (2013). Forward. In R. Guenther & G. Vittori (Eds.), *Sustainable Healthcare Architecture* (2nd edition). Hoboken, NJ: Wiley & Sons, p. xiii.

Gou, Z. & Xie, X. (2017). Evolving Green Building: Triple Bottom Line or Regenerative Design? *Journal of Cleaner Production* 153: 600–660.

Guterres, A. (2018). Remarks at High-Level Event on Climate Change. September 26. Retrieved from www.un.org/sg/en/content/sg/speeches/2018-09-26/remarks-high-level-event-climate-change (accessed July 30, 2019).

International Living Future Institute. (2014). *Living Building Challenge 3.0: A Visionary Path to a Regenerative Future*. Retrieved from https://living-future.org/wp-content/uploads/2016/12/Living-Building-Challenge-3.0-Standard.pdf.

Miller, E. (2018). 'My Hobby is Global Warming and Peak Oil': Sustainability as Serious Leisure. *World Leisure Journal* 60(3): 209–220.

Miller, E. & Buys, L. (2008). Retrofitting Commercial Office Buildings for Sustainability: Tenants' Perspectives. *Journal of Property Investment and Finance* 26(6): 552–561.

Moore, R. (2015). Walkie Talkie Review – Bloated, Inelegant, Thuggish. *The Guardian* (January 4). Retrieved from www.theguardian.com/artanddesign/2015/jan/04/20-fenchurch-street-walkie-talkie-review-rowan-moore-sky-garden

Thackara, J. (2007). Forward. In J. Chapman & N. Gant (Eds.), *Designers, Visionaries and other Stories: A Collection of Sustainable Design Essays*. London: Earthscan, xii–xvi.

WCED. (1987). *Our Common Future*. Oxford: Oxford University Press.

Wilding, M. (2015). London's New 'Sky Garden' Is a Symbol of Inequality. Retrieved from www.vice.com/en_au/article/dpwmdk/londons-sky-garden-public-space-192

Conclusion
Creating Great Places through Theory-Storming

Throughout this book, we have argued that to create great places designers must engage with evidence-based research and theory. Inspired by de Bono's thinking hats, we have proposed a new process – theory-storming – and envisioned a future where designers collaboratively think about a project or design decision through the lens of multiple theories. Just as *design thinking*, *design doing* and *future thinking* processes have become standard design tools, we have a similar vision for *theory-storming*. Imagine the fresh observations, insights and ideas that will arise if designers actively put on an affordances hat, prospect-refuge hat or biophilic design hat, and actively engage – individually or in groups – with the transformative possibilities of thinking theoretically. Approaching design challenges head-on using multiple theoretical lenses will foster inspiration and creativity, and lead to more effective urban design solutions for health and wellbeing.

Doing Health Policy and Design Differently

Creating great places that foster health and wellbeing, means challenging conventional practice and being open to new ways of doing things. Take a moment to consider what you would do if you controlled the healthcare system in your country. With your limited budget, what initiatives and changes would you prioritize – and why? Would you prioritize creating great places?

England's National Health Service (NHS) is doing just that. In collaboration with Public Health England, the NHS is creating ten 'healthy new towns' as demonstrator sites across the country. Started in 2016, the towns together will include approximately 76,000 new homes for 170,000 residents. Creating great places is increasingly vital to preventative healthcare policy and practice, with the NHS Chief Executive explaining they would 'kick themselves' if they missed the opportunity to ' "design out" the obesogenic environment, and "design in" health and wellbeing' (NHS England, 2016).

Figure 11.1 Painted stairs in Singapore serve as a visual reminder that creating great places is a journey.

Source: Robin Hickmott (Flickr, CC BY ND-2.0).

Design is now a central feature of the public health discourse, reflected in the purposely provocative title of a 2018 University of Oxford public seminar, 'Is Designing Healthy Communities the Right Response to an Overstretched NHS?' The answer, of course, is a resounding yes. Using both brownfield and greenfield sites, the Healthy New Towns Initiative has the unique opportunity to focus on healthy environments right from the start. The developments will incorporate dementia-friendly streets and create virtual care homes which use technology to facilitate access to healthcare, will designate fast-food free zones, and transform typically bland urban streets into adventure streets that incorporate incidental exercise and elements of fun as children walk to school (Siddique, 2016). These progressive ideas acknowledge what designers already know: the solution to many of our pressing public health challenges, from social isolation to obesity to climate change and a rapidly ageing population, lies in redesigning our built environment.

Our Moral Obligation as Designers to Engage with Theory

As policymakers begin to embrace design to answer these wicked problems, designers have a moral obligation to ensure the proposed answers are evidence-based and grounded in deep theoretical understanding. As we have argued throughout this book, thoughtful engagement with design theories and evidence has the power to positively transform everyday lives, creating great places where people thrive. We must make sure that our proposed design interventions are the best they can be.

One factor limiting this transformation towards evidence-based practice is that the myth of the creative genius dominates. Renowned architectural theorist Juhani Pallasmaa (2017) worries that an intellectual research-oriented approach to design might limit creativity and dull empathetic imagination, insight, and innovation. Historical geniuses of design, such as the ancient Greeks or Michelangelo and da Vinci, Pallasmaa argues, demonstrated a deeply intuitive, experiential and empathic understanding of materials, form, structure, detail, scale, image, orientation, climate, and place – engaging in the task of design without the insight offered by 'today's instrumentalized research' as 'thinking and feeling beings' foremost, 'not just intellectual problem solvers' (Pallasmaa, 2017, pp. 148–149).

Critically, these geniuses of design often conducted much first-hand empirical research themselves, through meticulous observation, deep self-reflection and exhaustive experimentation. Michelangelo's comprehensive anatomical knowledge, for example, was gained through serious study, public dissection of bodies and experimentation, making molds of muscles to understand and experiment with shape and form (Eknoyan, 2000). Catalan architect Antoni Gaudi made an upside-down model of the Sagrada Familia to test his structural theory, and may have tested his revolutionary designs for Park Guell at a psychiatric hospital where patients served as his artisans. Finish architect Alvar Aalto is renowned for his non-linear design method of deep reflection and hands-on engagement and creative experimentation with different materials (Pallasmaa,

2009; Burgen, 2011). Fundamentally, reflecting on the work practices of these design geniuses is a reminder that creating great places requires dedication – a commitment, willingness, and excitement for lifelong learning and experimentation, which includes a deep knowledge and appreciation of theory.

Reframing the Design Skillset, Being Both Creative Genius and Skilled Theorist

Design is both an art and a science. Empathic intuition, iterative non-linear cycles of design thinking, and the inspirational flash of creative insight – the 'ah ha moment' – should always be the critical building blocks of the design process. Few of us are as naturally talented, creative or visionary as Michelangelo, so contemporary design practice needs to be strongly grounded in evidence and theory. Solving the problems of the 21st century – a time of unprecedented urbanization and high-density living, climate change, population growth and ageing, and skyrocketing rates of disease – all demand a new way of thinking, planning and designing – one that positions theory and evidence-based approaches at the center of the design process.

Design decisions powerfully shape urban life and are intimately tied to our health and wellbeing. And so, just as the medical profession has evolved from anecdotal practices to a strong scientific knowledge base, so too must the practice of design evolve to become evidence-based. We have examined a range of classic design theories, concepts, research and practical real-world examples in this book, purposefully covering those that are international (for example, biophilic design in Singapore, Italy and the Netherlands; sustainable buildings in Canada and Australia; and how *genius loci* is guiding high-profile adaptive reuse projects in China); contemporary (for example, the universal design of the Library of Birmingham, to smaller scale sensory gardens for people with ASD and dementia); and all ranging in scale and scope (for example, reflecting on how engaging with evidence and theory might help improve the design of a bus shelter, a green roof, and an entire transport system).

What's more, by introducing the new process of *theory-storming*, the ideas in this book serve as valuable inspiration and a design theory toolkit for all design educators, researchers, practitioners, and students striving to create great places.

We hope this book starts a new, imminent dialogue, whereby designers openly discuss theories and cutting-edge research findings. And more importantly, we advocate for the transition towards evidence-based design practice that privileges informed processes and decisions. If we are to positively shape urban life, we must respect and engage with the transformative power of design, drawing on both the art and science of it, to create places which truly foster health and wellbeing.

Only then will we create great places where all people thrive.

References

Burgen, S. (2011). Gaudí May Have Used Psychiatric Hospital to Test Designs. Retrieved on 20 February 2019 from www.theguardian.com/world/2011/aug/12/gaudi-psychiatric-hospital-test-designs.

Eknoyan, G. (2000). Michelangelo: Art, Anatomy, and the Kidney. *Kidney International* 57(3): 1190 1201.

NHS England. (2016). NHS Chief Announces Plan to Support Ten Healthy New Towns. Retrieved from www.england.nhs.uk/2016/03/hlthy-new-towns.

Pallasmaa, J. (2009). *The Thinking Hand: Embodied and Existential Wisdom in Architecture*. Chichester: John Wiley & Sons.

Pallasmaa, J. (2017). Empathy, Design and Care – Intention, Knowledge and Intuition: The Example of Alvar Aalto. In C. Bates, R. Imrie & K. Kullman (Eds), *Care and Design: Bodies, Buildings, Cities*. Chichester: John Wiley & Sons, 138–154.

Siddique, H. (2016). Ten New 'Healthy' Towns to be Built in England. Retrieved from www.theguardian.com/society/2016/mar/01/ten-new-healthy-towns-to-be-built-in-england.

Recommended Readings

By necessity, describing six core design theories and four global priorities in one book has limited the scope and depth of our discussion. Therefore, we provide a brief summary of key books and theorists for further reading if you wish to delve deeper into a particular theory or idea. As there is a vast literature on these topics, the resources and recommended readings listed for each theory are limited to those that have most informed our thinking. We start with a short list of books we love, written by notable and emerging thought leaders from a wide array of disciplinary backgrounds including urban planning, sociology, environmental design, architecture, landscape architecture and journalism. While these authors approach the task of placemaking from different perspectives, each and every one of these books will resonate, inform and inspire designers to create great places where people thrive.

Books to Start with . . .

Bates, C., Imrie, R. & Kullman, K. (2017). *Care and Design: Bodies, Buildings, Cities*. Chichester: Wiley Blackwell.

This 12-chapter edited volume is a delight to read and deeply explores the relationships between design, care and cities. This thorough, accessible and beautifully crafted book encourages deep reflection about form and function, practice and theory, and offers a range of deep pedagogical, methodological and theoretical reflections from thought leaders across geography, sociology and design.

Carmona, M., Tiesdell, S., Heath, T. & Oc, T. (2010). *Public Places – Urban Spaces: The Dimensions of Urban Design* (2nd edition). Burlington, VT: Elsevier Science.

This wonderful book, designed as an introductory textbook, provides a very comprehensive introduction to the principles of urban design theory and practice. Full of relevant case studies, research and theory, this book emphasizes that urban design is – first and foremost – about and for people.

Cooper-Marcus, C. & Barnes, M. (1999). *Healing Gardens: Therapeutic Benefits and Design Recommendations*. New York: John Wiley & Sons.

This well-written, accessible and comprehensive resource draws on research, multiple case studies, site plans and photographs to demonstrate the value, design and impact of nature and healing gardens across different settings, including hospitals, hospices and nursing homes. Honestly documenting what works and what doesn't, this book is an extremely useful reference for anyone interested in advocating for, designing or managing therapeutic landscapes.

Gehl, J. (1987). *Life between Buildings: Using Public Space*. New York: Van Nostrand Reinhold Company.
Gehl, J. (2010). *Cities for People*. Washington, DC: Island Press.

Throughout his career, Danish architect and urban design consultant Jan Gehl has helped improve the quality of urban life by re-orienting city design towards the pedestrian and cyclist – creating (or recreating) cityscapes on a human scale. In his thoughtful and enlightening books, Gehl clearly explains the methods and tools he uses to reconfigure cityscapes into 'cities for people.' Drawing on photographs and examples from around the globe, Gehl reminds us to plan cities from a small-scale view, to consider the five human senses and focus on the experience at the speed of walking, rather than at the fast speed of riding in a car or public transit. In these must-read works, Gehl explains convincingly that 'first we shape the cities – and then they shape us.'

Goldhagen, S. W. (2017). *Welcome to Your World: How the Built Environment Shapes Our Lives*. New York: HarperCollins.

In this brilliant book, architectural critic, academic and writer Sarah Williams Goldhagen illustrates how the design of our built environment – our homes and urban settings – shapes our lives. With over 150 color photographs, and examples of the worlds' best and worst buildings, landscapes and cityscapes, Goldhagen draws on multiple perspectives (architecture, urban planning, cognitive psychology, neuroscience, politics) to argue that poor planning and design is negatively affecting our health and wellbeing. She then challenges us to leave a better built environment as our legacy. A must read, this insightful and powerful book is destined to become a classic.

Jacobs, J. (1961). *The Death and Life of Great American Cities*. London: Vintage Books.

American-Canadian journalist and activist Jane Jacobs (1916–2006), wrote this seminal book exploring what makes a great neighborhood. Drawing on many examples, including her own New York's Greenwich Village, she reflects on, and often criticizes contemporary thinking on urban planning. An essential framework for assessing the vitality and livability of all cities, there is a reason Jacobs's monumental work is required reading for urban planning and design courses around the globe.

Keedwell, P. (2017). *Headspace: The Psychology of City Living.* London: Aururm Press.

In this thought-provoking book, Paul Keedwell uses a psychologist's perspective to examine the effect of urban planning, architecture and interior design on our physical and mental wellbeing, productivity, and quality of life. Drawing on a large body of disparate research and international examples, Keedwell thoughtfully discusses how our built environment – our homes, neighborhoods, workplaces and hospitals – affects our health and wellbeing, drawing on examples from prospect-refuge and many of the other concepts and theories we discuss in this book, including play and work spaces, high-density living and healing spaces. This practical, accessible and eye-opening book demonstrates the power of good, thoughtful design.

Lynch, K. (1960). *The Image of the City.* Cambridge, MA: MIT Press.
Lynch, K. (1981). *A Theory of Good City Form.* Cambridge, MA: MIT Press.

Kevin Lynch's important works identify his normative theory of the city, exploring the intersections of purposeful activity, city form, and perceptions. Lynch (1918–1984), who studied with Frank Lloyd Wright at Taliesin and later obtained a Bachelor of City Planning degree from MIT, outlines how to evaluate the 'goodness' of cities, and what we might learn from utopian communities and 'hellish' images. His books are must-reads for reflective practitioners, scholars, and students, or anyone interested in the practice of urban design, urban morphological design theory, the use of cognitive mapping and focus groups, or how to shape the future of our cities.

Regnier, V. (2018). *Housing Design for an Increasingly Older Population: Redefining Assisted Living for the Mentally and Physically Frail.* Hoboken, NJ: John Wiley & Sons.

In a practical and engaging book, teacher, researcher, and architect Victor Regnier outlines how thoughtful design decisions can enhance the experience of daily life for older people in aged care and nursing home environments. The detailed case studies and photographs of specific design practices, as well as the identification of 20 key design decisions, makes this book an essential resource for aged care design. The only person to have achieved fellowship status in both the American Institute of Architects and the Gerontological Society of America, Regnier is a Professor of Architecture and Gerontology at the University of Southern California. Regnier's book is a comprehensive guide to designing for the world's ageing population.

Whyte, W. H. (1980). *The Social Life of Small Urban Spaces*. Washington, DC: Conservation Foundation.

In 1980, William 'Holly' Whyte published the findings from his revolutionary Street Life Project in *The Social Life of Small Urban Spaces* and accompanying film. Whyte's fantastic eye-opening work, defined by his charming humor and biting insight, motivates us to apply critical eyes at the everyday urban spaces around us and consider the variety of factors that combine to make them good public spaces or not. Project for Public Spaces continues his work around the world, with their website a wealth of information (see www.pps.org).

Books for Each of the Six Core Theories . . .

Theory 1: Affordance Theory

Gibson, J. J. (1979). *The Ecological Approach to Visual Perception*. New York: Psychology Press.

American psychologist James J. Gibson developed the concept of affordance over many years, with his informative 1979 book exploring how we see the environments around us (the surfaces, layouts, texture) and how the qualities of an object or environment communicate opportunities to do certain actions. The notion of affordances is critical in human factors and design, and this is one of the key texts.

Norman, D. (2013). *The Design of Everyday Things* (revised and expanded edition). New York: Basic Books.
Norman, D. (2009). *The Design of Future Things*. New York: Basic Books.

Donald Norman is a researcher, professor, and author of many wonderfully engaging, relevant, and sometimes funny books. Linking design and psychology, Norman advocates user-centered design and very clearly mapping the affordances with the design of everyday items and spaces. His works include fascinating discussions ranging from the design of door handles and light switches, to the perils and promise of smart technology and intelligent objects of the future, from cautious cars to cantankerous refrigerators.

Theory 2: Prospect-Refuge Theory

Appleton, J. (1975). *The Experience of Landscape*. Chichester: Wiley and Sons.

In this classic book, first published in 1975, Jay Appleton proposed and argued a new theoretical approach to landscape aesthetics, which included prospect-refuge theory. Although this theory references the days of hunter gatherers when humans needed to see out into the landscape while being protected from predators, today it has important implications for safety in public spaces, as well as placemaking interventions that involve people watching and performance.

Kaplan, R. & Kaplan, S. (1989). *The Experience of Nature: A Psychological Perspective*. New York: Cambridge University Press.

In this influential book, environmental psychologists Rachel and Stephen Kaplan offer a research-based analysis of the vital psychological role that nature plays in our lives. Their attention restoration theory (ART) asserts that people concentrate better after spending time in or viewing nature with this thorough and very accessible book serving as an invitation to think deeply about the important role of nature in our lives.

Theory 3: Personal Space Theory

Graziano, M. (2018). *The Spaces between Us: A Story of Neuroscience, Evolution, and Human Nature*. Oxford: Oxford University Press.

While not about the built environment, this contemporary book, written by a neuroscientist, provides deep, engaging, humorous and often personal insight into the science of personal space.

Hall, E. T. (1966). *The Hidden Dimension*. New York: Anchor Books.

Edward Hall coined the term proxemics, the study of space, with this critical book outlining people's perceptions of social and personal space – how we conceptualize, use and organize space. His reflective book outlines how intimate, personal, social, and public distances may differ depending on a person's cultural background, gender, age, and relationship with others, and is peppered with Hall's insights, personal experiences and research learnings.

Theory 4: Sense of Place Theory/Genius Loci

Norberg-Schulz, C. (1980). *Genius Loci: Towards a phenomenology of Architecture*. New York: Rizzoli.
Norberg-Schulz, C. (1997). *Nightlands: Nordic Building*. Cambridge, MA: MIT Press.

Classics in this field, the books by Norwegian architectural theorist and historian Christian Norberg-Schulz provide in-depth theoretical and practical design rationale for why we must 'dwell' with a site to find its *genius loci*. *Nightlands* is an especially evocative insight into how the distinctive Nordic architectural identity emphasizes a timeless, mythic relationship with nature – an example of *genius loci*.

Pallasmaa, J. (1996*)*. *The Eyes of the Skin*. New York: John Wiley & Sons.

Pallasmaa's books are exquisite. Often considered foundational texts in architecture, reading Pallasmaa's work is a powerfully personal reminder of the importance and impact of good design. Each and every page is thought provoking, succinctly identifying the critical dimensions of human experience in architecture and the importance of reflection. His books deserve a place on every bookshelf.

Theory 5: Place Attachment Theory

Altman, I. & Low, S. (Eds.) (1992). *Place Attachment*. New York: Plenum Press.

This edited collection is considered one of the critical texts on place attachment theory. Covering aspects ranging from childhood attachments, environmental memories, attachments with ordinary landscapes, to transcendence of place, many highly respected researchers contribute to this important work. In its entirety, the book considers the unique emotional experiences and bonds that people develop with places.

Manzo, L. & Devine-Wright, P. (Eds.) (2013). *Place Attachment: Advances in Theory, Methods, and Applications*. New York: Routledge.

Lynn Manzo, a professor in environmental psychology, and Patrick Devine-Wright, a researcher in human geography, have edited a comprehensive volume that presents the latest research on place attachment. The book focuses on theory, methods and application, to provide a critical overview of contemporary thought. Topics cover a range of relevant and timely issues such as placemaking, displacement, migration, civic engagement, and global climate change.

Theory 6: Biophilic Design Theory

Beatley T. (2016). *Handbook of Biophilic City Planning and Design*. Washington, DC: Island Press.

From the perspective of urban design practice, perhaps the most influential work in this area is by Timothy Beatley. His beautifully illustrated book covers a range of case studies from across the globe, and is a wonderful introduction to the concepts of biophilic urbanism, blue urbanism and world-leading design practice in this space.

Kellert, S. R., Heerwagen, J. & Mador, M. (2008). *Biophilic Design: The Theory, Science, and Practice of Bringing Buildings to Life*. Hoboken, NJ: John Wiley.

Stephen Kellert pioneered the literature in this space, with this wonderful edited book sharing twenty-three original, inspiring, and thoughtful essays by world-renowned scientists, designers, and practitioners, including Edward O. Wilson, Howard Frumkin, Tim Beatley, Janine Benyus and William Browning. Written for architects, landscape architects, planners, developers and building owners, this handbook is a valuable resource.

Acknowledgments

First and foremost, we would like to thank our family, friends and colleagues, for their understanding and support as we wrote this book. We especially acknowledge the valuable contribution of our writing coach and editor, Karyn Gonano – her support, encouragement and guidance has been invaluable. Undergraduate students Ama Hayyu Marzuki and Felicity Bruce, as part of a QUT Vacation Research Experience Scheme, sketched and formatted some of the images in this book – thank you both. Finally, thank you to the design practices, researchers and community members from across the globe for providing design inspiration and allowing us to use some of their images – we appreciate your generosity.

Index

Note: **bold** page numbers indicate tables; *italic* page numbers indicate figures.

Aalto, Alvar 179–180
Active Design Guidelines (Center for Active Design) 111
active lifestyles, encouraging 25
adaptive reuse projects 62, 180
Adelaide (Australia) 12
ADHD (attention deficit hyperactivity disorder) 2, 110, **134**
aesthetics 30, 59, 68, 71
affordances 1–2, 8–9, *8*, 13, 17–27, 99, 186; and age-friendly/inclusive design 27, **141**, 146, 150, 153, 154; and behavior setting/programming 9, 24–26; benefits of using in design 26–27; and children *see under* child-friendly design; and cues *see* cues; false 22–23; hidden 23; independent mobility as 121; and individual characteristics 18; multiple 25–26, 65; origins of theory 17–19; perceived/real 18, 22–23; and place attachment 71, 75; and positive/negative affordances 9; preventing 23–24; and prospect-refuge theory 29–30, 32; and salutogenic design 25, 105, 108–109, 110, 111, **112**, 115; and scales 18–19, *20*, 26; and sense of place/*genius loci* 26, 65; and sustainable design 170
age factor 9, 18, 31, 45, *see also* child-friendly design; children
age-friendly/inclusive design 2, 3, 7, 11–12, 99, 138–157, 185–186; and affordances 15, 27, **141**, 146, 150, 153, 154; and ageing population 11; and biophilic design 91, **143**, 152, 153, 155; bus shelter scenario 1, 99, 140, **141–143**; and bus shelters 155–157, *156*; and design theory 140, **141–143**, 151–153, 157; design tools/principles/processes for 145–149; and enablers/disablers 140–145, *144*; and personal space **141**, 153, 154; and place attachment **142**, 155; and policies 140, 145; and prospect-refuge **141**, 150, 153, 154, 155; and sense of place/*genius loci* **142**, 152–153, *152*, 154; and sensory gardens *139*, 150, *152*, 153–155; and universal design 145–146, *147*, 150, *see also* disabled people/disabilities; older people
aged care facilities 1, 46, 91, 150, 153, 155
aging population *see* older people
air quality 3, 48, 84, 121
airports 43, 46–47, **88**, 174
Alila Villas Uluawtu (Bali, Indonesia) **89**
Allen Lambert Galleria/Atrium (Toronto) **89**
alley activism 73
Altman, Irwin 67, 188
anecdotal evidence 4, 5, 180
Angawi, Sami 69, 70
anthropology 4, 6, 40–41, 44, 56
anti-loitering devices 118, 130
Antonovsky, Aaron 103, 115
anxiety 82, **112**, **134**
Appleton, Jay 28, 29–30, 187
apps 151
aquariums 84, **88**, 108

architectural identity 62–64
architectural journals 6
architecture 56, 57, 58, 59; Islamic
    69–70; Nordic 62–64
ART (attention restoration theory) 10,
    84, 187
art of design 1, 2, 5
art walks 108
ASD (autism spectrum disorder) *see*
    autism
astronauts 9, 47–48
Atelier Deshaus 62
Attenborough, David 163
attention deficit hyperactivity disorder
    (ADHD) 2, 110, **134**
attention restoration theory (ART) 10,
    84, 187
Auckland Design Manual 146, *147*
Australia *21*, 22, 40, 85, 88, 122,
    140; affordances in *21*, 22;
    age-friendly/inclusive design in
    140, 144, *144*, 149, 150–151,
    155, 174; biophilic design
    in **88**, 92–93; child-friendly
    design in 128, *129*, 130; sense
    of place/*genius loci* in 54, *63*;
    sustainable design in 12, 165,
    174–175, 180
autism 20, 45, 46, 138, 139–140,
    141, 151, 153, 154, 174, 180
autobiographical memory 77

B Team Initiative 160, 168
Ban Ki-moon 160–161
Bandung (Indonesia) 122, 175
Barcelona (Spain) 153, 179
Barnes, M. 184
Batbridge (Netherlands) 90, 94
Bates, C. 183
Bates Smart (architecture firm) 92–93
bats 94
Bayer, Vanessa 86
Be My Eyes app 151
Beatley, Timothy 62, 91, 188–189
Becker, C. 103
Bee Gees Way (Brisbane) 108
behavior setting 9, 24–26
belonging, sense of 75, 155
Benyus, Janine 85, 189
best practice 6, 12, 48, 92, 94, 119,
    122, 150
Bewitched (TV show) 34
biomimicry/biomorphism 12, 85, 87,
    89, 168, 173
Biophilia (Wilson) 80

biophilia/biophilic design 2, 7, *8*, 13,
    78, 80–96, 99, 180, 188–189; and
    30 Days Wild challenge 80; and
    age-friendly/inclusive design 91,
    143, 152, 153, 155; and attention
    restoration hypothesis 10, 84;
    and biomimicry/biomorphism 12,
    85, 87, **89**, 168, 173; and bridges
    89, 90, 94, *95*; and certification
    systems 84; and children 11,
    110, 120, 122–123, 124, **134**;
    and cities *see* biophilic urbanism/
    cities; and crime/violence 83;
    defined 80–81, 84; emergence
    of 84–90; and gardens 80, 87,
    88, 90, 91, 92, 94; and hospitals
    82–83, **88**, 90, 92–94; and need
    for connection with nature 80,
    81; and place attachment 70, 71;
    as positively disruptive 87; and
    prospect-refuge **89**; and salutogenic
    design 108, 109, 110, **113**, 115;
    and sense of place 87; and sensory
    experience 87, **88**; and sustainable
    design 169–173, **171**, *172*; and
    therapeutic value of nature 81–84,
    110; tools/strategies/core patterns
    of 87–90, **88–89**; and water
    features 85, 87, **88**, **89**, 91, 94,
    95; and workplace absenteeism/
    productivity 83–84
Biophilic Design Framework 87
Biophilic Design (Kellert/Heerwagen/
    Mador) 189
biophilic urbanism/cities 10, *81*, *82*,
    84–85, 90–91, 92
bioremediation 59, 61
Birkeland, James 167
Birmingham Library 151–153,
    152, 180
Bishan-Ang Mo Kio park (Singapore)
    91, 92
blind/low-vision people 138, **141**,
    147, 150; Braille signage for 140,
    152, 153; and technology 151
blood pressure 82, 84, 87
blue urbanism 62, 64, 91
body territory 44
Boeri, Stefano 85
Borgafjäll Hotel (Sweden) 64
boring design 107–108
Bosco Verticale (Vertical Forest,
    Milan) 85, *86*
Boys, Jos 145
Branson, Richard 160

BREEAM (Building Research
  Establishment Environmental
  Assessment Method) 153, 165,
  168, 174
bridges 10, **89**, 90, 94, 111; locks on
  68, see also Zalige bridge
Brisbane (Australia) *21*, **88**, *102*, 108,
  128, *129*, 144, *144*
Britain (UK) 80, 83, 122, 128, 149;
  Healthy New Towns initiative in
  177–179; sustainable design in
  165; universal design in 151–153,
  152, 180, *see also* England; London
Brown, Martin 167
Browning, William D. 87–90,
  88–89, 189
Brundtland, Gro Harlem 160
Brundtland Report 160, 163
Bruno-Kreisky-Park (Vienna) 50
building design 4, 9; age-friendly/
  inclusive 11, 138, 139–140, **141**,
  145, 146, 149, 151, 153; and
  aged care facilities 1, 46, 91, 150,
  153, 155; boring 107–108; and
  courtyards 22, 28, 52, **88**, **89**,
  93; and environmental impacts
  12, 163; hospitals *see* hospitals;
  offices *see* office buildings;
  and personal space 40, 41,
  46, 51–52; and programming
  24–25; and prospect-refuge
  28, 31, 34, 35; residential *see*
  residential buildings; and sense of
  place/*genius loci* 58, 59–64, 65;
  sustainable/biophilic *see* green
  buildings; and ventilation 70,
  84, 87, 153, 173; and work *see*
  workplaces
building footprint 12
Burra Charter 58
bus shelters 1, 31, 99, **141–143**,
  155–157, *156*, 180

cafes/cafe culture 35, 44, 51, 56, 72,
  111, **113**
Canada 12, 67, **89**, 173, 180
cancer 2, 3, 101, 105
*Care and Design: Bodies, Buildings,
  Cities* (Bates/Imrie/Kullman) 183
Carmona, M. 183–184
Casa Batlló building (Barcelona) 153
Center for Disease Control (USA) 107
Central Park (New York City) 4–5, 44
certification systems 84, 153,
  165–167, 168, 174

CFCs (child-friendly cities) 118–121,
  123, 124, 125, 127; and design
  theory 132, **133–134**; policy origins
  of 120–121; UNICEF/UNESCO
  initiatives for 120
chairs 22, *see also* public seating
Charleston (USA) 145
Chawla, Louise 120
Cheers (TV show) 44
Cheonggyecheon stream (Seoul)
  81, *82*
chess metaphor 1, *2*
Chicago (USA) 83
child-friendly cities *see* CFCs
child-friendly design 2, 3, 7, 11,
  37, 99, 118–135, *147*, 154; and
  affordances 18, 22, 25, 119, 122,
  125, 130, **133**; and biophilia 11,
  110, 120, 122–123, **134**; and child-
  friendly cities *see* CFCs; and *genius
  loci* 123, **133**, *135*; and healthy
  child development 125–127; and
  independent mobility 121–122,
  124, 130; and personal space
  approach 46, 48, 50, 122–123,
  125, **133**; and place attachment
  72, 76–77, 119, 123, 132, **134**;
  and play *see* play; playgrounds;
  and prospect-refuge 32–33, 37,
  122–123, 125, **133**; and safety/
  security 121–122, 124–125, 127;
  and sensory stimulation 130–132,
  131; and street design 122–123,
  123, 179
Child-Friendly Integrated Public
  Spaces (RPTRA, Indonesia) 127
children: discrimination against 118;
  participation in design by 120, 132;
  and personal space 46, 48, 50; and
  place attachment 72, 76–77; and
  prospect-refuge 32–33, 37; rights
  of 118, 120
Chile *41*
China/Chinese design 4, 49, 52,
  61–62, **88**, 180
circular design 12, 163–164, *164*,
  168, 175, 176
Circular Design Guide 164
cities 40, 80–81; child-friendly (CFCs)
  118–119; healthy 105–107; smells
  of 132
Cities for People (Gehl) 184
Cities and Streets for Kids 121–122
city councils 23, 61, 71, 72
Clancy, J. O. 87–90, **88–89**

climate change 4, 12, 71–72,
     161–163, 164, 180
Clinton Climate Change Initiative 167
Clinton, Hillary 43
coherence 3, 11, 104–105, **112**; and
     contextual factors for healthfulness
     105, **106**; and generalized
     resistance resources 104
color 12, 20, 22, 58, 93; and personal
     space theory 47
communication 44, 149
communities 4, **106**, **113**, **142**, **155**,
     167; and children 121, 127; and
     personal space theory 48; and
     prospect-refuge theory 32, 35, *see
     also* neighborhoods
community amenities 11, 107
community attachment/engagement
     70–71, 105, 107
community gardens *49*, *50*, 73, 91
Complete Streets concept 26
COOKFOX Architects' office (New
     York City) 90
cookie-cutter development 54,
     69, **142**
Cooper-Marcus, Clare 184
corporate social responsibility 160
courtyards 22, 28, 52, **88**, **89**, 93
cradle-to-cradle 12, 168, 175
creativity/imagination 1, 4, 13, 82
crime 5, 10, 32, 83, 124; deterrents,
     incorporated in design 34–35
crime prevention through
     environmental design (CPTED) 34
cues 6, 8, 17, 18, 25, 26–27, 33, 93,
     133, **170**; and age-friendly/inclusive
     design 146, 150, 153; mapping 20;
     matched to affordances 19–22,
     21; and personal space 41, 46; and
     salutogenic design 25, 105, **112**; to
     action 19, *see also* signage
cultural constraints 23
cultural diversity 12, 127
cultural factors: and *genius loci* 57,
     58; and personal space 9, 41, 44,
     45; and place attachment 10, 67;
     and visual cues 17, 18, *see also*
     socio-cultural context
Cuthbert, A. R. 7
cycling/cycle paths 3, 11, 18, 111,
     112, *114*; and blind corners 29; and
     child-friendly design 121, 122

da Vinci, Leonardo 179
Darling River (Australia) 85

Davidson, J. 154
daylight 88, 94, 105, 108, 153, 154,
     173, 175
de Bono, Edward 13, 177
*Death and Life of Great American
     Cities, The* (Jacobs) 35, 184–185
defensible space 34
degree programs for environment
     professionals 4
dementia 2, 12, 103, 138, 139–140,
     141, **142**, 150, 179; and mapping
     cues 20; and sensory gardens 153,
     154; and technology 151
density 12, 40, 81, 111, 127, 180, 185
depression 2, 82, 83, 101, 105
design awards 64, 65, 91, 92, 94, 111,
     151, 173, 174, 175
design charrette 13, 122
Design of Everyday Things, The
     (Norman) 186
design failures 12, 107–108
Design of Future Things, The
     (Norman) 186
design justice 12
design theory 1–2, 4, 6–7, 15,
     109, 111, 177, 179–180; and
     complexity of design challenges
     7; explanatory/normative 6; and
     global priorities 10–12, 15; and
     practice, gap between 13, *see also*
     theory-storming; *and see specific
     theories*
desire lines 23–24, *24*
Devine-Wright, Patrick 188
Dezeen 167
diabetes 82, 101
disabled people/disabilities 11,
     109, 138–140, 155; as central to
     design process 145; conditions
     encompassed by 138, 146, *147*; and
     enablers/disablers 140–145, *144*;
     global extent of 138; medical/social
     models of 139–140; and technology
     151; *see also specific disabilities*
domestic violence 10, 82
doors/door handles 19, 47, 146, 155
Dosen, A. S. 38
Dragehjelm, Hans 128
Dreiseitl, Herbert 91
dropped curbs 145
Dutch Design Awards 65

*Ecological Approach to Visual
     Perception* (Gibson) 186
8–80 Cities movement 150

Einsiedlerpark (Vienna) 50
Elkington, John 160
emotions 10, 13, 67, 68, 74
England 22, *49, see also* London
entrapment 33, *34*, 38
environmental autobiographies 77
environmental protection/care
    71–72, 160
environmental sustainability 69
Erskine, Ralph 64
ethical practices 4, 5, **170**
ethnic enclaves 74
European Union (EU) 167
Evelina Children's Hospital (London)
    93
evidence-based design 1, 2, 4–6,
    15, 35, 99, 119, 132, 149; and
    academic journals 6; as informal/
    unsystematic 5; and myth of design
    geniuses 179–180; and reliance on
    specific methods 5–6; and research-
    informed practice 6; salutogenic
    108, 111, 115; working towards
    12–13
Experience of Landscape, The
    (Appleton) 28, 29–30, 187
Experience of Nature, The (Kaplan/
    Kaplan) 187
Eyes of the Skin (Pallasmaa) 58, 188

Fallingwater (Frank Lloyd Wright)
    85, *86*
families 2, 43, 72, 118
farmers markets 107, 127
fashion 52
fast food 4, 101–102, 179
favourite place analysis 77
Fedrizza, Rick 164–165
Fialko, M. 73
Finland 48–50, *49*, 59
First Nations peoples 67
Fit City initiative (New York
    City) 111
footpaths 3, 11, 73, 87, *102*, 109,
    121, *see also* multi-use trails
Fortaleza (Brazil) 122
Foster, Norman 94
Frew Park (Brisbane) 128, *129*
'Friendly Bench' *49*, 50
Friends (TV show) 44
friendship 45, 72
future-focused design 57, 65, 177

Gaines, K. 154
gamification approach 108, 128

gardens 87, **88**, 92, 93, 94, 111, 184;
    cities as *see* Singapore; community
    49, 50, 73, 91, **113**, 168, **170, 171**;
    rooftop 151, *152*, 168; sensory 80,
    139, 150, *152*, 153–155
Gardens in the Bay (Singapore) 90, *92*
Gas Works Park (GWP, Seattle)
    59–61, *60*
Gaudi, Antoni 153, 179
Gehl, Jan 12, 18, 50, 107, 184
Gehry, Frank 51
gender 9, 31, 45, 50–51
*Genius Loci: Towards a
    Phenomenology of Architecture*
    (Norberg-Schulz) 58, 187–188
genius loci see sense of place/*genius
    loci*
gentrification 70
geography 4, 44, 56; social 6
Gibson, J. J. 17, 186
Gifford, R. 75
Global Designing Cities Initiative 122
global priorities 10–12, 15
Goldhagen, Sarah Williams 4, 12, 184
Goldsmith, Selwyn 145
graffiti murals 108
Graziano, Michael 40, 187
green buildings 83–87, *86*, **88**–89, 91,
    164–167, 180; and certification/
    performance benchmarks 84, 153,
    165–167, 168, 174; hospitals/
    healthcare facilities 82–83, **88**,
    90, 92–94, *92*, 108; and LBC
    167–168, 169, 173; and restorative
    sustainability 167; and Sustainable
    Development Goals 165, *166*
Green Man+ scheme (Singapore) 150
green prescriptions 83, 110
green roofs/walls 85, *86*, 87, **88**,
    90–91, 108, *161*, 169, **170, 171**,
    172, 173, 180
green urbanism 91
Guterres, António 161–162, 163
GWP (Gas Works Park, Seattle)
    59–61, *60*
gyms 110–111

Haag, Richard 59–61
habitat theory 30
Hadid, Zaha 35
Hajj pilgrimage 69
Hall, Edward T. 9, 40–41, 44,
    46, 187
Hamilton, D. K. 5, 6
Hampton, J. 73

Handbook of Biophilic City Planning and Design (Beatley) 188–189
Handler, S. 150
Hassell, Richard 91
hazards 29, 30, 31–32; incident/impediment 32
Headspace: The Psychology of City Living (Keedwell) 185
Healing Gardens (Cooper-Marcus/Barnes) 184
health 103–104; defined 103; as process 104
health-promoting activities 3, 10–11, 13; contact with nature 81–84, 87, 96, *see also* salutogenic design; well-being
healthcare facilities *see* hospitals
Healthy New Towns initiative (UK) 177–179
healthy/unhealthy eating 101–102
heart disease 82, 101
Heath, T. 183–184
Hediger, Haini 40
Heerwagen, J. 189
Heidegger, Martin 57
Helsinki (Finland) 48–50, 49, 59
Henderson, V. 154
heritage 58, 59–61, 69
Hes, Dominique 167
Hidden Dimension, The (Hall) 41, 187
hierarchies, spatial 20
High Line park (New York City) 9, 54; industrial heritage in 59; and prospect-refuge theory 35, 36
high-rise apartments 52, 85, 86
Hitchcock, Alfred 28
Hjerkinn (Norway) 62–64
home territories 44
home zones concept 122
homeless people 23, 48
Hong Kong 49, 50, 93
hospitals 10, 46, 107–108, 150, 184, 185; and biophilic design 82–83, 88, 90, 92–94, 92, 108
hostile architecture 23, 48
Housing Design for an Increasingly Older Population (Regnier) 185–186
How to Thrive in the Next Economy (Thackara) 163
Human Factors in the Built Environment (Nussbaumer) 47
human rights 118, 139

human spatial needs *see* personal space theory
humanitarian design 12

Ibiza (film) 76
ICOMOS Charter for Places of Cultural Significance 58
identity 68, 70, 73, **106**, *see also* sense of place/*genius loci*
Image of the City, The (Lynch) 185
Imrie, R. 149, 183
inactive lifestyles 4
inclusive design 33, *see also* age-friendly inclusive design
India 76, 146–149, *148*
indigenous people 10, 174–175
Indonesia 40, **89**, 122, *126*, 127, 175
industrial heritage 59–61, 62
'Influencer' Indi-Pacific INDIE award 175
Instagram 76, 80
interactional territories 44
interior design 56
international PARKing Day 72, 73
intimate distance 42–43, *42*, 47
intuition 4, 13
Ireland 174
Islamic architecture 69–70
Italy 58, 85, *86*, 120, 122, 180
It's a Wonderful Life (film) 69, 72

Jackson, J. B. 56–57
Jackson, M. 139
Jacobs, Jane 12, 35, 184–185
Jakarta (Indonesia) 40, 122, *126*
Japan 153–154
Jeffrey, C. Ray 34
Jencks, Maggie Keswick 93
Jones, E. Fay **89**
Jorgensen, A. 50
journals 6

Kahn, Louis 29, **88**
Kampung Admiralty (Singapore) 91
Kansai Rosai Hospital Garden (Osaka) 154
Kaplan, R./Kaplan, S. 84, 90, 187
Keedwell, Paul 153, 185
Keith, Lois 140
Kellert Biophilic Design Award 173
Kellert, Stephen 84, 87, 189
Kennedy, L. 110
Khartoum (Sudan) 58
Khoo Teck Puat hospital (Singapore) 88, *92*

Kitchin, R. 157
Kullman, K. 149, 183
Kuo, F. 83

landscape architecture/design 1, 4, 6,
  55, 56, 71; and overlay mapping
  method 5–6
landscapes 28, 30, 55, 56, 64;
  cultural/mythical 57–58, 64; threats
  to 71–72; urban 59 61, 60
Language of Space, The (Lawson) 47
Laobaidu coal bunker (Shangai) 62
Las Vegas (USA) 40
Law, R. 157
Lawson, B. 47, 48
LBC (Living Building Challenge) 84,
  167–168, 169, 173
Lee Kuan Yew 90
LEED (Leadership in Energy and
  Sustainable Design) 165, 173
Levitated Mass (Los Angeles Museum
  of Art) 89
libraries 44, 140, 151–153, 152, 155
Licka, L. 50
Life Between Buildings (Gehl) 50, 184
light 31, 88, 94, 105, 173
light therapy 105
lighting 25, 34, 48, 50, 107; controls
  20; day- 84
Living Building Challenge (LBC) 84,
  167–168, 169, 173
locks on bridges 68
London (UK) 12, 93, 94,
  111–115, 168
Long Museum west Bund
  (Shanghai) 62
Low, Setha 67, 68, 188
Lynch, Kevin 120, 185

McDermott, Kathleen 52
McDonalds 101
McDonough, William 167
Mace, Ronald 145
McHarg, Ian 5
MacKinnon Pass (New Zealand) 64
Mador, M. 189
Maggie's Centres 90, 93–94
Malaysia 88
Maller, C. 110
Manhattan (New York) *see* High Line
  park
manspreading 42, 44
Manzo, Lynn 188
Maoris 64, 67
mapping visual cues 20

maps 5, 120; smell 132
mashrabiya 69–70
Massey, Doreen 56
Matakana (New Zealand) 64
meaningfulness 56, 75, 104
Mecanoo (design team) 151
Mecca (Saudi Arabia) 69
Medina (Saudi Arabia) 69
Melbourne (Australia) 40, 54
Melbourne Royal Children's Hospital
  92–93
memory 10, 56, 57, 58, 59,
  61–62, 74, 125, 132, 154–155;
  autobiographical 77
mental health 3, 83, 103, 138, 146
Michelangelo 179, 180
Microlibrary initiative (Indonesia) 175
Middle East 69–70
Milan (Italy) 85, 86, 122
Milburn, L.-A. 6
Minsheng Wharf (Shanghai) 62
MIT building (Gehry) 51
Miyake, Yoshisuke 153–154
mobility 11, 50; and children
  121–122, 124, 130
Moore, Rowan 168
Mork and Mindy (TV show) 17
Moscow (Russia) 54
Moses bridge (Netherlands) 90,
  94, 95
mosquito device 118, 130
multi-use spaces 25–26
multi-use trails 102, 112–113,
  114, 115
Mumbai (India) 76

NASA 9, 47–48
national parks 20, 81
Native Americans 67
nature, human connection with, *see*
  biophilia
Nature Lab (Pittsburgh) 169–173
neglect 5, 73, 91, 157
neighborhoods 12, 18, 28, 72–73;
  and children 121; and Complete
  Streets concept 26; gentrification
  of 70; healthy 107; and place
  attachment 70–71, 72–73, 74, 75,
  see also communities
net-positive approach 160, 167, 169,
  175, 176
net-zero approach 160, 165, 167,
  169, 173
Netherlands 48, 90, 94, 122, 180;
  Zalige bridge 55, 63, 65, 95

New urban Agenda 145
New York City (USA) 28, 124;
    biophilic design in **88, 89**, 90; Fit
    City initiative in 111; High Line
    park *see* High Line park; parks
    in 4–5, 33–34, *34*, 46, **89**, *119*;
    Project for Public Spaces 12
New Zealand 64, 67, 146, *147*
Newman, Oscar 34
Next Architects 55, 63, 65, 94, *95*
NHS (National Health Service)
    177–179
Nightlands: Nordic Building
    (Norberg-Schulz) 62, 187–188
Nivala, J. 57
Norberg-Schulz, Christian 57, 58, 62,
    187–188
Norman, Donald 17–18, 19, 20, 186
Norway 23, 62–64, *63*, *see also* Oslo
Norwegian Wild Reindeer Center
    Pavilion 62–63
Nussbaumer, Linda 47

obesity 2, 3, 25, 82, 101–102,
    103, 178
Oc, T. 183–184
office buildings 19, 22–23, 90; and
    personal space 47, 51–52
Oizumi Ryokuchi Park (Osaka) 153
older people 2, 109, *139*, 140, **141**,
    142, *147*, 149–151, 185–186;
    and 8–80 Cities movement 150;
    and falling/fear of falling 150;
    growing number of 149; and
    intergenerational playgrounds 125,
    150, *see also* age-friendly/inclusive
    design
Olmsted, Frederick Law 5, **89**
open space design 1, 12
openness 61, 62, 71
orientation 12
Osaka (Japan) 153–154
Oslo (Norway) 12; Airport 174;
    Opera House 62, *63*
Osmond, Humphry 46
Oswald, M. J. 38
Our Common Future (Brundtland
    Report) 160
overlay mapping method 5
Ozdemir, A. 45

Paley Park (New York City)
    33–34, *34*
Pallasmaa, Juhani 58, 179, 188
panoramas 31

Paramit Factory (Malaysia) **88**
Paris (France) 35
parks 11, 18, *21*, 71, 91, 121, 128,
    133–134, *135*, 153; desire lines
    in 23, *24*; gyms in 110–111;
    intergenerational 125, *131*;
    miniature (parklets) 73, *73*; and
    personal space 44, 45, 48–51,
    49; and programming 25; and
    prospect-refuge theory 33–34, *34*;
    and social justice 168
participatory design 12, 122
pathogenic model 103
pedestrian areas 35, 121, 122–123
pedestrian bridges *see* bridges
Pennsylvania (USA) 82–83, 85
people-watching 9, 35, 38, 109, 187
performance 9
personal space **8**, 13, 40–52, 71, 99,
    187; and age-friendly/inclusive
    design **141**, 153, 154; and animals
    40; and children 46, 48, 50,
    122–123, 125, **133**; continuing
    importance of 52; and culture 9,
    41, 44, 45, 52; and dense urban
    settings 40, *41*, 43; and gender 50;
    and Hall's spatial taxonomy 41–43,
    42, 44; and individual differences
    45–46, 48, 50–51; and interior
    design 46–47; and materials 47;
    and NASA space stations 9, 47–48;
    origins of theory 40; and place
    attachment 71, 75; and prospect-
    refuge theory 50–51; and public
    parks 44, 45, 50–51; and public
    seating 44, 46–47, 48–51, *49*; and
    public transport *42*, 43, 44, 52;
    and salutogenic design 108, **112**;
    size/regulation/flexibility of 44–46;
    sociofugal/sociopetal 46–47; and
    street design 108; and sustainable
    design 169, **170**; and territoriality
    44; and Trump/Clinton 43; and
    workplaces 47, 51–52
*Personal Space: The behavioral Basis
    of Design* (Sommer) 46–47
personal space bubbles 40, 42, 45,
    48, 52
personal/interpersonal distance *42*,
    43, 45, 46
phenomenological research 77
Phipps Conservatory and Botanical
    Gardens (Pittsburgh) 169–173
physical activity 25, 91, 155; and
    children 110, 125, 179; and

salutogenic design 101, 103, 106, 110–111, **113**
Pittsburgh (USA) 12, 169–173
place attachment 7, *8*, 10, 13, 56, 65, 67–78, 99, 107, 188; and affordances 71, 75; and age-friendly/inclusive design **142**, 155; benefits of 75; and biophilic design 70, 71; and children/child-friendly design 72, 76–77, 119, 123, 132, **134**; and communities/neighborhoods 70–71, 72–73, *74*, 75, 77; designing for 77–78; development of 73–75, 76–77; and emotions 67, 68, 74; and environmental care 71–72; and ethnic enclaves 74; and everyday/special places 69–71; and *genius loci* 70, 76; and gentrification 70; and locks on bridges *68*; and Middle Eastern holy cities 69–70; origins of theory 67–68; and personal space theory 71, 75; and prospect-refuge 70, 71, 75; and proximity 74–75; research methods for 77; and safety/security 72–73, 75; and salutogenic design 105, 107, 108, **113**; and social connections 72–73; and sustainable design 72, **171**; typology of 68
Place Attachment (Altman/Low) 67, 188
Place Attachment: Advances in Theory, Methods and Applications (Manzo/Devine-Wright) 188
place creation 73, 74
place intensification 73, 74
place meaning 56
Place and Placelessnes (Relph) 56
place, power of 2–4; and mental health 3–4; and quality of life/healthy living 2–3, *see also* sense of place/*genius loci*
place realization 73, 74
planning 2, 4, 7, 50, 73, 180, 183, 184, 185; and child-friendly design 118, 120; and prospect-refuge 33, 37; and sense of place/*genius loci* 56, 60, 65
play 11, 18, 25, 37, 50, 61, 120, 125, 126, *135*; importance of 127–130; and risk 128, *129*; traditional games *126*, 127
playful city 130

playgrounds 1, 18, 71, 93, 111–115, 127; adventure 128, *129*, 130; intergenerational 124–125, 150
plazas 1, 23, 25
politics 56, 57, 59
pollution 3, 85, 124; and bioremediation 59, 61
Polman, Paul 160
Pontevedra (Spain) 121
Pope, Alexander 55
post-traumatic stress disorder (PTSD) 45, 46
Power of 10+ 25–26
Prague (Czech Republic) 58
Pritzker Architecture Prize 52, 61
privacy 9, 19, 46, 47, 93
probabilistic functionalism 33
programming 24–25
Project for Public Spaces (New York City) 12, 25–26
people-watching 9
Prospect Park (New York City) **89**
prospect-refuge 7, *8*, 9, 13, 28–38, 99, 187; and aesthetic 30; and affordance theory 29–30, 32; and age-friendly/inclusive design **141**, 150, 153, 154, 155; and biophilic design **89**; and children 32–33, 37, 122–123, 125, **133**; and cycle paths 29; and entrapment/refuge balance 33–34, *34*, 38; and freedom of movement 31–32; and habitat theory 30; and hazards *see* hazards; and health/wellbeing 32–35; and High Line park 35, *36*; and human evolution 28; importance of 38; and light 31; origins of theory 28–30; and perception of danger 32–33; and personal space theory 50–51; and place attachment 70, 71, 75; and placemaking/social engagement 35–37; and probabilistic functionalism 33; prospect/refuge balance in 30–32; and research 37–38; and safety/security 28–29, 32–34, 38; and salutogenic design 109, **112**, 115; and shelter concept 31; and surveillance 34–35; and sustainable design 169, **170**
proxemics 9, 40, 41, 44, 52, 187, *see also* personal space theory

psychology 4, 67, 104; and affordance theory 17–18; environmental/ ecological 6, 56; and personal space 44, 45
PTSD (post-traumatic stress disorder) 45, 46
public distance 43
Public Places – Urban Spaces (Carmona/Tiesdell/Heath/Oc) 183–184
public seating 9, 108, 109, **112, 141,** 153, 155, *156*; and *genius loci 63*; and personal space 44, 46–47, 48–51, *49, 52*
public territory/zone 44, 47
public toilets 64, 150–151
public transport *42*, 43, 44, 48, 180

quality of life 2–3, 11, 12, 149

Rear Window (film) 28
recreation spaces 50, **170,** *see also* parks
recycling 163–164, *164*
Redström, Johan 7
Redwoods Forest (Rotorua, New Zealand) 64
Regnier, Victor 185–186
Relph, Edward 56
renewable energy 72
research-informed design *see* evidence-based design
residential buildings 35, 85, 86, 91, 154, 155
RESTORE project (EU) 167
retrofitting 11, 115, 144, 167
Reynolds, Malvina 54
Riley, R. 75
rituals 69
rivers 57, 62, 65, 81, *82, 102*; pollution in 85
RO&AD Architects 94
Rome (Italy) 58
running 3, 25, **112,** 115
rural areas 85, 122, 155
Russia 54
Ryan, C. O. 87–90, **88–89**

safety/security 11, 28–29, 32–34, 38, **170**; and child-friendly design 121–122, 124–125, 127; and CPTED/defensible space 34; and place attachment 72–73, 75

Saint Basil's Cathedral (Moscow) 54
St. Johann Park (Vienna) 50
Saliba, R. 70
Salk Institute, La Jolla, California (Kahn) *29*, **88, 89**
salutogenic design 2–3, 7, 10–11, 99, 101–115; and affordances 25, 105, 108–109, 110, 111, **112**, 115; and biophilia 108, 109, 110, **113**, 115; and coherence *see* coherence; future of 115; and *genius loci* 107, 108, 111, **112**; and global health crisis 101, 115; and healthy cities 105–107; and mind–body balance 103; and multi-use trails 102, **112–113**, *114*, 115; and obesity/ unhealthy eating 102; origins of 103–104; and pathogenic model, compared 103; and physical activity 101, 103, 106, 110–111; and place attachment 105, 107, 108, **113**; and placemaking strategies 107–109; and prospect-refuge 109, **112**, 115; six key elements of 104–105; and sustainable design 167, **170**; theory-driven 111–115
Santiago (Chile) *41*
Satherley, S. 60–61
Saudi Arabia 69
scale 58, 61; and affordances 18–19, 20, 26; and prospect/refuge 31; and territoriality 44
Scannell, L. 75
schools 11, 46, 121, 125
Scotland 54
Seamon, D. 73
seashore 81
seasonal affective disorder 105
Seattle (USA) 9
self-esteem 75
selfie-gaze tourism 76
Selwyn Goldsmith Award 151–153, *152*
sense of place/*genius loci* 8, 9, 52, 54–65, 99, 123, 180, 187–188; and affordances 26; and age-friendly/inclusive design **142,** 152–153, *152,* 154; and biophilic design 87; and child-friendly design 123, **133,** *135*; in Chinese design 61–62; and cold places 64; comparison of terms 54–57; critique of 56–57; of everyday

objects 64–65; and future-focused design 57, 65; and historic/iconic buildings 58, 59; as human need 56; and industrial heritage 59–61, *60*, 62; as intangible/messy experience 56, 58–59; and memory 56, 57, 58, 59, 61–62; natural/man-made elements in 57–58; and Nordic architectural identity 62–64, 188; origins of theory 57–59; and place attachment 70, 76; and salutogenic design 107, 108, 111, **112**; and sustainable design **170**, 174–175; three core pillars of 56
sensory experience 12, 56, 58–59, 87, **88**, 130–132
Seoul (South Korea) 81, *82*
serotonin 105
7 Senses Foundation (Australia) 130
Shackell, A. 94
shade 3, 70, 104, 108, **113**
Shandong province (China) 49
Shanghai (China) 9, 62, **88**
Shannon Airport (Ireland) 174
Shepley, M. 5, 6
SHUT OUT (Australian Government's disability review) 140
sidewalks 22, 23, 26, 31, 35, 107, 108, *109*, 111
Sigala, M. 76
signage 11, 22, 109, **133**, *171*; and age-friendly/inclusive design 140, **143**, 150, 152, 153; and natural cues/actions 19
Singapore 10, *81*, 90–91, *92*, 150, *172*, *178*, 180
single-use 26
site-specific design 4, 5, 35, 52, 174, *see also* sense of place/*genius loci*
skateboarding 23
Skye, Isle of (Scotland) 54
Skygarden (London) 168
Skyrise Greenery Incentive Scheme (Singapore) 90–91
Smart Growth America 26
smoking 101
Snøhetta (architectural firm) 62
Snøhetta (Norwegian mountain) 64
social capital 4, 84, **113**
social distance *42*, 43
social impact perspective 12
social inclusion 11, **141**, 149, 160

social interaction 103, 122, **170**, *172*; and age-friendly/inclusive design **141**, 144, 155; and biophilic design 84, 91; and personal space theory 45, 46, 48, 51
social justice 70, 105, 168, 169
Social Life of Small urban Spaces, The (Whyte) 35, 186
social media 76, 80
social offerings 70
socio-cultural context 1, 12, 45, 56, 138, 174
sociofugal/sociopetal space 46–47
sociology 4, 6, 44, 67; urban 56
Söderström, O. 146, 154
sole practitioner designers 7
Sommer, Robert 44, 46
Sørensen, Carl Theodor 128
South Africa 124, 127
space stations 9, 47–48
Spaces Between Us, The (Graziano) 187
Spain 121, 153, 179
spinal cord injuries 140, 146–149, *148*
Spurlock, Morgan 101
Stewart, James 28, 69
Stockholm (Sweden) *161*
street design 26, 108–109, *109*, 179
street furniture 11, 109, 122, *see also* public seating
street life 35, 56; and alley activism 73, *see also* neighborhoods
stress 3, 11, 82, 105
Sullivan, W. 83
Suomalainen, Timo/Suomalainen, Tuomo 59
Supersize Me (documentary) 101
surveillance 34–35
sustainable design 2, 3, 7, 84, **89**, 99, 160–176, 180; and affordance 170; and airports 47; and biophilic design 169–173, **171**, *172*; and buildings *see* green buildings; and circular design 12, 163–164, *164*, 168, 175, 176; and climate change 12, 71–72, 161–163, 164, 169; and design theory 169, **170–171**, 176; emerging trends in 167–169; and global initiatives 160; and LBC 167–168, 169, 173; and materials 124; net-positive approach 160, 167, 169, 175, 176; and net-zero approach 160, 165, 167, 169, 173; and personal space 169, **170**;

and place attachment 72, **171**; and prospect-refuge 169, **170**; and salutogenic design 167, **170**; and sense of place/*genius loci* **170**, 174–175; and trees 19; and triple bottom line 12, 160, 168, 175, *see also* green roofs/walls
sustainable development 89, 160, 162, 165
Sustainable Development Goals 160, 165, *166*
Sweden 18, 64, *161*, *172*
Sydney (Australia) *21*, 22
systems thinking 12

tactical urbanism 12
Tear Drop Park (New York City) *119*
Temppeliaukio Church (Helsinki) *59*, 64
territoriality 44, 47, 48
Thackara, John 163
theoretical lens *see* design theories
Theory of Good City Form, A (Lynch) 185
theory-storming 7, *8*, 13, 31, 99, 177; and age-friendly/inclusive design 140, **141–143**, 157; and child-friendly design 119, 122, 125, 132, **133–134**; and salutogenic design 102, 108, **112–113**
thinking hats 13, 177
30 Days Wild challenge 80
Thorncrown Chapel (Eureka Springs, Arkansas) 89
Tiesdell, S. 183–184
toilets 64, *144*, 150–151
topography 54, 57, 87, **170**
Toronto (Canada) 89
tourism, selfie-gaze 76
traffic 26, 32, 37; and child-friendly design 121–123, *123*; and cues *21*, 22; measures for slowing 11; and older people crossing roads 150
Trancik, R. 56
transdisciplinary approach 7, 111
trash bins 20
trees 18–19, 25, 52, 87, 90, 93, 94, **134, 142**
trip hazards 150
triple bottom line (3BL) 12, 160, 168, 175
Trump, Donald 43

Tumbling Bay Playground (London) 111–115
Turkey 45

Ulrich, Roger 82–83
UNESCO Growing Up in Cities initiative 120
UNICEF CFC initiative 120, 125
United Nations 149; Brundtland Report 160; and climate change 160–162, 163; Habitat III 145; Sustainable Development Goals 160, 165, *166*
United States (USA) 9, 40, 45, 67, 107, 120, 124; affordances in 20, 22, 24; age-friendly/inclusive design in 144–145, *144*; biophilic design in 82–83, 85; community attachment in 70–71; sustainable design in 164–165, *see also* New York City
universal design 145–146, *147*, 150, 151–154, 180; award for 151; and sensory gardens 153–154
Urban Arts Projects (Australia) **88**
urban biodiversity 84, 85, 90, 91
urban design 1, 4, 7
urban heat island effect 87, 90, **170**
urban smellscape aroma wheel 132
urbanization 18, 40, 80–81, 122

Vaandrager, L. 110
van Rijswijk, L. 38
Vancouver (Canada) 12, 173
VanDusen Botanical Garden (Vancouver) 173
Vaux, Calvert 5, **89**
ventilation 70, 84, 87, 153, 173
Vienna (Austria) 50
vistas 31
visual cues *see* cues
Vitruvius 146
Voce, Adrian 128–130

walking 11, 84–85; and child-friendly design 121, 122; and cues 20, *21*; and salutogenic design 107, 108, *109*, 110, 111, *see also* footpaths
Walter, R. 94
Walumba Elders Centre (Australia) 174
Wang Shu 52, 61–62
Washington Square Park (New York City) 46

water 62, 65; and biophilic design 85, 87, **88**, **89**, 91, 94, *95*, *see also* rivers
Watkins, D. H. 6
wayfinding 20, 121, **142**, **143**, 153, 154, 155
weather **89**; and shelter 31, 32
Weeds (TV show) 54
Welcome to Your World (Goldhagen) 184
well-being 3, 12, 13, 50–51, 67, 75, **106**, **141**, 177–179, 181; and contact with nature 81–84, 96; and prospect-refuge theory 32–35; and sustainable development 160, *see also* salutogenic design
WGBC (World Green Building Council) 165
wheelchair users 28, 91, 138, **143**, 145, *148*, 152, 153, 154, 157
WHO (World Health Organization) 3, 103, 105–107, 127; on age-friendly/inclusive design 138, 149; Healthy Cities initiative 106–107
Whyte, William H. 12, 35, 48, 186

wicked problems 3–4
Wilding, M. 168
Wildlife Trust 80
Williams, Robin 17
Wilson, Edward O. 80, 81, 84, 189
WOHA (architectural firm) **89**, 91
Wong Mun Summ 91
woonerf (Netherlands) 122
workplaces 9, 47, 51–52; and biophilic design 83–84, **88**
World Architecture Network Sustainable Buildings Award 174
World Architecture News Small Spaces Awards 64
World Economic Forum 164
World Green Building Council (WGBC) 165
Wright, Frank Lloyd 85, *86*, 185

Young, Lyndsey 50
youth 2, 4, 50, 121

Zalige bridge (Netherlands) 55, *63*, 65, *95*
zoos 40